AT THE EDGE OF EMPIRE:
THE LIFE OF THOMAS B. GLOVER

For the peace activists of Nagakaski

AT THE EDGE OF EMPIRE:

The Life Of Thomas B. Glover

Michael Gardiner

BIRLINN

First published in 2007 by
Birlinn Limited
West Newington House
10 Newington Road
Edinburgh
EH9 1QS

www.birlinn.co.uk

ISBN 10: 1 84158 544 0
ISBN 13: 978 1 84158 544 4

British Library Cataloguing-in-Publication Data
A catalogue record for this book is available from the British Library.

Typeset by Hewer Text (UK) Ltd, Edinburgh
Printed and bound by ScandBook AB, Smedjebacken, Sweden

Contents

List of Illustrations

Acknowledgements

The opinions in this account do not reflect those of the sources I have consulted, or those who have helped with the writing. But for their generous time, advice and encouragement, I would like to thank: Alex McKay, Brian Burke-Gaffney, Anne Malcolm, Billy Watson, Loraine Noble, Ian Watson, James Flett, Tom Glover, Alan Spence, Duncan Rice, Neville Moir, Alison Rae, Kenny Redpath, Lee McRonald, Graham Donaldson, Yamaguchi Masahiro, Sugiyama Shinya, Kyoko Gardiner, Bill Cooper, Geraldine Cooke, Lisa Moylett, Ishihara Chikae, the librarians at Nagasaki Prefectural Library and at their photo archive, the librarians at the Queen Mother Library and Special Collections at Aberdeen University, the librarians at the National Library of Scotland, the librarians at Nagasaki Atomic Bomb Museum and at their photo archive, Nagasaki Tourist Board, Brig o' Balgownie Rotary, Chris Henry and the staff at the Museum of Scottish Lighthouses.

ONE

Dejima

E arly afternoon, 19 September. At 33 degrees, the weather is typical for Nagasaki. The wisterias are a lilac deep enough to cling to the clothes. The dragonflies are aircraft circling the ponds. The cicadas are deafening. Cicadas only sing for a few weeks, then fall from the trees and cover the ground like walnut shells. They have to sing deafeningly to be heard over the mobile phones.

Below, a view of a long channel leading into a bay. Down there the protagonist sailed into Japan, on 19 September. 1859 was not a year of typical weather. The dragonflies were subject to delays, the cicadas were too confused to sing themselves to death, and the passengers of Thomas Glover's ship had no view of the city, because the fog was too thick. On a clearer day, Glover would have seen lush mountains crowding in over him, an island chain funnelling him into the harbour, and off to the east, Nagasaki city centre, which will be officially off limits until the last few years of his life.

This is the scene looking down from the Glover Garden, set around the cruciform house which was his, and later became a tourist attraction. Here, the turmoil of the 1860s is suggested, its civil wars, its assassinations, and its intrigues. A busload of tourists stroll past, some turning the bells of flowers upwards to their noses. The tourists talk to one another, making a point of not listening to the young guide: they've earned the right not to.

What the guide might be trying to explain, as she passes the imperious European-looking house on the hill, is something like this. Thomas Glover had a hand in the education of some of the samurai – the ruling caste of Japanese society – who would become influential politicians after the change of government in 1868. He sold the Japanese Imperial Navy its first great ships and the equipment to become self-sufficient. He was the country's first major industrialist in the European sense. He was involved with the project to create Japan's first mint. He founded the first modern domestic brewing company, which later became Kirin. He helped set the scene – the guide is less likely to be saying – for an Anglo-Japanese relationship that ensured alliance in World War One. With his son, he introduced trawl fishing to the country. He came, it says in the garden brochure

> to Nagasaki in 1859 and established Glover & Co., a trading business and shipping agency. Later he was instrumental in the introduction of shipbuilding, coal mining, railways and various other modern industries to Japan. He was also a staunch supporter of the young samurai and feudal clans rebelling against the feudal government, and in that way he played a vital role in the turbulent political changes in Japan at the time of the Meiji Restoration.

The word staunch flattens Glover's life into one spent dedicated to forces understood in anachronistic terms as pro-democracy. But, as a freetrading entrepreneur, many of his actions were improvised, inconsistent, and dictated by changing circumstances. Still, this mini-biography has also been the version of the Glover story usually told in Scotland. Glover was modern, he inspired *Madam Butterfly*, he was staunch.

Glover himself might have humphed at this. His version of the story might have been a bit more raw.

He was born into a middling position in a big family. He had few educational opportunities, was rowdy in school, and was possessed of a restless desire to make himself heard, which was as likely to get him into trouble as to bring him success. When an opportunity to leave home came up, it was obvious to him that if he stayed, he would end up in the shadow of his more educated older brothers. He grew up around the smell not of wisteria but of herring, which sucked in fishermen from around Northern Europe. He befriended foreign traders around harbours, and early in life learned to associate strange ships with opportunity. A gruff personality, financial ambition and sheer luck would turn him into a lynchpin of modern Japanese government. He was willing to take great risks to achieve his ambitions, and he developed a knack of putting himself in the right place at the right time.

Soon after his own lifetime Glover disappeared from public view. This wasn't because he didn't have high standing in Nagasaki: by the time of his passing he was seen as an asset on a national level. Diplomatic histories bypassed the lives of traders in their memoirs, and traders didn't write much. Soon after his death his adopted homeland was starting to look like an enemy of the country of his birth. Only in the early 1980s was it realised that the early days of modern Japan could be related to a Scot.

But the haiku – modern/Butterfly/staunch – made to avoid any talk of violence can come to look like a form of aggression in itself. In Japan it is better understood that past war and present friendship are not mutually exclusive: anyone who has visited the atomic bomb museums in either Hiroshima or Nagasaki will have seen how horrifying atrocities can be remembered in an atmosphere which encourages calm and internationalism. The atomic bomb museums are amongst the friendliest and most outward-looking spaces in the country.

And Glover didn't succeed by obeying protocol. His straight-talking nature got negotiating with the samurai who were waiting to behead him when he arrived in the harbour down there in September 1859. He spent much of his life looking out from under these trees at this harbour. He made his livelihood here, as the town filled with ships, some of which he had built himself. The first few years of Glover's stay in Japan are the part of his life best remembered, often the only part remembered. His late teens and twenties were lived at a frantic rate that couldn't be sustained indefinitely and had to crash. For Olive Checkland, 'Glover is a good example of a man who found the excitements of the Japanese trade more hazardous than he had bargained for.' The familiar young Glover of 1859 to 1865 was far from home, often in desperate company, and much more lonely than his ability to network implies. His level of activity during this period demonstrates less a feeling of being staunch than a feeling of being lost.

Glover fact-finding represents a relatively new field, and a cultural comparison a non-existent one. After the first scattered journalistic forays into Gloverology in Scottish newspapers, the first serious book-length account was Brian Burke-Gaffney's *Hana to Shimo: Gurabakei no Hitobito*, (1989). In the UK, Alex McKay's *Scottish Samurai* (1993) broke the field and became the authoritative record, the product of years of painstaking research. In 2001 Naito Hatsuho published a massive record of Glover's movements, *Meiji Kenkoku no Yosho: To-masu B. Guraba– no Shimatsu*, which remains by far the most complete book written on him. McKay, Burke-Gaffney and Naito are the pioneers in Glover scholarship and their labours over primary material make a work like this possible. A lot of new material has been discovered since then, but rather than being exhaustive, it combines a look at Glover's life with repitched stories of his times.

McKay's book was, as they say, timely: despite Glover's involvement in Japanese government and technology, there remained an odd silence surrounding him in official histories of Japan. As early as July 1984, the Keio University economist Sugiyama Shinya had been expressing surprise that 'no substantial study of [Glover's] business activities seems yet to have been made' – a lack he partly answered in 1993 with his own *Meiji Isshin to Igirisu Shonin*. Glover's diplomat friend Ernest Satow had set the tone early by leaving him out of his important memoirs of 1921, even though the two had worked out pro-samurai strategies with global implications. After this, things went quiet for decades. Glover failed to get a mention by any of the contributors to Hugh Cortazzi's *Victorians in Japan* (1987), which charts the progress of important foreigners in the Meiji period. He doesn't appear once in the *Cambridge History of Japan: The Nineteenth Century* (1989), which runs to over 1,000 pages, and is otherwise thorough on political movements. Nor, for that matter, does he appear in Hamish Fraser and Clive Lee's *Aberdeen 1800–2000: A New History* (2000), over 500 pages itself.

And before Naito Hatsuho's huge volume, little reliable material was published about Glover in Japan. The garden, with its flower-watching tour parties, has been known as a peaceful place with wonderful views over city and sea, not as a centre of research. His story is important to Japan, but this is not to say that he is simply revered. The city of Nagasaki has been in a tricky position, since although not every act of Glover's career was as wholesome as they might like, vital revenue comes from a form of tourism that shows the era as one of movement forward. Since 1957, when Mitsubishi gave Glover House to the city of Nagasaki, the city has used the garden as a taste of the west, echoing the free trade principles of Glover himself. It features authentic western houses, built by an architect who had never left Japan, filled with models of period furniture; the original contents having been cleared out.

Today, with its quiet winding paths teeming with cats, the area of the garden is an oasis in the city. Nagasaki is one of Japan's most attractive cities, but like all Japanese cities is short on public space. The garden looks down on another oasis, the Dejima harbour boardwalk, where various chain cafés and bars are now lined up. In Dejima, I made waiters sheepish about their English, without speaking. This is typical for medium-sized cities: sometimes it's easier to go along with the semaphore and the pointing. This was the relationship that Glover perfected, one he helped to introduce, and it has never gone away. One belief is that Glover conducted all his dealings in the native language. In fact he dealt almost entirely in English, gradually slackening his study of Japanese – and this increased his value amongst internationally minded samurai rather than decreasing it, just as it does for foreigners today, when it is still common for English conversation instructors to pretend to have no Japanese to increase their popularity.

It's easy to see why Glover spent most of his life in this city. Nagasaki is, by Japanese standards, open, spacious, and leafy. There really is something historical beneath the Historical. World-changing things really did take place here. The traders of the 1860s did look down from these luxurious western-style houses on the hill onto ships in the channel, and those ships did stop here on their way to battles that would dictate how people would be governed for centuries. Foreign traders did bolt themselves into the house of William Alt next door, after finding themselves in the eye of a war between rebels and allied foreign forces. Settlers' houses were torched without warning, collaborators were assassinated around them, and huge amounts of cash did change hands.

For over 50 years Glover struggled to make Japan modern, as in the first epithet of the memorial haiku. What is missing from the brief accounts of Glover's legacy is how modern is easy to confuse with better. For Mohandas Gandhi, for example, the modern was not a necessary and natural step, but a sign of indebtedness to Europe. The leader of what became the world's most populous country spent much of his latter years spinning cotton. A lot of Asia still actively avoids the modern, in its common sense of global-isation with unfettered capital. But in a country that had been strongly restricted for two centuries, Glover found the most Europhile market he could have hoped for. In newly opened Japan, becoming modern was quickly defined as chasing a cultural and economic ideal already reached elsewhere. A central example remains language, as in the semaphoring waiter catching up with my silent English.

Before I could answer even this question, there was the problem of Glover's nationality, which paradoxically threatened to hide some of the most substantial information. When my own nationality was discovered, answers seemed to appear before the questions were asked. Gathering information began to feel like celebrating an alumnus for a school magazine. Because Glover was Scottish, I was exhibiting my pride. Was I? Was he?

I must have been muttering, because a garden groundkeeper looked up from his hoeing. He looked up at the clear sky sliced by the trails of aircraft bringing more tour parties, then nodded to me. I said something about how Glover is always described as Scottish. He smiled and went back to hoeing. No, I said, listen:

Glover is almost always described as a Scot, and almost never as a Briton. The stress on nationality has become a kind of moral duty. But to describe someone at national level is a conscious choice — and in Scotland's case is a particularly active choice, since 'British' is a definite category, while 'Scottish' is indefinite. There is no Scottish body equivalent to the Foreign Office. The word 'Scotland' does not appear on any passport. At the time of writing, there is no Scottish state. Scottishness resists definition because it isn't an official status, it's an elective identity. People choose to be Scottish. To say that someone is Scottish is not to state a fact, but to make a judgement.

For some people, usually those who see themselves as liberal, being born within the borders of the nation is enough to qualify as Scottish. Few of these people, however, would see themselves as sharing a national heritage with their neighbours whose parents are from Poland. Nor would most accept that if they moved to Canada they could no longer have Scottish children. For others, Scottishness is about parentage. But this is a circular explanation, since parents' nationality depends on their parents', which depends on their parents', and so on forever. Besides which, the first thing we find out about Glover's father, Thomas Berry, is that he was 'English'. If we go by the parentage argument, Glover was a Half-Scottish Samurai. Other people think that Scots become Scots through environment. But Glover spent 52 years of his 73-year life in Japan. He was born in Fraserburgh, quite safely in Scotland, much of his childhood was spent in Bridge of Don, near Aberdeen, and he may have spent three formative years at two of his father's posts near Grimsby, but this means that he spent only a total of 15 to 18 of his 73 years in Scotland.

This was a central question, since national pride is always somehow involved in the Glover story. I showed the gardener both versions of the garden brochure, and pointed out how the descriptions of the man differed. In Japanese, the term to describe Glover remains eisho, meaning both English merchant and British merchant (ei connotes both Britain and England). For visitors, his success is inextricable from his being a kind of English gentleman (the duality of ei) – a typology still large in the popular imagination. It is only in the English version of the brochure that he becomes a Scottish merchant. His statue in the garden in Nagasaki had him as English until it was very visibly changed, probably in 1999. When I asked the garden manager about it, he didn't remember the inscription ever having been altered. Despite the heavy scrape marks on the inscription, he didn't seem keen on the subject of the inscription at all, and pointed me back towards the views.

Unsurprisingly, the re-inscription of Scottishness on the statue has been tacitly claimed as a moral victory. A cutting from the (Aberdeen) *Evening Express* of 6 January 1999 describes one couple protesting too much by 'tak[ing] no credit':

> Mrs. Sunley said 'We only found out when we were sent a postcard by our friend Kazuko Takeshita which shows "Englishman" on the plaque changed to "Scotsman".'
> 'She knows the mayor of Nagasaki and mentioned it to him when we told her about the mistake.'

One reason for the alteration is doubtless the phrase attributed to Alex McKay, but probably originating with newspaper headline-writers of the 1980s. McKay's *Scottish Samurai* has been influential in Nagasaki and was prominent in both English and Japanese translation on the bookshelf in the garden manager's office.

The gardener chuckled in a way that told me he was bored stiff. He bent down to tend a row of pansies. After a few seconds, he straightened, looked pensive, and told me that he didn't know much about the Scotland stuff, but that if I wanted to find out about Glover, there were other ways. This part of the city had been left relatively intact by the atomic bomb, which had hit further east. And it had, after all, been less than a century since Glover had died. He took out a notebook from the pocket of his overalls, and leafed through it, then made notes on the last blank page. He tore the page out and handed it to me.

I almost trod on his flowers to take the page from him, then stepped back and unfolded it. It was a list of phone numbers.

TWO

The Deep North

On 24 July 1827, Thomas Berry Glover, a young Englishman of strict self-improving vision, entered the recruitment office of his local coast-guard. The service was relatively new, but there were plans for its expansion, and it was a solid job with prospects. He spoke with confidence and was offered the position.

Early in life Thomas Berry knew that he wanted to serve his country and to have a large family. During his career, the scope of the coastguard widened significantly. It fell under the powers of the Admiralty in 1856, in part as a result of the Crimean War which ended in that year, and became a reserve naval force. In photographs Thomas Berry is usually seen dressed in a suit or in his uniform, straight-backed. He soon cultivated the thick beard of the sea salt, which went white in middle age. He rose through the service steadily, especially since he was willing to move around. His patriotism and single-mindedness seemed almost to drive him to seek isolation and he started his career posted to the unthinkable location of Portsoy, Aberdeen-shire.

Thomas Berry Glover took up this post on 6 February 1828. Like his more famous son, being stationed in foreign parts only encouraged his libido: despite his isolation, he found his way into local society quickly enough to marry Mary Findlay of Fordyce, seven years his junior, just over a year into his tenure, on 3 July 1829. In marriage Mary Glover was given to shawls, headscarves and brooches, recalling the look of Queen Victoria, and spent much of her time indoors with her growing family. In the year after their marriage the first of the six Glover brothers, Charles Thomas, was born. William Jacob followed two years later, then James in 1833. Thomas Berry was promoted in 1835 to the position of chief officer at Fraserburgh, where the Thomas Glover Foundation is based today, and where speculation about Thomas junior's early years remains folklore.

Less remote than his first posting, the Fraserburgh job allowed Thomas Berry Glover to live with his wife and three sons in the aptly named Commerce Street, looking down onto the busy harbour. It was here, probably at number 15, that the next four children were born: Henry Martin, the only child not to survive beyond infancy, our Thomas Blake on 6 June 1838, and after them Alex Johnston and Martha Anne. If the house was indeed number 15, it was destroyed by bombing during World War Two.

At the time, Fraserburgh was a successful mercantile area, and Thomas Blake was born into a businesslike atmosphere: not only did he come into the world in Commerce Street, both witnesses on his birth certificate were bank clerks. But as the fifth son in a busy household, born too late for family funds to give him the same schooling as his brothers, he soon became restless. During infancy the port at the bottom of Commerce Street insinuated itself into his imagination. During childhood he watched his older brothers set up in Aberdeen as shipping clerks and determined to outdo their sound but unspectacular ambitions. Alex would be Thomas's closest playmate during childhood and would develop something like the same wanderlust as Thomas, later accompanying him on many of his foreign ventures.

In the 1840s Fraserburgh had a population of about 3,000, swelling to three times this during the herring season. Even so, it was primarily a trading port rather than a fishing port, and was connected via timber and other trades to Prussia, the Baltic countries and Russia, whose ships came and went. Fraserburgh residents stress the possibility that the children stayed here throughout Thomas's childhood, though it has often been assumed that his father took him to England at the age of six when he accepted two consecutive postings near Grimsby. Absence from or presence in Fraserburgh makes a significant difference to the Thomas Glover story, since it may be that in the passage between infant and boy lies the key to his later ambition and his ease with foreigners. Billy Watson, an art teacher in the town, has imaginatively suggested that the style of Broch windows of the time, topped with a radial semi-circle, resembles that of the Nagasaki Glover Garden house, Ipponmatsu, though Glover had minimal design input. Even more imaginatively, the unicorn which tops the statue in Fraserburgh's Saltoun Square, signifying hope, bears a similarity to the fabulous giraffe later used as a symbol of Glover's Kirin beer.

At the end of the street the younger Glovers ran errands for foreign sailors and tried to banter with them. This didn't arouse in Thomas or Alex any aptitude for foreign languages, but it did put them at ease with the bustle of international trade. They also witnessed the passage of large amounts of cash between the merchants and, in season, the fishermen, and understood that money could be earned in short periods. Thomas Berry Glover had told Thomas and Alex enough stories to make sure they knew that the seas which brought sailors from the Baltic were dangerous, but they could also see that these currents brought money.

The most significant Fraserburgh influence in the life of the adult Thomas, and a strong indication that he stayed in the town, was the building of a patent dock in the port during his infancy, in 1842. Designed for the construction and repair of ships, the dock was built in pieces in Aberdeen and shipped in, and was a major project for a town of Fraserburgh's size. The plans for the dock were drawn up by Robert Stevenson of the Stevenson engineering empire. Although Thomas was only four, as the coastguard's son he was certainly aware of the fuss over the dock, which hung in the air for years. His father, in his coastguard's post from 1835 to 1844 in a town of 3,000 people, was thoroughly acquainted with the project during its various phases. One of Thomas Blake's most successful projects in Japan, perhaps his single most important technological achievement, would closely resemble this patent dock.

Fraserburgh was known for another two activities close to the mature Thomas Blake Glover's heart: smuggling and political mischief. Some locals claim that Bonnie Prince Charlie plotted the '45 in Warld's End, a street near the harbour. One major Jacobite renegade, Lord Glenbuchat, certainly 'hid out' in the town – in fact he walked around freely without anyone giving him away – and organised various, mostly far-fetched, anti-Union schemes. A century later, it was a semi-official part of Thomas Berry's job to stop smuggling, but in practice a certain amount of contraband was permitted amidst the throng of trade. Soon, his fifth son would be engaged in a similar form of smuggling in a country beyond his imagination.

From 1844 to 1847 Thomas Berry Glover lived near Grimsby, first and very briefly in Sutton, and then in Saltfleet. As the Brochars say, it is possible that Glover senior went alone to England as a career move, leaving his family until promotion brought him back. As it happens, the conscientious but long absent father has since become a common figure in Japan. After his Fraserburgh appearance in the 1841 census, Thomas Blake turns up in the Bridge of Don 1851 census with no record between, leaving open both the possibility of his staying in Fraserburgh and going to England. But so persuasive is the influence of Broch culture in the later Thomas Blake's life, particularly the slipway and the maintenance of local contacts, that it is quite possible that Thomas Berry left the young children with their mother in the north-east.

Suggesting that he was indeed missing his family from afar, in 1847 Thomas Berry Glover's move to Collieston in north-east Scotland signalled a permanent return to the region. The station was an outpost separated from the nearest city of Aberdeen by the daunting distance of ten miles. There was a practical reason for his move back north: his older sons were nearing an age where they would require some steering in life, and the question of their schooling soon prompted another request for transfer, to a more urban station in the area. In his infancy Thomas Blake had attended the local parish school, in the huge and unruly class of a Mr Woodman in Saltoun Place, Fraserburgh, which allowed him to give vent to his boisterous nature without learning much. His father wanted him city-educated, a choice that would be vindicated, since it was in a more metropolitan setting that he would appeal to the future employer who took him to the Far East.

Thomas Berry's final posting was as chief coastguard in Oldmachar, now Bridge of Don, near the rapidly expanding city of Aberdeen, where the family moved in November 1849, to live in a large terraced house. In November the next year, after a gap that suggests his birth was unplanned, the now middle-aged Thomas Berry saw the appearance of his youngest son, Alfred.

Although Oldmachar was then slightly separated from the city, the landmarks of Old Aberdeen were visible from the house, in particular the university and St Machar's Cathedral. Oldmachar was, and remains, a well-to-do area with a growing population, in 1849 about 30,000. An official account from the time describes it as spacious and comfortable:

> This parish rises in a gentle slope from the sea, and though there is no eminence in it that deserves the name of a mountain, its surface is beautifully diversified by rising grounds. The windings of the Dee and the Don, the manufactories, and the woods on the banks of the latter, some detached clumps of planting on the rising grounds, interspersed with a number of gentlemen's seats and villas, – together with the various prospects of the sea, the rivers, the cities of Old and New Aberdeen, and the villages of Gilcomston and Woodside, – give a pleasant variety to the general appearance of this parish.

Thomas Berry watched as his younger children spent their early years playing in and around the River Don, or in the beaches to the east, while his older sons were making their way in the Aberdeen shipping business. He colluded with Thomas and Alex to conceal their swimming in the river from their mother, since some of its currents were notoriously treacherous. The real miracle, of course, is not that the boys avoided drowning in the Don, but that they avoided hypothermia.

Like most local children, the Glover children also enjoyed playing around the harbour, as Thomas and Alex had done in Fraserburgh. Thomas would later recall running down Market Street to watch 'the arrival of some foreign vessel, and spend hours running by the ships'. One formative event was the arrival of Queen Victoria in Aberdeen harbour on her way to Balmoral in September 1848 – Thomas Berry took his family to watch her arrival. And Marischal College was visited by Prince Albert, where Charles, then at the College, saw him in person. Throughout their lives the boys remained strongly monarchist: into the 1900s, often the worse for wear, Thomas would still be raising a glass 'to the queen'. The response to the 1848 visit shows how British monarchist pride fitted into the prosperous cosmopolitan atmosphere of Aberdeen for aspiring families like the Glovers.

Aberdeen and its environs have long stretches of beach, as the record of the 'gentle slope from the sea' suggests, and the seaside, the river at Oldmachar, and Aberdeen harbour made up a triangle of maritime play-grounds for the younger children, Thomas, Alex, and Martha. Both the Fraserburgh and Aberdeen residences provided easy access to attractive beaches which were then often used in a promenade style familiar to us from English resorts like Brighton, strange as it now seems given the weather. The Glovers often took their younger children on walks along the beach. The port of Aberdeen in the mid nineteenth century was home to a high proportion of foreigners, and later Thomas would send some very foreign foreigners to live in the city just as his father retired. Just over 100 years later, the discovery of oil would bring a new wave of business-minded incomers – some with a Texan version of the pragmatism that Thomas used in business – and the university, Scotland's second oldest, has increasingly attracted students from around the world. Today EU expansion again links Aberdeen to the Baltic, as Polish communities are becoming prominent in parts of the city. Scotland's third city has always been more multicultural than its map location suggests.

It was important to Thomas Berry that his sons grow up as self-supporting as he had himself. He gave them some experience in hunting in the mountains inland. Thomas and Alex showed an early prowess with firearms, presciently given that guns would become Thomas's main source of income in his twenties. It was also natural in Aberdeen for the children to learn to row, sail and navigate, and Thomas Berry made sure that Charles, William and James were proficient in seacraft before Grimsby, and Thomas and Alex after his return. Charles would later commission, and James captain, ships that Thomas Blake sold in Japan. Even as they grew too old to play by the sea, all remained aware of the sea's opportunities and dangers. In 1853 Thomas Berry was involved in the rescue operation of the *Duke of Sutherland* in Aberdeen harbour, in which 16 lives were lost. His participation was seen as an adventure by the young brothers, and didn't put them off a maritime life.

As hard as he worked to set up his children, the size of the Glover family meant that only the first three Glover brothers were able to go to Aberdeen Grammar School, one of the county's most prestigious institutions. After the bedlam of Fraserburgh, Thomas Blake attended the Gymnasium, the Chanonry House School, in Aberdeen, from 1851 to 1854, as a day pupil. Without the funds to send him to the Grammar School, this would be as far as his education would advance. The Gym was a genteel and conservative institution favouring the Classics, literacy and numeracy, and religious studies. The site of the old Gym has now been swallowed up by the campus of the University of Aberdeen, which holds most of the few mementoes of the school that remain. While Thomas was not an outstanding pupil, one of the students he would later help to smuggle out of Japan would become a star at the school in the 1860s. Despite his middling academic talent, Thomas Blake did absorb the Gym's stress on hard work and piety, and its aspirations for its students. A boarder of the time gives a flavour of the institution by describing a typical day:

> . . . School-work proper commenced at *8.45*, and continued with short intervals until *12.30*; dinner at *1.15*; classes again at *2*; dismissal at *4.15*; [and for boarders] tea at *5*; preparation classes from *6* to *8*; supper at *8.30*; prayers immediately after; and bed by *10*p.m. concluded the work of five out of the seven days. Saturday was a holiday, except that we had a drawing class from *8.30* to *10.30*a.m. On Sundays, we were allowed to go to any church we pleased in the forenoon; but in the evening we all went to 'Govie's' chapel some distance off. We were expected to take notes of one or other of the sermons we heard, which were handed in to 'Govie' or the tutor at 'good-night'.

Thomas Berry was a supporter of this religious discipline, which was often by rote and not open for discussion – the boarders felt privileged to go to 'any church they pleased' for half of each Sunday. Thomas Blake would continue to think of himself as a Christian, by default if not always from principle, and despite some of his un-Christian pursuits in Japan, he remained quietly pious throughout his life. The public school atmosphere of the Gym also comes through here in the sense of camaraderie. And the strongly Protestant spin of the sermons instilled the work ethic common amongst many Scottish imperial adventurers of the time. The same memoirist suggests that the Gym was the kind of school used to sending graduates to overseas appointments:

> Curious stories could be told of 'our boys' . . . of some of those who slept in the same dormitories meeting accidentally in the wilds of Africa, and on the shores of China, proving that the world is not so very big after all.

Thomas Berry had been right if he thought that his move to Oldmachar would give the boys global opportunities.

For financial reasons, only the eldest son, Charles, was able to progress from the Grammar School to Marischal College, Aberdeen University. His attendance from 1844 to 1848 was a sign of prestige for the family, and at this point the self-improving father felt that he had made it. A son at university was definitely a social step up. It's tempting to think that Thomas Blake might have wanted to pursue his education further had funds allowed, but there are no indications that his practical mind was suited to the academic disciplines of the day. If anything, Thomas's practicality marked him out for a career of entrepreneurism, where a Scottish university education of the 1850s would have been more generalist and moral. As well as being strongly Protestant, the Gym was also Anglophile in its practical emphasis, a stance that is sometimes described as threatening Scottish general thought – the tradition of linking various studies through philosophy or first principles. The apex of the Anglicising movement in Scottish education is usually seen as being the Education Act of 1872, passed not long after Thomas and Alex had finished their studies.

The elderly Thomas Blake discounted any idea that his success had been related to academic ability. He may not have been gifted, but nor did he get into any serious trouble, despite his boisterousness. He fitted well into the public school scheme of things at the Gym, which would come in useful in a gentlemanly later life of semi-diplomacy and mask his brusque manner and short temper. Trained under the Gym's work ethic, the young Glovers were expected to succeed in a way that was both financially canny and self-improving, perhaps even in imperial regions formal or informal, like the newly opened China described by the Gym's diarist. Most importantly, in this tradition Christian piety and individual ambition were far from mutually exclusive: both fell under the umbrella of improvement.

Thomas Berry's older sons set up in Aberdeen as shipping merchants, and ship clerking was working well for them by the time Thomas and Alex finished at the Gym. Thomas followed, briefly, but his school years had shown him to be unsettled and slightly overshadowed by his more educated brothers. His pique became a spark of tenacity, and tenacious Aberdeen boys of gentlemanly education were in the sights of scouts for the growing Scottish overseas trading companies, particularly the Far Eastern giant Jardine Matheson.

Although Thomas Berry had engineered the possibility of opportunity for his sons, he was as surprised as the rest of the family when number five son got the call from Jardine Matheson. Thomas's overseas opportunities were seen by the brothers in the same self-improving light as their father had seen his own career rather than, in more modern terms, the chance to encounter other cultures, and it would be anachronistic to view Thomas as setting out with the idealism of a gap year student. Connection to a large concern like the East India Company, Dent & Co. or Jardine Matheson, was another step up in the strict Victorian class system. The Jardine Matheson boys might even be described as maritime lads o' pairts – though the Glover family was too prosperous for the substantial rise of at least one of their sons to have seemed unlikely. Thomas Blake's wilfulness had been difficult to academicise but was easy to turn into business imagination, and he had felt stultified by the prospect of spending his entire life in one place, a mood vividly recreated by Alan Spence in his novelisation, *The Pure Land*. What happened in the couple of years between the Gym and the Jardine Matheson headhunting remains unclear, but for at least some of the time Thomas worked as a shipping clerk in James George's office in Marischal Street, Aberdeen. He was certainly involved in some minor aspect of shipping business, and was less than satisfied.

What trading houses like Jardine Matheson were looking for were boys of high ambition who showed strength of character useful in negotiation and who were willing to spend years away from their families. In Thomas Blake's case, the scouts may have been masons: one of the buildings in the Glover Garden complex in Nagasaki is a masonic lodge, and there is a close system of business contacts running through his career. Jardine Matheson invited Thomas to interview sometime in early 1857 at the age of 18, and not long after he was posted to China.

Glover is not noted, though, in the *China Directory* – a gazetteer covering the whole of East Asia and produced in Hong Kong – until 1861, when he had been joined by brother James. By this time Thomas had been in the Far East for almost four years. By the time of the 1861 census of Oldmachar, Thomas Berry's household consisted of himself and his wife, a staff of two, who would probably have lived locally and come every day, daughter Martha, and the only 'scholar', or juvenile, the young Alfred. Between the 1850s and Thomas Berry's retirement in 1864, all the other surviving sons of the family had joined their father in maritime trades: from Charles down to Alfred, they were all either shipping clerks or had taken to the sea on business.

Thomas Berry was both saddened and relieved when his fifth son jumped at the chance of employment by Jardine Matheson in China, at the time a hugely lucrative part of Britain's informal empire (territory unoccupied but subject to trading treaties advantageous to the settlers). He had recognised the possibility of at least one son drifting abroad and realised the scale of the opportunity. He had had them well educated, and knew that aspiring Aberdeen boys made good emissaries. The city, after having played an important but largely unsung role in the Scottish Enlightenment, was becoming a key point of the British empire in a way it hadn't in the previous century, or even in the previous decade. In December 1850, when Thomas Blake was nine, the city had been joined to the capital of the imperial homeland by the opening of a new railway station.

The new Jardine Matheson employee who left Aberdeen was growing into, as Naito Hatsuho says, 'a five foot six, 34-inch chested man, weighing 130 pounds'. He had a moustache from his early twenties and thinning hair from not much later. W.B. Mason recalls him as being '[e]ndowed with a fine physique and a courtly manner that captivated Japanese and foreigners – men and women alike'. Most accounts have him as well-built and handsome, though this description may have something to do with protocol and something to do with apologia for his womanising. Alan Spence also makes him a reader of Burns, hinting at the same magnetic character of the méchant. In all the photographs that remain – Glover took lots of family pictures, mercifully, since he left no journal and few proper letters – he is always well-groomed and well-comported. In middle years, he was typically seen in a three-piece suit with watch-chain and later a light two-piece suit and straw boater, resembling a British colonial governor.

The happy tragedy for Thomas Berry was that every surviving brother would follow Thomas Blake around the world. Soon after Thomas Berry retired, even the young Alfred took the trip as soon as possible. Even the lone daughter Martha, who had stayed with her father until his death, ended up in Nagasaki in 1889 – the last of the siblings to arrive. Martha married James George in 1861, but widowed, moved back in 1867 to her parents' home at Braehead, the house Thomas Blake had by then bought for them. The oldest brother, Charles, a model shipping clerk when the younger brothers were finishing the Gym, would prove invaluable to Thomas Blake's Japanese projects in the years around the restoration of the Japanese emperor under a new government in 1868. It was Charles who commissioned the building of the three huge ships by Alexander Hall & Sons of Aberdeen that would form the backbone of the new Japanese Imperial Navy and for which Thomas Blake would become celebrated. Charles also helped with the bit-by-bit construction of the Kosuge Slipway which allowed ships to be worked on in the water, recalling the Fraserburgh dock of 1842. When Charles died of cancer in Aberdeen in 1877, he was relatively unknown in Britain, despite his role in the establishment of the Japanese Imperial Navy and his management of several Glover projects.

The brother below Charles, James Lindsay, born in 1833, went to China in 1859 and, as far as we know, then to Japan in August 1861, the year that Thomas was officially listed in the *China Directory*. Thomas's reluctance to register himself in the *Directory* before this point may hint at the dubious status of his business partner, and James may have triggered his registration. James returned to Aberdeen in 1864, but died a year later, aged 35. Alex also set sail for China, then Nagasaki in 1863, to join his closest brother. Alex helped Thomas build Guraba Shokai, Glover Trading, and became Thomas's greatest confidant in business. William Jacob Glover, born in 1832, captained a number of ships to Japan. He was in the wreck of the first ship built for the Japanese in Aberdeen, the *Satsuma*, in 1864, but survived and joined Thomas in his political activities of the mid 1860s before returning to Braehead. The baby of the family, Alfred, born in 1850, outdid the youthfulness of Thomas's emigration by arriving in Nagasaki in

1867. He worked in the office of Thomas's Takashima mine, for the well-known Nagasaki firm Henry Gribble, and later for Thomas's sometime collaborator Holme Ringer. Alfred was active in Nagasaki life, founding its St Andrew's Society (British loyalists, despite the name).

All of the surviving Glover sons had left Aberdeen for China and Japan by 1867, three years after their father had retired and might have expected to have his family around him. It was the kind of success a parent longs for and dreads. Having spent so long preparing a path for his sons, he had to watch as they took up opportunities on the other side of the world.

THREE

Chinese Whispers

T he reasons for Jardine Matheson's appointing Thomas Blake Glover are not documented, even in their own records, and may have involved exotic handshakes. We don't know. We do know that Thomas was performing well enough in Aberdeen alongside Alex and James to seem a good bet for the company. He was likely, after an education at the Gym, to be politically loyalist and good at keeping out of trouble. From boyhood he had an invaluable gift for cunning, as numerous Fraserburgh fishermen found out.

Glover's reputation as a hard worker would remain with him throughout his life. He was described by an early Jardine Matheson colleague as 'resourceful and capable'. The company's choice proved to be a good one, initially. When he was shipped to Shanghai, his reaction to his most trying times would be to throw himself into his work. Sickened by the smells of the harbour, insecure, often hungover, he reacted by getting his head down. Nor was Sunday exempt in this non-Christian country, a shock to some of the boys from more puritan backgrounds. Glover was also perfect in being untouched by any ideals that might get in the way of trade in the fierce world of imperial business. Jardine Matheson operated a merciless version of free trade in China, and had become something like an East India Company for the Far East, largely run by Scots.

When Glover chose to go to China neither he nor the company had any idea that he would eventually travel further east. When he left Aberdeen, he had no idea where Japan was. His emigration followed the end of the Second Opium War (1856) when Britain and other western powers struggled to enforce free trade on China. The infamous Scottish imperialist Lord Napier had been sent to Macao as a troubleshooter as early as 1834, and William Jardine of Jardine Matheson had lobbied the British government to fight the First Opium War. When the war was only a month old, Jardine sketched out a plan for a new economic order. Following the Nanking/Nanjing Treaty on 29 August 1842, which formalised Chinese concessions to trade after the First Opium War (1839–42), the country

opened five ports to western trade, including Shanghai, and Jardine Matheson
& Sons established themselves in the new formal colony of Hong Kong.
Hong Kong would remain a long-term base in the Far East for Jardine
Matheson, a staging point for Scots in the Far East, and a touchstone for
Glover in his dealings. Although China was not occupied, the country was
routinely reminded that it was in no position to resist aggressive trading.
Lord Palmerston (Henry Temple, Third Viscount Palmerston), who would
become known for his uncompromising foreign policy, became Prime
Minister in 1855, a position he held for a decade, with a brief interregnum
in 1858/9. He sent a subduing eight-boat attack to China in 1856, a year
before Glover arrived.

Glover's passport was granted in August 1857. There is no definite record
of his date of travel, but ships travelling east left Southampton on the 10th
and 26th of each month, and since he received his passport on 14 August,
it is unlikely that he was on the ship that left on the 26th. He probably
left on 10 September. He arrived in Shanghai on 25 November 1857. This
was his first intercontinental sailing, and the indications are that it was far
from smooth. Arriving in Hong Kong after a passage of two and a half
months, he relaxed briefly with the traditional Scottish pursuits of drinking
and accounting, before sailing into Shanghai through the Yangtzee.

The morning of 26 November 1857 in Shanghai was the first time Glover
woke up to a truly foreign atmosphere. Unfamiliar sounds and the scent of
aniseed and seaweed floated on a sharp windless air. On the quay, Cantonese
mixed with European languages including Broad Scots. By now over his
seasickness, it must have struck him how far he had come from home. From
the outset, he dedicated himself to his work with a sense of bravado, trying
to look at least as tough as the coolies, as he termed the native workers.
The young Glover was lean and muscular and probably slightly imposing
to native eyes.

Shanghai sprawled along a long urban coastline which went under the
generic name 'the Bund', a term coined by British colonials in India. Forced
into unequal trade, in 1857 the city was undergoing a period of rapid
change. Parts of it were under de facto foreign control, where foreign traders
were protected by French and British armies in makeshift citadels ringing
the foreign quarters. Under a state of semi-occupation, Shanghai was a
desperate city, though relatively safe for British merchants. The more entrepreneurial Chinese were accepting of incoming merchants, and were ready to
trade in almost any products beyond the 'big three' of silk, tea, and opium.

The city also had domestic problems, in the form of the Taipeng rebellion, which saw huge numbers of Chinese poor pushing eastwards into the city – largely due to China's loss of power after the Opium Wars. To the 19-year-old Glover, the situation was one of confusion on all sides. He concentrated on the cargoes that were offloaded in front of the makeshift offices, sometimes venturing to harangue the local dockers, who looked at him with bemusement. Shanghai was filling with foreign companies and representatives like him, young and ambitious. Most found their feet quickly, or made a show of doing so. Voraciously profit-driven, they were soon pushing for a version of free trade even more advantageous to the settlers, seeing their own government as being too lenient on pockets of native reticence. Some cavaliers even began talking about access to the mysterious and newly opened nation to the east, to the muffled sighs of the Foreign Office.

Throughout the 1850s foreign speculators in Shanghai had been trading everything that would turn a profit, but opium remained foremost. In her celebrated account, Harriet Sergeant describes the newly opened city:

> In its early years as an international city, Shanghai resembled a colonial outpost. After the Treaty of Nanjing in 1842 trading houses like Jardine Matheson and Dent & Co. dispatched young and healthy men to open branch offices. Along the edges of the Whangpoo, on land covered with mulberry trees and ancestral graves, they built comfortable houses with arched verandahs and red-tiled roofs. They planted their compounds with tulip trees, roses and magnolias. Behind lay the merchants' godowns (warehouses) and homes for the Chinese assistants. The larger firms had two or three partners, eight or ten foreign clerks and fifty or sixty Chinese staff. They dealt principally in silk, tea and opium. Opium clippers arrived from India and, as a gesture to the drug's illegality in China, discharged their contents into hulks lining the Whangpoo before clearing customs.

As spring 1858 wafted in, the Bund got warmer, and began to stink. The entire harbour area had become an open market. For the hours after work, there were knots of ex-pat bars and drinking clubs, and 'recreation' districts offering prostitution to foreign sailors. Lurid stories can be told of child prostitution in the Shanghai of the time, but the sex industry was only expanded to service foreigners, and fell perfectly into line with the Newtonian laws of supply and demand seared onto the retinas of speculators like Glover. He was under as few illusions over the recreation districts as he was over the token gestures towards smuggled opium. Both existed because the money was now needed by the Chinese. Suddenly alone, the young Glover developed a lifelong habit of paid women, although a mild one compared to some of his workmates, especially the short-termers who made their profits and ran. An opium habit was something he never developed, otherwise his career would have finished in Shanghai, as it did for some of the boys. But there is something ironic about the status of Jardine Matheson boys if we compare it to today's vilified position of the dealer in opiates, especially heroin. Glover was, of course, still only 19 or 20, driven by ambition, and didn't think too much about his cargo – but the same is true of heroin dealers today. A vital part of his work for Jardine Matheson was to check the crates of imported opium, write inventories, and prepare the product for distribution.

Almost all the foreigners tried opium – the drug was not yet stigmatised, at least amongst the middle classes – but Glover remained too driven by self-improvement to get drawn into opiate daydreams. The prevailing understanding of free trade demanded the expansion of the market to new customers.

This was a place in which, as far as Glover knew, he would be making his long-term home. But while looking forward to the possibility of a lucrative future, he became dissatisfied with the routine of working, drinking and prostitution. His workmates were of the same type, though most lacked his ambition. In a Peter Pan-like atmosphere away from the grown-ups, Glover avoided opium, but he did adopt the habit of hard drinking common to the young men. Shanghai was a place of great opportunity, but also one of great loneliness and uncertainty, and few wholesome outdoor pursuits or days off in which to pursue them. The sudden loss of home comforts fuelled the traders' addictions, as did the 'lack of western women' as it is sometimes put, as if discussing the copper market. The stress of profit-making was constant: a willingness to seek out trading loopholes was the reason these characters had been chosen. These emissaries were like the wide-boy currency traders of 1980s London, and it would be fitting if a film were made of Glover's life with the lead played by Ewan McGregor, who also played the over-caffeinated bad boy of Singapore finance, Nick Leeson, in James Dearden's film *Rogue Trader* (1999). Making a profit in 1850s Shanghai was shooting fish in a barrel, though the money would soon seem minor compared to what would be found further east.

Even before Glover reached Shanghai, rumours had begun to circulate of the opening of a country yet further away. The American Commodore Matthew Perry's 'black ships' had forced their way into Shimoda in central Honshu in 1853, leading to the Convention of Kanagawa on 31 March 1854, at which were agreed the opening of Shimoda, Perry's point of attack in Shizuoka in the middle of the biggest island of Honshu, and Hakodate in the northern island of Hokkaido. For the Shanghai traders, the fascination of the new country to the east was also what made it such a difficult prospect. Japan proved much more resistant than China in the face of enforced free trade by the four big nations – Britain, the US, France and Russia – and had strongly opposed being 'opened' in 1853. The government at this point consisted of a ruling group, the bakufu, led by the shogun, who formed a de facto national executive that claimed to represent the emperor, but which was resisted by other daimyo, or clan leaders. The daimyo considered themselves more loyal to the emperor, and pushed for his restoration. Rebel activity was particularly strong in the southwest, on the island of Kyushu, and had a strong base in Kyushu's northwestern city, Nagasaki, where Glover would soon be headed. Palmerston never tried his Opium War gunboat tactics on Japan in the 1850s: Japan would have tried to resist his advances by military means, though would undoubtedly have failed. In all, Japan received the attentions of far fewer diplomats and businesses than China.

But to the traders of Shanghai, Japan's reputation for danger seemed to corroborate the idea that gains were to be had. Still, until the late 1850s everything had been guesswork: having pursued a policy of sakoku, closed borders, for over two centuries, the country was a black hole which no traveller could enter, and from which no native could escape. Defections were extremely rare and punishable by death without trial, often by ritual suicide. Little was known about the country's legal and social structures, except that they were unforgiving of transgression. Unsurprisingly, many of the laddish Shanghai traders found this system of summary justice perversely appealing. As Consul Rutherford Alcock salaciously observed, '[t]he severity of the Japanese laws is excessive, the code is probably the bloodiest in the world; for death is the penalty of most offences'.

During the era of sakoku, Dutch was the only western language widely spoken in Japan, in the small strip of free land, Dejima, whose boardwalk is now an oasis lined with chain restaurants. In the early nineteenth century, rangaku, Dutch Studies, had exerted its power over seigaku, Chinese Studies, encouraged by figures like Philip Franz von Siebold, a Nagasaki doctor and botanist who compiled huge studies on Japanese culture and promoted the use of the Dutch language. But during the 1850s and 1860s both Dutch and Chinese suddenly crumbled under yogaku, studies of the west in English. There remain stories from the time of travellers who studied Dutch to make the trip to Japan and were surprised to find themselves addressed in a language they couldn't understand. As it happens, the first recorded English teacher in the country was a half-Scot half-Inuit called Ranald Macdonald. He arrived in Japan before 1854 but was popular enough amongst the locals to be spared the death penalty, and fascinated some samurai with broken tales of technologies like steamships and telegraph, helping to prime the market for Glover and his colleagues.

After the 1854 opening, and having had one eye on the Chinese Opium War, Japan was a country going through a speedy process of fiscal preparation for military defence – the first time in centuries it had had to spend any significant money on a foreign policy. Japan's efforts nevertheless only emphasised the technological gap, and came too late to prevent the country's acceptance of the Ansei Treaties (Unequal Treaties/Ansei Keiyaku), a group of agreements with foreign powers to open its ports from 1859. The Ansei Treaties represented the same kind of economic process as had been imposed on China, but without gunboats, at least in the beginning. Even after aggressive interpretations of the Nanjing Treaty, the Euro-American traders in Shanghai had continued to lobby for an even freer trade environment. Glover contributed to this activism, and it is from his devotion to total free trade that his early acquaintances with ambitious rebel samurai in Japan developed, even though it would seem that his interest in opening the country was directly opposed to their interest in protecting it. Ironically, later in life, he would campaign to overturn the Ansei Treaties to give the Japanese empire a chance to compete.

In 1858 the British government lent its voice to the pressure of the Shanghai traders and forced a trade agreement onto the Japanese shogun. A wary diplomatic corps was dispatched to Japan. As Consul Rutherford Alcock recalled:

In consequence of the treaty entered into with the government of the Tycoon by the Earl of Elgin in 1858, it became necessary to establish a permanent diplomatic mission in Japan; and it was yet early in the spring of the following year when I received, at Canton, the first intimation of my appointment as its head. To me as to the rest of the world probably at this period, Japan was but a *terra incognita*.

When trader gossip about the unknown land began to mount in Shanghai, Glover became interested. He was already weary of the routine and squalor of Shanghai's makeshift marketplace. Despite the dangers, he was ready to move on, to the new profits which seemed inevitable. As a grafter, he was also starred by the company, who wanted to see him progress. Never a great reader, he was nonetheless keen on the guidebook *Nippon*, then circulating amongst the Shanghai traders, and he attended lectures on Japan by the law professor S.W. Williams. When Alcock's 'treaty entered into with the government of the Tycoon' brought the eastern horizon within reach, he was amongst the first to request transfer.

Japan had been approachable for only about five years when Glover arrived. The country's non-political classes perceived that something was happening. Shocked by the flood of white faces, but kept more or less ignorant of the workings of government, they didn't grasp the importance of the opening. The bakufu had been suddenly awoken by the appearance of the American black ships in 1853, and had dithered in its response to American Commodore Matthew Perry until it was clear even to their own samurai, both loyalist and rebel, that they were powerless against a western military attack. The bakufu's lack of international influence, realised too late, was viewed with a sense of vindication by Japan's rebel samurai, who had long been pushing for openness to foreign military technology within an attitude of joi. Joi is often transliterated as 'Expel the foreigner!', complete with exclamation mark, but jo derives from cleaning or wiping, and i is difference, suggesting 'ethnic cleansing' as a translation. Nevertheless joi had a double aim of maintaining ethnic purity and aspiring to foreign logistics, meaning that the joi rebels were more willing to be 'open' than the recognised government. The rebels were always destined to be on Glover's side, if he could find a way to negotiate with them.

The British had followed the Americans in the few years after 1853 and were central in negotiating the Ansei Treaties. The French who, until a rapid conversion at the last minute before the imperial restoration, were the only major supporters of the bakufu, were nevertheless not far behind, securing a trade agreement on 9 October 1859. In the same year, Jardine Matheson started to allow the most promising of their volunteers to move into Japan. Although the Ansei Treaties weren't supposed to take effect until 1 July 1859, Glover's early Jardine Matheson mentor Kenneth Ross Mackenzie moved to Nagasaki in the New Year, to do more of what he had been doing AWOL in inner China, dealing on the fringes of the law in silk, tea, and now, from Okinawa, sugar. In moving to Japan early, Mackenzie had become one of the illegal aliens subject to beheading if discovered, without recourse to his own government.

Mackenzie, like Glover, viewed himself as a moderniser of the east in terms of free trade at any cost. Then as now, modernisation in a new market meant sweeping aside any political system which got in the way of the set-up of the new firms. The bakufu were instantly disliked because of their ingrained truculence in the face of foreign trade. The fact that Mackenzie invited Glover to help him in Japan suggests that Glover had been, like his mentor, aggressive, entrepreneurial and probably operating well outside the law in China. Glover arrived in Nagasaki on 19 September – safely after the legal beginning of the Treaties – by which time Mackenzie had already been living there illegally for some time, and had had some of the richest pickings.

After the enactment of the Ansei Treaties, the small Dutch area of trading concessions, Dejima, had become part of the wider kyoryuchi, or foreign settlements. Throughout sakoku, there been occasional but regular envoys to China, which tend to get forgotten in histories of western modernisation – in part because of the later Japanese policy of datsua, or deliberate separation from an Asia perceived as backward. During the 1860s period of rapid Japanese expansion, Chinese traders were often more prominent and more successful in the foreign settlements than western ones. The Chinese were amongst the pioneers in commerce and culture, even though when we say pioneering we often mean western.

On 19 September 1859 the weather around Nagasaki was not typical. The whole bay area was covered in a fog thick enough to cause Glover's ship to slow down to keep its direction on the way into harbour. Nagasaki-bound ships snaked in through an island chain to land at Dejima, and one of the qualities which made Nagasaki a key territory from the opening to World War Two was this physical concealment: the harbour is protected by the archipelago, as well as being banked on three sides by long and steep mountains. (But explanations of the city's military importance, as concretised in the Mitsubishi shipyards, as a reason for the 1945 atomic bombing are misleading: targets were chosen primarily for experimental reasons including population density.) Though Glover would have sensed the outline of these mountains when he first sailed into Japan, nerves on edge, he didn't see much of the country on the first day. Even with the boldness he had brought from Fraserburgh, approaching Dejima he likely questioned his own wisdom. With samurai lying in wait, it was quite possible that he wouldn't last the night in Nagasaki.

The fog helps to explain why people figure larger than landscape in Glover's first sense of the country. His impressions were immediate and practical: when he was able to pick out the harbour he was struck by the concentration of the workers going about their business, the orderliness of the town, the slated roofs, and the temples. It was far from the pandemonium of Shanghai. Deep in fog which concealed assassins real and imagined, the city was eerily quiet.

For the European reps who managed the 'coolies', there was little gentility in what was still frontier territory. Alongside Glover's respect for Japan's upper political echelons there was a casualness in dealing with manual workers which only increased his feeling of sympathy for samurai. Samurai had been trained to see themselves as natural occupiers of a managerial caste, and Glover had been educated into a comparable class tradition at the Gym. So although every first impression was of danger, samurai would be kin in a natural elitism. Still, during his first few weeks and months, Glover found himself constantly dodging samurai of both bakufu and rebel loyalties, not knowing where an attack might come from next.

Glover didn't record the event of his landing, but by a happy coincidence Consul Alcock, with a habit of boarding-school diarism, also arrived in a mysterious fog, though later and under the cover of the Foreign Office:

> even under a cloudy sky the entrance [to Nagasaki] was not devoid of beauty. Island after island comes into view as the bay is entered, many very picturesque in form. As the ship moves farther up the bay, the town of Nagasaki is seen lying at the farther end, clustering at the foot of a range of hills, and creeping no inconsiderable distance up the wooded sides. *Decima* [Dejima] to the right fixed the eye – a low, fan-shaped strip of land, dammed out from the waters of the bay, the handle being towards the shore, and truncated. One long wide street, with two-storied houses on each side, built in European style, gives an air of great tidiness; but they looked with large hollow eyes into each other's interiors, in a dismal sort of way, as if they had

been so engaged for six generations at least, – and were quite weary of the view.

Similarly for Richard Brunton, the Aberdeenshire engineer later employed by Robert Louis Stevenson's family to rebuild Japan's system of lighthouses with a nudge from the invisible hand of Glover: 'Nagasaki, a specially interesting port with a harbour entirely backed by lofty hills, is one of the world's most beautiful, even as it is the safest in the world.' Brunton landed in relative peace after the 1867–68 civil war had been settled. For Glover arriving in September 1859, safe was not a word which came to mind.

Now a veteran trader of 21, when Glover found reliable ground in Nagasaki, he re-engaged with a community populated by the hard core of the traders, those who had been willing to take the early step from China. Disorientated and defensive, he again buried himself in work. His first letter to Jardine Matheson Shanghai is dated 22 September 1859, only three days after he arrived. He took to the diet – a mixture of Chinese, local and imported European food – without problems, and probably with some relief: local Japanese food is amongst the healthiest and most various in the world. He moved into a house owned by the company in October in the new kyoryuchi, and was employed as clerk to Mackenzie, who soon characteristically moved east to Yokohama to test the market there.

The traders of 1859 arrived in the first non-Chinese, post-sakoku ships to come to the country legally, and were an object of wonder, if not welcome, to all the natives. For years, Glover would operate in a climate in which joi attacks were common, undertaken by the many rogue samurai who, having lived their lives in isolation, found the Ansei Treaties inconceivable. The anti-bakufu samurai especially, opposing their own government, were loath to recognise any contracts with the outside world. Still, some of the attacks were for legitimate reasons of local law, for example trespassing or insulting daimyo, laws often ignored by outsiders. The British Foreign Office was used to getting its own way abroad further west, and had few qualms in putting its traders in the front line. From a safe distance, Rutherford Alcock ordered ships from China to deliver a pacifying attack in mid December 1859, only provoking 'terrorist' counter-attacks on European houses, churches and interpreters, European or native, and endangering his own country's merchants.

For a year the sporadic attacks escalated, then one of the first major assaults on the British in Japan came in July 1861, when the Edo (Tokyo) Legation was sacked by several dozen samurai, who injured and almost killed the Legation secretary Laurence Oliphant and consul George Morrison. In darkness, Morrison fought off samurai of unknown allegiance with a pistol, and was saved by a single oak beam above his head as he crouched, later emerging to see a deep sword cut in the wood. The shogunate were embarrassed, not for the first time, about failing to protect British diplomats, as the terms of the Treaties demanded. The Kyushu traders felt the tremors: there would be no such embarrassment if they were attacked. During the summer of 1861, many of the traders moved their socialising from the makeshift drinking clubs to their own rooms, and drowned their fears in Dejima Dutch courage. The Foreign Office was duly outraged at an attack on their own representatives, which was reported in the *Nagasaki Shipping List* of 20 July:

> We have heard a report and endeavoured, but unsuccessfully, to trace its source in this place, that there has been a serious disturbance at Kanagawa . . . That the residence of the British Consul had been violently broken into by about forty armed men – that they had been resisted and defeated, but that in the scuffle some wounds had been received by the English party. Mr. Oliphant, as we heard, was severely wounded on the wrist.

The emerging Anglophone press did little to instil calm after the Legation attack. It was all good copy, and, as the news developed, the *Nagasaki Shipping List* became more worked up:

> The noise which aroused the sleepers and awakened all to the impending peril was a determined effort to burst open the main door, upon which (as described) the blows fell like the discharge of musketry. A legion seemed to be at the work. I should think, if there was time for any sensation, those who appreciated the reality of the attack must have felt the cold hand of death – and such a death – upon them! Japanese assassins, reckless of their own lives, seldom leave their work unfinished, and here they were with clamour and yell within a few paces of their destined prey . . .
>   . . . The darkness, intensified by the flashes from the pistol, rendered it difficult for the assailed to see their enemies or the effect upon them; but it is certain that the retaliation blows, intended to be *avenging*

blows, were struck, the latter retreated by a side passage, leaving drops
of blood and bloody finger marks upon their track. They kicked down
the screen of the room from which they were fired upon and in which
there was a lamp burning, evidently to lighten their way down the
passage: and passing another bed-room one of them must have entered
it; a book upon the table was cut through – the mosquito curtains
were cut across as with a razor, and a pine bed-post two inches thick
was broken by a blow which *cut* an inch deep into it: the mattress
was also thrust through in a most malicious manner. By this time,
which must have passed quicker than the narration, the six occupants
of the building were assembled in the verandah beyond the drawing
room, entirely ignorant of the numbers of their assailants or the direction in which they would come, anticipating only a final struggle and
immediate slaughter. Of the six, one was completely disabled
[unarmed], and amongst the rest were only two revolvers and two or
three swords – one a dress sword, – not a bad weapon for a single
encounter, but less serviceable against a rush of heavily armed foes . . .
there would be space for fighting at close quarters and from the darkness
the assassins could be fired upon as they approached through the
lighted room. But to the surprise of all, they did not come and silence
soon ensued.

Speed, blades and ruthlessness are all typically recurring motifs in British
descriptions of Japan of the time, brought together here in the tone of an
adventure thriller. Ernest Satow, a diplomat who would become one of
Glover's longest-standing allies, was more balanced about the attack, filling
in a background of anti-foreign action during Glover's time leading up to
the one on the Legation, attacks which had been missed by the Foreign
Office because they hadn't been aimed at Brits:

In November [1859], a Chinese servant belonging to the French vice-
consul was attacked and killed in the foreign settlement at Yokohama.
Two months later, Sir R. Alcock's native linguist of the British Legation
was stabbed from behind as he was standing in the gateway of the
British Legation in Yedo [Edo/Tokyo], and within a month more two
Dutch merchant captains were slaughtered in the high street at Yokohama.
Then there was a lull for eight or nine months, till the French Minister's
servant was cut and badly wounded as he was standing at the gate of

the Legation in Yedo. On the 14th January, 1861, Heusken, the Secretary of the American Mission, was attacked and murdered as he was riding home after a dinner-party at the Prussian Legation. And on the night of July 5 occurred the boldest attempt yet made on the life of foreigners, when the British Legation was attacked by a band of armed men and as stoutly defended by the native guard.

After the attack, Consul F. Howard Vyse 'call[ed] . . . for the British Community to be calm' in the *Nagasaki Shipping List* of 31 July 1861. Vyse was, like the Victorian British colonial administrator of legend, perpetually calling for people to simmer down, even with katana trained on their heads. Glover held his nerve better than most, with the aid of long, distracting working days, and his willingness to accustom himself to foreignness, which often puzzled the diplomats who had come through a school system keeping them far from anything like a Russian fisherman in Fraserburgh.

The overwhelming sense of danger of those first few years was made especially troubling by the fact that joi was not exclusive to the rebel clans: bakufu loyalists were also prone to breaking their own shogun's treaty promises. Any Japanese nobleman was dangerous, and there was no way of knowing which samurai to avoid. The two sets of loyalties seemed locked into an unholy alliance incomprehensible to the foreigners: there was a kind of contest between samurai of the bakufu and the rebels to prove who was more joi and therefore more loyal to the emperor. The bakufu insisted that its ruling samurai in Kyoto were the true protectors of the country's purity. But unprotected trading firms, including the Nagasaki branch of Jardine Matheson, continued to be in danger from both sides. The Brits would receive an even greater shock in May 1863 when the Edo US Legation was burned down entirely, with little trace of a culprit, and therefore little food for the hysteria of the *Nagasaki Shipping List*. Extraordinarily, Glover would soon harness the joi energy of the very samurai responsible for this arson and, through a combination of rhetoric and brazenness, squeeze their anger into the mould of British free trade.

FOUR

A Chancer

It was never a childhood ambition of Glover's to go to Japan. Before Shanghai, his knowledge of the country, like that of most Britons, was next to nil. China was dangerous enough to unsettle his mother, who was relieved to see her older sons educated and safe. Thomas was now further away from home than any of the family had ever thought he would be, and, despite his boldness in going east, in his early twenties his goal was, like the other Jardine Matheson boys, to get rich and stay alive doing it, then get out.

He had volunteered for the trip to Japan early, and the reference for his passage had arisen from an encounter with the veteran entrepreneur Kenneth Ross Mackenzie, a fellow Scot already notorious in the Far East for his casual attitude towards trade agreements. Mackenzie's bending the rules didn't trouble Jardine Matheson. Their connection to him was increasingly loose, they were used to turning a blind eye, and their profits depended on not knowing exactly what was going on. Mackenzie met Glover in Shanghai, probably in a drinking house, and soon realised the younger man's ambition. Together, the two became smugglers and traders in the big three products – silk, tea and opium – accustoming Glover to lawbreaking in a way which would soon see him embroiled in Japanese politics.

Mackenzie was both a sage and a liability. When Glover arrived in Nagasaki, Mackenzie was waiting for him at the docks, nominally to protect him but making the situation even more dangerous. Summers in Kyushu are very humid, and, although by mid September it would have been cooling, it would still usually clear 30 degrees in the daytime. In September 1859, had been a long hot summer, and samurai on both sides were restless. Especially in the west of Japan, midsummer is hot enough to encourage a kind of craziness, made more extreme by small rooms, hard work, and, for the western agents, formal dress. In later life, during the hottest part of the summer, Glover would take to escaping to the peaceful mountain temple area of Lake Chuzenji, now known as the popular tourist spot of Nikko. His Nagasaki house Ipponmatsu was positioned to catch mountain breezes, and was much bigger and more airy than most Japanese houses. As soon as electrification came, it would be fitted with ceiling fans. But for the whole of his life in Japan, stepping outside during the hottest couple of months would layer his whole body with perspiration, and, in July and August, cause an exhaustion of the brain which made it hard to think straight. The early autumn of 1859 was dangerous, but in a way it was the best time of year for him to arrive, since midsummer was farthest away. But when the summer of 1960 came, the Aberdonian Glover had never felt anything like it. There emerged an element of abandon in his engaging lethal samurai in conversation in the outdoor seasons of the following years.

By the terms of the Ansei Treaties, Shimoda and Hakodate remained open. Kyoryuchi in Yokohama and Nagasaki were to be fully opened later in 1859, Niigata on the Japan Sea coast (facing Russia) in 1860; and Hyogo (later Kobe), officially at least, in 1863. Shimoda was to close six months after Yokohama had opened. Right of entry to the kyoryuchi was given to the four big powers – the US, Britain, France and Russia – and the kyoryuchi were set up to have extraterritorial status, meaning that they remained legally foreign territory. Nagasaki, with its history of Dutch traders and its proximity to China, immediately become the most vibrant of the Ansei ports. Athough foreign-controlled, the kyoryuchi were as wild as the Japanese territory outside, except that their outlaws couldn't be touched by Japanese rules, at least without risking the anger of the shogun. In the kyoryuchi, of course, the traders made up their own laws as they went along.

The rules of sakoku, under which both Japanese defectors and foreign sailors landing in Japan were to be put to death, were also changed by the terms of the Ansei Treaties. But before the Treaties allowed entry on 1 July 1859, concession hunters had no rights. Even so, Kenneth Mackenzie hadn't waited. A chancer of repute with a slender but muscular build and an expression set to permanent affront, Mackenzie taught Glover much of what he knew about Japanese rules, and how to avoid them. Glover wasn't reckless enough to take on pre-Treaty Japan. As dangerous as the bakufu would make Japan in the early 1860s, pre-July 1859 foreigners like Mackenzie were goldfish in samurai-infested waters, unprotected either by their adopted homeland or by their own Foreign Office.

Prior to the construction of the foreign settlement, Mackenzie clandestinely rented a house near Myogyoji, a building which was also the French Consulate (he even briefly acted as French Consul, showing the fluidity of the early brokers' allegiances). In addition, he rented the property at Oura lot 15 in his capacity as an agent of the Peninsular and Oriental Steam Navigation Co. (P. & O.). As soon as there was an official foreign presence in the Nagasaki kyoryuchi, Mackenzie headed its first fire service. In the tiny world of pre-concessionary Japan, he was a key player. His desperado taste for fortune appealed to Glover, who followed him at a safe distance. Mackenzie took on the role of mentor to some of the young traders in those early years, Glover now amongst them.

But while samurai were a constant danger, relationships amongst the Britons themselves were far from perfect: the traders, as well as having alcohol-fuelled in-fights, were often mistrustful of the diplomatic service, seeing them as sneaky public school boys, while the diplomatic service were equally, if more eloquently, suspicious of traders, seeing them as profit-seeking cowboys. The head rustler in this Japanese western was Mackenzie himself, unbeloved of the Foreign Office, suffered wearily by the settlers, and assumed to have teamed up with Glover in Shanghai for 'patriotic' and perhaps masonic reasons. Mackenzie was by this time a Far Eastern veteran who had been working in partnership with his brother C.D. Mackenzie in Shanghai in their company Mackenzie, Brothers & Co. since as early as August 1850. Four years later he moved his tea interests to Hankow, where he expanded his plans and moved into smuggling proper. He was listed as a Jardine Matheson representative in Shanghai in autumn 1858, and official records have him arriving in Nagasaki from Shanghai on 9 January 1859, aboard the *Egmont*, six months before the Ansei Treaties deemed it lawful.

Already known for his adventurous deals in inner China, Mackenzie was even more aggressive in business than Glover, though he lacked the personal ambition to deal directly with the samurai. It was the less urbane Glover, rather than the Edinburgh-bred Mackenzie, who tried to engage samurai when they came across them in the pathways of the concessions. Because of Glover's tendency towards rebel meetings, Mackenzie sometimes felt he was following his junior partner into more dangerous waters, which appealed to his interest in extreme trading, but not his pride. The rebels, with a code of honour the foreign traders only partially understood, maintained an image of terror, the engagement with them giving Glover and Mackenzie an advantage over most traders. Both realised that dealing with rebel samurai was illegal, and until the mid 1860s, the British Foreign Office was seen to have nothing to do with rebels and talked up their terrorist image. One diplomat is typically sweeping in his characterisation of native terrorists of both stripes, despite a lack of first-hand knowledge:

all of a certain rank [samurai] are armed with two formidable weapons projecting from their belt; swords, like everything else in Japan, – to our worse confusion – being double, without much or any obvious distinction between military and civil – between Tycoon's, officers', and Daimio's retainers. These are the classes which furnish suitable types of that extinct species of the race in Europe, still remembered as '*Swash-bucklers*' – swaggering, blustering bullies; many cowardly enough to strike an enemy in the back, or cut down an unarmed and inoffensive man; – but also supplying numbers ever ready to fling their own lives away in accomplishing a revenge, or carrying out the behests of their Chief.

Another reason for the pair's success was that in politically unstable Japan, Nagasaki quickly developed a reputation as a centre for exchange. Hearing of growing rebel activity, daimyo and high-ranking samurai came to the city from throughout the southwest from the end of the 1850s to study seamanship, trade and logistics. When the rebel clans started buying foreign warships in 1861, having recognised the need to modernise their armed forces to avoid a western walkover in the manner of Opium War China, Glover took note – though it would still be a while before he would move into shipping in Japan with much success. It was the combination of Nagasaki's newly international status, the joi samurai need for arms, Glover's own mercantile ambition, and the outlaw behaviour of his mentor, that made Nagasaki the perfect place for him to be.

The Glover–Mackenzie partnership had a semi-formal basis within Jardine Matheson, which encouraged this kind of pairing between old hands and apprentices. All Far Eastern merchants required significant company investment to kit them out, transport them, and train them – Alex McKay has estimated the figure at £300 – so were chosen carefully, as the young Glover was frequently reminded by Mackenzie. Mackenzie also helped Glover over any ethical problems he might have had with cargoes like guns and drugs. Mackenzie, although less inclined to talk back to samurai, was an arch-pragmatist, manipulating any corruption he came across, administering bribes where they were needed, and priding himself on local knowledge. He was an ally to the bakufu when there was a profit to be turned – to the extent of becoming French Consul – while dealing with the clans, playing one side against the other. His methods of dealing with powers as they existed in practice rather than recognised states, and relying on cheap native labour with foreign management, would be replicated in the early part of Glover's career. His meeting Glover off the boat at Dejima in September 1859, when the Ansei Treaties were only weeks old and there was still a hangover of legal joi action, had only made Japan seem even more threatening, and Glover's short life expectancy was partly attributable to the state of the country, and partly to the company he kept.

When he found semi-permanent lodgings about a month after his arrival, Glover registered as a clerk with the British Consulate in Nagasaki. Since he was Mackenzie's partner, and both members of a partnership couldn't apply simultaneously, he didn't participate in the first application for concession land, but was given Oura lot 21 in the next. Despite this disappointing start, he built up his business interests quickly: when a Chamber of Commerce was set up in the city in June 1861, he was elected, at the age of 23, along with Robert Arnold and William Alt. His early rejection from the concessions only made him more determined in real estate investment – perhaps, in the end, more determined than he should have been. By the end of 1864, his company owned 20 lots.

As in Shanghai, the frontiersmen continued to urge their diplomatic representatives towards ever more extreme versions of free trade. Some adopted belligerent attitudes towards samurai in general, but in particular towards bakufu samurai, whose ingrained habits from the era of sakoku seemed to be suffocating trade. Carrying on their Shanghai lifestyle, some paid for their attitude with their lives. For a few, like Glover, a carefully pitched antagonism towards the bakufu provided common ground with the rebel samurai, though at the beginning there was no easy way to communicate this attitude. For most foreigners, the rebels were simply to be avoided: under no governmental compunction, they seemed even fiercer than the bakufu.

The insight that dawned on Glover throughout 1861 and 1862, was that the rebel clans, looking to modernise before their government, were likely to overthrow the bakufu sometime soon. His dealings with the rebels were not primarily for reasons of principle: for the traders, there was little to choose in terms of civility between the bakufu and the rebel clans. And the year of 1862 had seen increasingly frequent terrorist attacks. But the desire to further open the country, and the sense that, given the abundance of resources and cheap labour, great opportunities would open up, put him on the side of the rebels early, and encouraged him to greet them, with some trepidation. Dangerous as this was, other reps recognised it as a bold move towards new trading possibilities, raising Glover's esteem in the kyoryuchi. Since the Ansei Treaties, like most traders, Glover and Mackenzie had expressed their frustration at having their deals through Jardine Matheson blocked by the bakufu. Appreciative of the encouragement, Glover nevertheless toned down Mackenzie's behaviour. As soon as May 1860, about a year after the Nagasaki opening, a trader reckoned to be Mackenzie was involved in a wrangle in Minami Yamate with a samurai of unspecified clan, from whom he was trying to buy a caged bird. Glover restrained Mackenzie as he saw the samurai tensing as if for combat, indicating that he hadn't wanted to sell the bird at all. The samurai passed the cage to Glover and walked away, and the bird flapped in Glover's office for a couple of days before he could offload it.

Most of the other traders avoided direct engagement, having seen their colleagues threatened in the street. These traders were of the retire-by-30 school and accepted that their profits were likely to be short-term and high-yield. Then as now the standard in new territories was to suck the new market dry and then leave, and Glover, despite his precocious diplomacy, was not exempt from this kind of short-termism. Later on towards the end of the civil war between the rebels and the bakufu, on 3 April 1867, the Kanagawa British Consul F.G. Myburgh recalled the time after opening in a letter to Harry Parkes:

> The success attenting to the first opening of the ports in China and Japan brought into the commercial field a larger number of adventurous men with little or no capital, eager to make rapid fortunes and quit the scene. These imported into business a sort of gambling spirit, which soon gave rise to a degree of competition and reckless speculation which the trade could not possibly sustain, while the banking establishment to make matters worse afforded them accommodation to an unwarrantable extent in the belief that as before it was only necessary to touch anything to turn it to gold.

Glover's fierce desire for self-betterment, which he held onto even more tenaciously far away from home, both competed with and found a similar amorality in bushido, the samurai code. But during these early years, Glover found no general alliance between himself and the rebel clans, only friendly pockets in tea-houses, and later in the drinking clubs which were often in the houses of well-to-do samurai, where he would follow the crowds unless they looked like turning. Despite similarities of outlook, the exchanges don't show deep respect for bushido on Glover's part: he watched samurai use their elite status, and this appealed to his pragmatism. Samurai were not like martial arts experts or religious leaders: their authority was hereditary rather than earned, and their use of it was ruthless.

Similarly, rebel samurai never believed that Glover had gone into trading for honour or adventure. Despite his long-term achievements, his business behaviour in Japan until the late 1860s was, like Myburgh's 'adventurous men', aimed at amassing a fortune quickly, and he traded with the bakufu and the rebels. Quite often before he finally put his weight behind the rebels just before Restoration, he admitted that turning to their side was purely strategic. In his novelisation Alan Spence has Glover traumatised by a British attack on the rebels in 1863 to the extent that he sets himself the aim of toppling the bakufu: this is a neat storytelling twist which connects just cause and a traumatic insight into his own country's policy, and is partly based on information in Alex McKay's *Scottish Samurai* which showed that the profits of a Glover deal with the bakufu were passed on to the clans. Glover did pass on all sorts of financial and technological help and loans to the rebels after 1863, and certainly he was siding with the rebels after the Battle of Kagoshima in 1863, but the battle wasn't a turning-point, and didn't stop him dealing with the bakufu. And what happened with the $30,000 described as being passed on from the bakufu to Satsuma was that in August 1865, Glover intercepted and siphoned off three-quarters of a bakufu payment to Jardine Matheson which was never his money to loan in the first place. This was a worrying foretaste of how he would play fast and loose with Jardine Matheson money, after the more pensive traders had cashed in their chips.

So Glover was always an economic rebel, but only gradually and sketchily a political one. Between 1864 and 1867 he provided the bakufu – who were trying to neutralise the rebels – with three ships, an unknown amount of land guns, and enough silver bullion to dent the Chinese silver monopoly. In his youth – at the time of Restoration he was only 29 – the work ethic and the bottom line remained paramount, appropriately for someone with his education, his training in the cut-throat world of Shanghai, and his desire to come to a country as potentially deadly as Japan. Nevertheless in the early years from 1859 to 1863 he consolidated rebel acquaintances, becoming trusted by some, even escalating to close relationships with the daimyo, seeing them almost as heads of a local chamber of commerce. The rebels recognised Glover as a pragmatist who could be of more use to them than to the bakufu, and only during 1863, when he began to harbour terrorists, did they develop a political bond.

Increasingly feeling in the shade of Glover's popularity, Mackenzie became more tenacious in his pursuit of new trade. As well as the staples of tea, silk, seaweed and opium, he pushed towards the thoroughly modern business of foreign exchange, and the two men dealt in any weak currencies which came their way, playing on the natives' inexperience the field. In particular, they bought Japanese currency in Yokohama and sold it where it was more valuable in Nagasaki. In the beginning the Japanese were forbidden from using the Mexican silver dollar, the common currency of the time, and, when eventually the local currency, the ryo, was linked to the dollar, there was initial confusion over exchange rates. Mackenzie and Glover seized on the chance to make profits of up to sevenfold. Rutherford Alcock commented on the predatory new forex market with the reproving tone of the diplomat: 'ultimately . . . [the Japanese] altered their gold coinage to the European standard, but not too late to prevent large exportations and much mischief'. Mackenzie decided to return to his old trading ground of China as soon as 18 June 1861 — a move which perhaps denied him the place Glover was to take in history — and was replaced by his junior colleague as Jardine Matheson's chief agent in Nagasaki. This was Glover's first promotion: it gave him leeway to act as entrepreneur using company money, which he did with the enthusiasm of his mentor.

Newly independent, Glover began to use his local status accordingly. He set up Guraba Shokai as an independent company with fellow trader Francis Groom, and by early the next year his brother James had joined the company. Soon after, he set up another precocious partnership with Alt and Arnold. Today the Alt house is one of the three which feature in the Glover Garden, along with Ipponmatsu and the residence of the tea merchant Frederick Ringer. It was in the Alt house that some of the traders, including Glover, hid out during some of the most fearful joi times of 1862, expecting at any minute an attack by fire or sword.

When Mackenzie was leaving for China, the Nagasaki Jardine Matheson offices were just being finished at Oura lot 2. This building would become the headquarters of the new Guraba Shokai. Mackenzie also bought land at Minami Yamate for a house for Glover. The land for Ipponmatsu was a parting gift, and on 18 June 1861 Mackenzie made his plans for his successor's accommodation clear to James Whittall at Jardine Matheson's Shanghai branch:

After great delay and much trouble I obtained a large and beautifully situated hill lot held upon very easy terms as to annual rent which Mr. Glover will cause to be planted and will therefore build a bungalow upon it at a cost of $800 and which he is instructed to hand over to you . . .

Ipponmatsu, symbol of Glover's life in Japan, was built by Koyama Hidenoshin in the style of how he imagined western houses should be. Glover himself had little to do with the design, though along with the houses of Alt and Ringer, it has been promoted by Nagasaki-shi from the 1950s as authentically western. The houses are a strange fusion of types, designed by a local architect who was gifted but guessing about styles he had never seen. Ipponmatsu is a cruciform, luxurious, extensive and furnished in a quasi-western manner. It was a huge house for a young man. It was also perfect for entertaining, for projecting an image of success, and the type of place in which he could plot and form a circle of business contacts around himself. It is worth noting, though, that although Ipponmatsu is splendid and seems perfectly placed on the hill overlooking Nagasaki, its site was not at the time reckoned to be prime real estate, but was in the mid-range price bracket of the concessions.

Glover's mercantile interests after Mackenzie continued to feature the big three products, with silk sinking to the bottom. He also began to act as a financial guarantor for various rebel Satsuma han (clan) dealings, indicating an early, shaky trust between him and Satsuma elders. The first business to which Glover turned his own entrepreneurial hand was the manufacture, rather than trading, of tea. This might seem disingenuous in a country already known for its tea production, but Glover had noticed that in Japan's humid climate only green tea could be produced, leaving a demand for dried tea of the black type, known in Japan then as today without irony as 'English tea'. So even in a tea-producing country, a neighbour of China, tea production became a viable business for Glover. Refiring tea for sale as English tea became his first independent business success, conducted with Jardine Matheson under the aegis of the new Guraba Shokai.

The building of the tea-firing plant took place in two stages: first the exoskeleton was constructed, then the firing pot itself, completed in June 1862. After the first stage Glover sent tea samples to Jardine Matheson Shanghai, with which they seemed pleased. After the second stage he was ready to produce English tea for a clientele of ex-pats and curious natives. At some point after the distribution of the finished product, however, Jardine

Matheson became dissatistified with the quality, and in late 1863 Glover realised that current demand wouldn't cover the costs of the large, mostly Chinese, labour force. Tea-firing never made him much money, but it did get him recognition as an entrepreneur, as well as a trader, and it put him into collaboration with lifelong business associates, notably Ringer, whose daughter joins the story later. The success of a scheme as audacious as selling tea in a tea-producing country also gave Glover the confidence to diversify. And as well as cementing brother James into the concern, it encouraged the up-and-coming Edward Harrison to join in September 1862. The following year Francis Groom became the company's Shanghai representative, and Harrison its Yokohama representative.

These first entrepreneurial steps were taken after long and intensive training under Mackenzie, and after his mentor had helped him into the iconic residence known to this day as Glover House. The two never forgot the bond they had formed in the jumpy streets of early kyoryuchi Nagasaki. Mackenzie had a job waiting for him when he returned from China in 1869 after a period of disappointing returns, and he accompanied Glover's own period of speculation to its conclusion, unsteady as he was. It is appropriate that it was in Ipponmatsu that Mackenzie passed away, on Guy Fawkes Night 1873.

FIVE

At the Edge of Empire I: Greater Britain

W hen Glover arrived in Japan, the country was in a state of turbulence far greater than anything he had seen in Shanghai. It wasn't only arguments between rebels and bakufu over whether to open up to outside technology: there was also a mutual resentment between the rebel samurai themselves. The story of the emergence of modern Japan is of how from the late 1850s to the late 1860s, rebels came to see the common enemy of the bakufu as more immediately pressing, embracing outside technologies to defeat them together. To outdo the flailing bakufu, they increasingly looked to the European incomers – or at least their technology. Soon Glover was foremost amongst these incomers, to the annoyance not only of the bakufu but also of the British Foreign Office. By the middle of 1863, he was drinking with Ito Hirobumi, one of the Choshu samurai responsible for the torching of the Edo Legation.

For outward-looking rebels, the way had been shown by ronin, or masterless samurai, in the 1850s. Ronin had cast off the collaborative tendencies of their clans and set out travelling as political agitators, sometimes mercenaries, usually against impossible odds, and ending in premature death. (Today the word ronin is used less glamorously for students who have failed university entrance tests and have to wait a year.) By 1860, ronin influence had started rippling through the big clans. When Satsuma bought the ship *England* in 1861, it signalled an important precedent – a single han had bypassed the bakufu, nominally their ruling government, and acted like a state. Rival han had no choice but to assume similar powers. This threatened an arms race between the two big rebel clans of Kyushu, Satsuma and Choshu, which could only be headed off by some kind of agreement. Glover had the sale of the *England* on his mind throughout his dealings with Mackenzie and Guraba Shokai. He watched the next year as the bakufu, pressurised by the west, loosened its regulations on the import of ships. By September 1864 he was making his first shipping sale in Japan, when Jardine Matheson asked him to offload the *Carthage*. From here on, his background in shipping was duly noted, and he and Jardine Matheson agreed to split the profits from brokering.

By now Glover had realised that although the bakufu were nominally protecting the power of Emperor Komei in Kyoto, the emperor was effectively a prisoner of the ruling faction. He understood that rebel han were not trying to depose the emperor, but trying to restore his power as they saw it. In strict samurai ethics the place of the emperor was that of a human deity: only after World War Two was it laid down by the Macarthur Constitution – targeting the 1889 Constitution which had stated that the emperor is sacred and inviolable – that Japan must be a secular state (and it has become, arguably, the most secular state in the world). The often heard comment that Japanese secularism shows a casual attitude to spirituality represents a quite new idea: at the time that Glover arrived, the competition amongst samurai was to show the greater devotion to the emperor.

Over the long period of closure until 1853, the bakufu had settled into a custom of stifling rebellion by demanding an annual pilgrimage for the payment of tax to the central capital of Kyoto – a long way from Kyushu on worn roads which disappeared for long stretches. The bakufu had also stipulated that the families of the taxpayers had to be left behind under the eye of local representatives. This annual journey was supposed to underline deference to the emperor, but really propped up the old political system by holding taxpayers' families as security against any temptation to organise. Taxation had become a system of institutional kidnap. This system was stable, in its senile way: it was based on respect for tradition over present conditions, tradition that reached so far back it resembled natural right. No one could remember any other form of government.

Since both sides of the Japanese conflict were supposed to be loyalist, Glover's support for the rebels was not really for structural change of the political system. Rebels wanted to replace one form of total samurai control with another, one more advantageous to the outward-looking contacts Glover had made far from Kyoto in the first couple of years. And as he watched, the rebels looked increasingly serious in their political intentions. If they could be helped into government – as seemed a real possibility from a Kyushu perspective – the bakufu stranglehold over trade would be over, and the new government would be captive customers for any product – particularly, after their long period of closure, arms. Thus the business ambitions of one Scot conjoined with the loyalties of a few dispossessed samurai became pivotal to the development of today's Japanese government. The more astute diplomats of the early 1860s, as much as they disdained Glover's methods, also recognised that the coming trade environment could be highly beneficial. In China, free trade had come about by force: in Japan, it seemed to be happening internally with the help of a few enthusiastic foreign importers.

Sometime during 1863 Glover managed to befriend not only Satsuma but also the feared Choshu clan, including Ito, later the first prime minister, and Inoue Kaoru, later the first foreign minister – both architects of the Legation arson. Both of these joi samurai would become members of the Choshu Five group of samurai, which Glover is often credited with smuggling abroad. Despite the Legation attack, from 1863 Ito became both a friend and a foil to Glover, a relationship which would remain, in various forms, throughout the course of their lives. Ito's slight build belied his power as a ruthless strategist. When he went abroad that year, he cut off his topknot and grew a moustache, and as a statesman he was rarely to be seen without a suit and a steely expression. His rapid conversion set the pace for that of Japan as a whole.

The early 1860s saw the peak of influence, on Ito and Inoue amongst others, of the rebel scholar and joi ronin samurai Yoshida Shoin. Despite Glover's guarded advances towards Ito, Choshu in general remained dangerous, and he continued to steer clear of most of them until as late as 1866, remembering the terrifying times of 1862 and 1863, particularly both summers, spent hiding in the house of William Alt from samurai imagined to be mostly Choshu – though no one knew for sure. Yet, since they were the most aggressive, Choshu were potentially the most useful to Glover, because, war-minded as they were, they had grasped the importance of modern arms. Glover was beginning to see his future not simply in brokering warships for rebel clans, but also in selling small firearms for domestic use. He was already anticipating a civil war and, after it, a national rearmament.

Ito and Glover got to know one another cautiously in the bars and tearooms of Nagasaki where samurai threw their weight around, and by the time of Ito's defection to Britain were talking politics amicably at Ipponmatsu. As a Choshu confidant, Ito represented an exception to Glover's early preference for Satsuma, who seemed more ready to suspend the joi element. By Aberdeen standards Glover had never been a drinker, but in the tensions of early 1860s Nagasaki, sociable drinks at the club quickly turned into drinks to steady the nerves. During stressful spells, such as the summer of 1863, Glover would wake up in Alt's house with a back complaint which, he now realised in the comfort of Ipponmatsu, suggested a pummelling of the organs rather than bad bedding. He developed a taste for sake early, and it didn't help that samurai were proud of their drinking ability. (Sake has just over the alcohol content of wine and is drunk more quickly.) Ito in particular, despite his head for statecraft, had a reputation for boozing and womanising. The traders, far from home, deadline-pressed, and in constant danger, drank even more than they had in China. Diplomats were as impatient with the hard-drinking atmosphere as they were with any hint of a Brit going native. Consul Alcock for example, a fount of dubious anthropology, found the drinking habits of his temporary new home barbaric:

'The Japanese are perfectly ignorant of alcohol.' There may be a difference of opinion as to what constitutes alcohol, but '*Saki*' seems to me an excellent imitation; and, if it is meant that the Japanese are innocent of intoxication – a noisy, dangerous, and pugnacious intoxication, I am sorry truth compels me to say there never was an assertion of fact more signally refuted by practice.

Meanwhile language remained a problem: for the first few years communication was mostly conducted in broken English taught by the few Japanese who had returned from abroad. The interpreters were put in as much danger as the negotiators. Despite myths to the contrary, Glover's general Japanese stayed fairly basic for most of his life, and he never developed any noticeable literacy. Within a few years he accepted that his skills lay elsewhere and also that Japanese desire for his English language was in his favour, as samurai were struggling to internationalise.

Neither did most of the diplomats get far beyond broken Japanese, with a few exceptions such as Ernest Satow, who always took seriously the native language of his post. Most were too used to colonial Indian thinking, especially after the organisation of the exams for the Civil Service of the East India Company in 1855, which moved attention away from Greats in the Oxbridge syllabus and helped to solidify the canon of English Literature: the natives were from this point supposed to be glad of the civility bestowed by Good English. For a British diplomat in this atmosphere to have spoken Japanese could almost have been seen as a sign of cultural weakness. One function of informal empire, with no occupying role, was to share the fruits of Anglophone civilisation with the world. Throughout Asia and then Africa, the move to a cultural, as opposed to martial, model of imperialism was beginning to push English as a global language. If Glover had been granted a scholarship to an Oxbridge college as a youth and then joined the Foreign Office, he would probably have kept his distance and never approached unknown samurai in broken Japanese, and never have made the rebel connections which put him at the centre of public life.

Another value of Choshu was their competition with Satsuma to run a post-bakufu regime. A mini-arms race meant commissions for James Mitchell's 'Aberdeen Yard' (in Nagasaki), turning the port into an outpost of Aberdeen shipping. Mitchell, a natural friend to the homesick Glover, was ex Alexander Hall & Sons, long-term Glover family collaborators based in Aberdeen, and had been advertising in the *Nagasaki Shipping List* since 18 September 1861. For the diplomats, whatever happened, the country seemed unlikely to roll over in the face of free trade as had China, and any prodding was liable to be answered with more terrorism. While Japan might usefully act to counter Russian interests in China, there dawned on the Foreign Office, slowly, the extraordinary danger that the country might also become hostile to European imperialism as a whole. Glover and Satow were seeing these plans hatch in the eyes of Ito and Inoue as the two prepared to defect.

In 1863 Glover began to turn activist, as far as the less terrifying Satsuma were concerned. As Britain looked more liable to move in militarily, he hid the rebels from the pro-bakufu British forces, sold them weapons (contravening British trading rules), and gave them accounts of European systems of politics. He was suspected as a spy – reasonably, since he was providing arms to groups regarded as terrorists by both his own state and to the government with which it had a shaky treaty. He showed great prescience in seeing which way political power would go, but he was not a natural political agitator. Other subjects of the British empire, from Ireland to India, had often shown the kind of bravery now being shown by rebel samurai, and supporting rebels of this type would have been out of the question for the Glovers. Here his behaviour was much more pragmatic: if the clans could stop fighting one another long enough to topple the bakufu and if he could position himself as confidant to enough of the new government's central figures, he would have unlimited influence and access.

The trigger for the chain of events which would eventually unite the clans and lead to Restoration, was a samurai attack (or defence) which became known as the Namamugi Incident, after the settlement in Kanagawa where a party of four English dignitaries were challenged returning from a meeting in Yokohama on 14 September 1862. At this point foreigners had no legal right to travel outside the concessions, land under the jurisdiction

of the daimyo. More significantly, the party was cutting across the path of
the daimyo's representative, Hisamitsu Shimazu, which was forbidden even
for the Japanese. The four were signalled to move aside by the party of the
daimyo, and when they failed to do so, were seized upon by the daimyo's
guards. Charles Lennox Richardson was killed, and another two in the party
badly injured. Mrs Borrowdale, whose sliced hat proved that she had ducked
just in time, galloped away in a state of agitation to take the news to the
Consulate. The Consulate was duly outraged and dispatched the Yokohama
guard. As Satow describes it:

> On the 14th September a most barbarous murder was committed on
> a Shanghai merchant named Richardson. He, in company with a Mrs.
> Borradaile of Hongkong, and Woodthorpe C. Clarke and Wm.
> Marshall both of Yokohama, were riding along the high road between
> Kanagawa and Kawasaki [the border of today's Kanagawa-ken and
> Tokyo-to], when they met with a train of the *daimio*'s retainers, who
> bid them stand aside. They passed on at the edge of the road, until
> they came in sight of a palanquin, occupied by Shimizu Saburo, father
> of the Prince of Satsuma. They were now ordered to turn back, and
> as they were wheeling their horses in obedience, were suddenly set
> upon by several armed men belonging to the train, who hacked at
> them with their sharp-edged heavy swords. Richardson fell from his
> horse in a dying state, and the other two men were so severely wounded
> that they called to the lady: 'Ride on, we can do nothing for you.'
> She got safely back to Yokohama and gave the alarm. Everybody in
> the settlement who possessed a pony and a revolver at once armed
> himself and galloped off towards the scene of slaughter.

As well as a mass foreign hunt around the scene of the crime, the incident
provoked a report to the Admiralty by Edwin St John Neale, calling for
punitive action from the British government. F. Howard Vyse dispatched
HMS *Ringdove*, and, with the weariness of the imperial toff, again asked for
calm in the foreign community. The incident suggested anything but calm.
There would be several killings in 1863 in Yokohama and Osaka which
didn't provoke such a strong reaction – nor can Namamugi be seen as a
specifically anti-foreign attack, since a native attempt to cross the path of a
daimyo on Japanese territory would have been dealt with in the same way.
Rather, the seriousness of the situation was because of the social status of

the party attacked. Diplomatic wheels moved slowly to find a suitable outlet for British outrage.

Eventually the British government made a formal demand for $100,000 compensation, plus $25,000 for the families of the killed and wounded. The amount was never itself of great importance, but it was enough to disable Satsuma for the time being. The demand, though, threw the shaky Britain–Satsuma–Choshu–bakufu balance. If the injured British parties were considered nobility by their own people, so was the Satsuma daimyo by the Japanese. It was outwith the imagination of either Satsuma or the bakufu to pay compensation to protect the daimyo's own thoroughfares. The bakufu were now feeling the effects of the growing power of Satsuma. They were in an impossible situation – they couldn't put responsibility onto the local daimyo, since their tottering regime demanded the pretence that Satsuma had no independent power. But nor could they go to war with the British Navy. The bakufu stalled, and Satsuma called their bluff by making no move at all. Since the British government could only recognise the authority of the bakufu, the bakufu had to decide whether to protect their own internal enemies or accept that their power had been eroded and leave Satsuma to defend itself. The British and French governments, although imperial rivals, consolidated to pressure the bakufu, and Glover and the other foreign traders realised that war was becoming inevitable.

Glover was both excited at the economic path opening up before him and anxious at the thought of the coming violence. Shanghai had shown him the capabilities of the British armed forces. In these nervous times, his behaviour turned from gruff to abusive. On 21 February 1863 a charge of beating a messenger 'half to death' was laid against him by the Nagasaki governor. Glover was almost certainly culpable of cruelty against the messenger and didn't deny it. There are few recorded cases of Glover beating his servants, but they were well used to being shouted at. On this occasion Glover embarked on a contradictory two-leg defence, first claiming that he had been in the company of his brother James at the time, and second, counter-attacking the Japanese authorities for meddling in kyoryuchi affairs after it had been agreed that the concessions were not subject to national law. In the end he settled, and was relieved to drop the matter as war drew nearer, and the issue of where to place himself relative to the Satsuma army became a practical conundrum.

As the situation tensed up, Glover's letters to Jardine Matheson Shanghai began to reveal his unease. On 6 May 1863, he wrote: 'there is no alternative but hostilities'. On the 16th, '[w]ar now appears inevitable and the communities are leaving the port with their valuables'. Ten days later, 'owing to political troubles Trade is almost completely stopped'. On 24 June, the panicked shogun attempted to close the Ansei ports entirely. Would Glover put to sea with the British Navy or stand beside his new Satsuma allies? Or would he simply stay in Ipponmatsu and threaten to alienate both sides? By this time, though, he had come to the attention of the Foreign Office for trading in arms with the rebel clans, and from the summer of 1863, he would be remembered as a supporter of the rebels. The US ship *Pembroke* arrived in Nagasaki harbour on 8 July 1863, and there was a long lull. Perhaps, he thought, the British had made their threat and dropped the matter of the attack. But on 13 August the bombardment began.

Kagoshima is a medium-sized city in the far south of Kyushu, dominated by a sometime active volcano on Sakurajima. Clouds drift across the upper reaches of the mountain, much as they do across Fuji san. It is one of Japan's castle towns, dominated by the residence of the local daimyo, in this case of the rebellious Satsuma. This southernmost point of the southernmost major island had a culture and a government separated from the rest of the country, and was independently minded. But there was nothing much battle-like about the Battle of Kagoshima, as it became known, in which the British Navy fired on the wooden town with large cannon, only receiving the occasional hit in exchange. Some within the bakufu would have been content to see this stronghold destroyed, though their pride was damaged by the strike on Japanese territory and the fact that they couldn't keep their own clans under control. Satsuma's arch-rival Choshu, meanwhile, began to imagine the same thing happening to them all too easily.

It didn't take much of an attack to reduce the capital of the government pretenders to splinters. Its houses were made of timber with no protection, and its city was unwalled and largely unarmed. A few Glover-brokered guns were used by Satsuma in the exchange, but they had the effect of throwing gravel. In all, about 400 heavy shots were fired by the British Navy. It augured badly for Satsuma that its refugees creeping up the eastern coast of Kyushu also received friendly fire from a ship from Nobeoka han (today's Miyazaki). But in the confusion and destruction that followed the battle, there was a change in the way the big clans viewed the west. The daimyo had had no idea they would be so thoroughly outgunned. Despite his support for Satsuma, Glover could see the walkover coming, which was one reason for his pre-Kagoshima anxiety.

Foreign offices in endangered parts of Kyushu had been moved to ships in the bay for safety. Glover stood with Satsuma samurai on the defences until just before the actual battle, at which time he was moved to a British ship. This was enough to assure the clan of his loyalty, and he would have their trust until Restoration. He may have been moved because Satsuma samurai feared for his safety, or because he was helping refugees off the shore, or, less honourably, because he was worried about being accused of treason if he stayed. Right up till the bombardment began he had helped the Satsuma troops prepare their ramparts. In his final interview of 1910 he recalled of early August 1863:

> The authorities found out [about hiding rebel samurai] and tried to capture them. In my garden at night they were carrying guns, pretending to look as though they were trying to shoot birds. They came in the night and went away in the night.

The Satsuma counter-attack caused the destruction of eight allied ships, including three foreign-built steamers. It cost thirteen lives, ten on the *Euryalus*, two on the *Coquette*, and one on the *Perseus*. Added to the *Pearl*, *Argos* and *Racehorse*, there were 50 casualties at sea. It was nevertheless a punitive strike rather than a battle, and British rhetoric painted the reprimand in schoolmasterly terms: where, after the Namamugi Incident, on 16 October 1862, the Foreign Office had called for a 'severe lesson' to be dealt out, when the attack finally came, the *Japan Commercial News* described it as a 'glorious battle of civilisation and humanity'.

Although Satsuma were right in claiming that it didn't have to respond to British pressure over Namamugi – it was a problem for the state government which had failed to keep them under control – it probably would have reacted directly had it felt it had enough weapons to make a stand. Satsuma strategists saw the strike less as a human disaster – we have no idea how many lower-caste Japanese died – than as a learning experience for samurai. After the attack Godai Tomoatsu, Satsuma envoy to foreign clans, was positively looking forward to rearming on the new scale he now perceived would be needed, thrilling at this 'new and decisive form of warfare'. From late 1862, when it had become clear a fight was likely, the clan had aimed to mass arm as quickly as possible, but Kagoshima had proved them to be unrealistically slow, and put Glover in position as broker of the new weapons. Godai wanted 100 Armstrong cannon immediately after Kagoshima, with the promise of many more to come. From now, the way forward for the Glovers would be arms.

In a sense Satsuma had been squeezed by both sides of the British presence, the governmental and the mercantile: the British Navy had exposed their weakness, and the traders would supply the arms to help them catch up. The rebel samurai, after centuries of sakoku, accepted this with great stoicism and looked to superior British logistics. In particular Glover and the arch-strategist Godai hit it off immediately. Godai was, after all, hand-picked to negotiate with 'outsiders', though this usually meant people outside his clan. Of all Glover's samurai friends, Godai was probably the most consistently loyal. Before Kagoshima they sailed to Nagasaki together under the British flag. Glover hid Godai in the wake of the battle, and they began talking about rearming for the future. In Godai, Glover found the 'best qualities of samurai' without the 'untempered mettle' of joi.

As far as Glover could see, Satsuma's, if not yet Choshu's, joi had receded significantly after Kagoshima, as the clan embarked on a military rebranding led by Godai. Godai also recognised that the ideological platform of the bakufu was wobbling as the sonno (respect for the emperor) joi of the samurai in the capital of Kyoto itself was descending into anarchy. In 1863 Emperor Komei even made an announcement of his displeasure, which made bakufu samurai claims to sonno seem absurd. The rebel clans were beginning to look like the real monarchists, and monarchism without joi was where Glover's heart lay.

Despite modest successes refiring tea and trading staples, between 1860 and the decisive engagements of the Restoration struggle in 1867, arms became by far Glover's most profitable product. As Satsuma re-formed themselves with his weapons, he took more daring risks to procure guns. Making the short journeys to the Shanghai market, he was now having to dodge the Royal Navy as well as the bakufu. Aged 25, he had become the central broker in Satsuma's, and potentially Choshu's, reorientation towards the stance of 'western knowledge, eastern wisdom' encouraged by Confucian samurai teachers in the shigakko, the fundamentalist schools of their time. If he could make the two clans cooperate, he would be arming an entire nation.

Guns fetched higher and higher prices, and between 1863 and Britain's U-turn on Restoration in 1866, Glover routinely broke trade laws to procure them, in a way that incurred the disdain of British diplomats – with the exception of Ernest Satow, who recognised that Glover understood more about the ambitions of samurai than did the Foreign Office. Satow's own arrival in Japan had been at the most incendiary time possible: aged 19, he took up his position within a week of the Namamugi Incident. He was appointed as interpreter to Admiral Küper on 'pacifying' missions, and early the following year became interpreter at the Consulate in Yokohama. A genuine linguist in a world of quasi-scholars, Satow would be invaluable in negotiations with the floundering bakufu in the mid 1860s. He also made his pro-rebel opinions felt in the press, influenced by Glover at times but seeing for himself that the bakufu were falling. In *The Japan Times*, he declared that the power of the shogun 'was a shadow and his power a mockery'.

The British armed forces, with Indian and Chinese experience, felt that a stable trade environment could be achieved only by pacifying all of Japan's rebel clans, and turned to Kyushu's other powerbrokers, Choshu. Their war against Choshu would be a much more drawn-out affair than Kagoshima and would have the unexpected catalytic effect of drawing both clans together. On 25 June 1863 the *Pembroke* opened fire on Shimonoseki, the Choshu stronghold located where Kyushu meets Honshu. The *Pembroke* was counter-attacked by two European-built warships belonging to Choshu forces. The next day, the French naval steamer *Kienchang* was fired on by rebel Japanese artillery at Shimonoseki, and after a lull, on 11 July, the 16-gun Dutch warship *Medusa* was also fired on, killing or wounding nine.

On the morning of 16 July, in a parallel grand punitive strike, the American frigate USS *Wyoming* sailed into the Straits of Shimonoseki and fired on the rebel fleet. Over two hours, the *Wyoming* sank one enemy ship and damaged another two, causing 40 Japanese casualties and itself suffering 14 crew dead or wounded. This bombardment was followed by a French landing force of 250 men, who attacked the town of Shimonoseki. The British vessels *Julius, Encounter* and *Pearl* were also involved in the action, coming from Shanghai, Hong Kong and Yokohama. Twice now Britain and France had been on the same side, even though the Foreign Office was more or less neutral about its loyalties, while France was still supporting the bakufu. It may be that, in this case, the French rationale was that they were attacking territory belonging to the legitimate government they supported but which was illegally occupied by the clan rebels. For Britain, it was simply a punitive attack. While Godai and his Satsuma comrades were being held in Nagasaki, the increasingly agitated Glover escaped to Yokohama. The island of Kyushu had finally become too dangerous. Nevertheless, both Glover and Godai were supplied during this time with money by the Satsuma daimyo Shimazu Saburo, suggesting that both saw themselves as fellow outlaws on the run from the British forces.

Like Satsuma, Choshu realised their own defeat and the loss of civilian life as necessary lessons in modernity. Choshu stepped up defence as a priority, not for a war with the incomers, but with the central government, who would have been relieved to see the clan crushed by the foreigners. But Choshu were stubborn, and the battle over the Straits of Shimonoseki dragged on through 1864 as they attempted to enforce a blockade. In a Jardine Matheson letter of 27 August 1863, Glover was already reporting that 'the Prince of Cho-shiu ha[s] stopped all junks coming to Nagasaki by the Shimonoseki route'. Throughout the rest of 1863 and the first half of 1864, the clan remained closed to foreign shipping. Rutherford Alcock discussed with the other foreign powers the feasibility of a joint military strike, and all were soon making preparations for a combined movement. In the Straits, fifteen British and four Dutch warships lay in wait ominously, with the threat of more to come from Hong Kong. Still Choshu refused to buckle in view of the allied demands and even attempted another attack in July 1864, firing on the US steamer *Monitor* when it entered the harbour for supplies. Finally, a multinational ultimatum was issued, threatening military force if the Straits were not opened.

On 17 August 1864, a squadron consisting of nine British, five Dutch, three French, and one US warship, together with 2,000 soldiers, steamed out of Yokohama to forcibly open the Straits. The two-day bombardment that followed on 5 and 6 September was, as with Kagoshima, intended to destroy the clan's military capability. During the two days of the attack on Shimonoseki it rained steadily over Kyushu, and Guraba Shokai offices were flooded. The 'Battle' was clouded in confusion, and the figures of dead and wounded are unknown. The rebel Choshu forces finally surrendered on 8 September, and US Minister Pruyn included an extraordinary demand for $3,000,000.

The Shimonoseki bombardment was followed by scattered Choshu counter-attacks, which were in turn met by further allied military force. Choshu knew they were fighting a losing battle, but the US could also have done without a prolonged engagement, fighting its own civil war at home. When the bombardment had become inevitable, Japan's most famous ryugakusei, or students abroad, the Choshu Five, had rapidly returned from England to their comrades, and set up an arms distribution network via Glover, which would soon shift its sights from the allied attack to the central government. Though shocked at the carnage, Glover began to supply the war economy he had hoped for. Within two years, through the Choshu diarist Kido Takayoshi, the clan had bought up to 4,000 Minie rifles, with the promise of thousands more. According to Kido, '[i]f Choshu would send a vessel directly to Shanghai to buy rifles, Glover will do everything in his power to buy and load as many guns as we want; he seems to be deeply committed to us on this matter'. Kido's impressions confirm Glover's growing social status through post-Shimonoseki arms sales: '[t]his man is the wealthiest of all foreign merchants who have come to Japan; and he is on intimate terms with ministers and consuls'.

But Glover was amoral, fickle and lacking in the finesse the diplomats took for granted. During the confused years of the wars, he was still making friends in scattergun fashion, and was unsure how long he would stay in the country to witness the effects of his arms sales. He had recognised even before Shimonoseki that while Satsuma were the most approachable and the most ambitious of the clans, it would be tough to get the powerful and ruthless Choshu on his side. In any potential Saccho (Satsuma–Choshu) alliance, moreover, Satsuma would aim not only to ruin the bakufu monopoly but also to overpower its ally after the bakufu had been toppled. During the wars Satsuma were already trying to work out how to prepare for overseas trade as a single-clan led state. This created a tricky administrative problem for Glover, if not an ethical one. As Sugiyama Shinya puts it:

> Glover thought that it was important to keep on friendly terms with Satsuma, since Satsuma was likely to become the biggest trader in Japan in the near future . . .
>
> As a young man himself, he may well have sympathised with the enthusiastic radicals who wished to reform Japanese politics. Yet to see this as a dominant characteristic of his activities is to overlook their fundamentally pragmatic, business-orientated nature. Glover seems to have strengthened his relationship with Satsuma, for example, not because he supported the idea of the emperor's sovereignty, but simply because Satsuma was anxious to develop foreign trade on its own account.

During the Satsuma and Choshu conflicts, Godai was particularly vocal in his new-found Europhilia. But even prominent Choshu samurai had come to reconcile joi with the need to educate themselves abroad, and the Choshu figures who had defected and returned had been Europeanised to a degree that surprised their comrades. The Choshu Five, as they became known, were Ito Shunsuke, later Ito Hirobumi, Prime Minister, Inoue Monta, later Inoue Kaoru, Foreign Minister, Yamao Yozo, who would train in seamanship at Anderson's College, later Strathclyde University, and work in the Clyde shipyards, Endo Kinsuke and Nomura Yakichi, later Inoue Masaru. Yamao returned to help found the Imperial College of Engineering, later the University of Tokyo, today still Japan's most prestigious educational institution.

Because of the attack on Shimonoseki, the Five's most important politicos, Ito and Inoue, cut short their celebrated visit to Britain. But this would prove to their personal advantage as they would remain in Japan throughout its most difficult period of redefinition between Shimonoseki in 1864 and Restoration in 1868, and secure for themselves the new executive's top two jobs, even though Satsuma had appeared to be the stronger faction. The journey of the Five, however, can't be counted amongst Glover's great achievements, since he was not, as is usually stated, responsible for their defection. Rather, the Choshu Five were hustled onto the boat of S.J. Gower of Jardine Matheson Yokohama by a Mr Weigal. Glover certainly supported Ito and talked politics with him, but he remained wary of all Choshu samurai throughout 1863, feeling that strong Choshu relationships could lose him the 'valued trust' of the primary faction of Satsuma. Despite a great number of repetitions in Glover guides, his not being the smuggler of the Five is no longer in dispute: he didn't claim it in his famous 1910 interview, and Ito Shunsuke's own biography makes it clear that it was Gower rather than Glover who took him to the ship. Naito Hatsuho's 2001 study corroborates Andrew Cobbing's extensively researched account of 1998, which offers a thorough summary of the inception of the story of Glover as the mastermind of the Choshu Five's escape. It is worth quoting at length:

> The long-standing claim that Glover engineered the escape of the first Choshu students presents an interesting case study in the making of a myth. The idea first appears in the early 1900s, mentioned by William Griffis in 1906 in his notes on the memoirs of R.H. Brunton . . . A Mitsubishi official called Uematsu who looked after Glover's house in Tokyo had also heard that the Scottish merchant helped Inoue and Ito escape abroad [as explained in a newspaper obituary of Glover]. The idea was further popularised by M. Paske Smith in *Western*

Barbarians in Japan and Formosa in Tokugawa Days 1603–1868 . . .
[t]hrough repetition, this version of events has now become widely
accepted, particularly among English [language] readers.

Japanese primary documents written by the Choshu students themselves . . . demonstrate in some detail that their escape was entirely
the work of S.J. Gower, the Jardine Matheson & Co. representative
in Yokohama . . .

Furthermore, on 26 June 1869, Kido Takayoshi recorded in his
diary: 'I went to see the Foreign Settlement with Inoue Segai to see
the Englishman Gower. At the time that the policy of expulsion of
the barbarians [that is, the policy of joi] prevailed, Inoue, Ito, Yamao,
and I consulted him in secret about going abroad. He readily consented
to help us; and we entrusted the arrangements to him' . . . [i]n 1865,
Ito did ask Glover to help him escape abroad again, but was persuaded
to stay in Japan and help pave the way for the opening of Shimonoseki
to overseas trade.

Glover and Gower often disagreed over politics, stubbornly and sometimes
childishly, and are unlikely to have seen eye to eye over the students. On
30 June 1869, Kido complained: 'Glover and Gower once had two entirely
different opinions about politics here; and both communicated their ideas
to us for the sake of our country. They differed in every particular.'

When the Choshu Five travelled to London in 1863, it was the first time
for over 200 years that a high-ranking Japanese group had been able to go
to another continent and import knowledge, making a reality of the ronin
samurai ideal of the 1840s and 1850s. Although Glover was not responsible
for the smuggling of the Five, he did approve and became an advocate to
Jardine Matheson to pay their expenses in Britain. Their boarding the ship
would be a defining moment in the shift from a samurai code to an imperial
one. They left from Yokohama on the *Pegasus* under the care of a Captain
Barstow on 12 May, at a cost of about 1,000 ryo each. Their trips lasted over
four months and were extremely rough in parts. Unaccustomed to sea travel,
all became famously seasick. Even tougher was the fact that they were disguised
as ordinary British sailors, their new shipmates conspiring not to see anything
unusual in this, and were addressed as the lowest order of seamen. They also
had to do the work of rank and file sailors, galling to young men who saw
manual labour belonging naturally to the lower castes – though of course an
English gentleman of the time would have felt the same.

In Shanghai the Five were hidden on an opium ship, amidst some confusion, and Ito was surprised to find the group split up. He and Inoue left the other three and went on ahead via Singapore, Bombay, Aden and Alexandria, arriving in Southampton on 21 June 1863, where they were met by a stranger who introduced himself as Thomas Glover's brother James. They proceeded to London the next day with James Glover, and if Thomas had been disoriented in the alien land of Nagasaki, his culture shock was mild compared to that of these five students, coming from a country in which there had been no reliable accounts of the world beyond the Chinese coast for centuries. They were soon introduced by William Matheson to Professor Alexander Williamson, a chemist of the Royal Academy and University College London, and wandered the wide streets of the capital, watching the crowds.

It is a sign of the influence of Jardine Matheson that the company was able to secure an appointment for the students with the Foreign Office. Ito and Inoue took the opportunity to press the anti-bakufu case to a government that seemed bound, in this modern land, to see reason. But as the officials listened politely, it dawned on the samurai that the British Foreign Office was less interested in ethical concerns in its semi-protectorates than in their smooth management. Soon after they buried their disappointment by going about their fact-finding mission, taking the route later associated with Gandhi from London to the Manchester factories. None had read the recent pioneering study by Friedrich Engels: none was prepared for the underside of a modern class society, where the living conditions of workers and managers were even more starkly differentiated than those between samurai and lower castes in Japan. In this tough world, Ito began to understand the motives behind Glover's ambition to leave and make his fortune. Despite Jardine Matheson's influence with British government, their brief visit was not spent courting dignitaries. Ian Nish has pointed out that where British visits to Japan tended to be concerned with engagements with diplomacy among the elite and observations of quaint oriental customs, Meiji Japanese visits to Britain concentrated on studies of manufacturing and the military. As they returned to the news of the shelling of Shimonoseki, Ito and Inoue reflected on how imperial Britain's modern version of military logistics was linked to a national identity which saw itself, despite the country's own inequalities, as having a mission of justice. During the strike on their capital, they helped to organise a network of weaponry in European fashion, with one eye on the coming struggle against the bakufu, and recognised that it would involve significant social changes.

Ironically in Britain itself, the time of the trip of the Choshu Five was one in which imperial expansion was not always seen as an advantage, and many in the House of Commons were pushing for a more cultural – rather than martial – attitude towards empire. In October 1864 Prime Minister Gladstone cut the war budget, though the consolidation of China remained important. In 1868 Charles Dilke's *Greater Britain* recorded this shift in policy by suggesting a new kind of imperialism which spread an absorbent form of cultural Britishness, rather than going to the trouble of governing land. In Westminster, it was often argued that occupying colonies was a drain on funds, and that countries should be persuaded to bid for membership of the British franchise themselves. The formal land mass of the British empire even briefly contracted. The Japanese luminary of the Meiji Enlightenment and later Glover collaborator, Fukuzawa Yukichi, would later make the same arguments against land expansion of the Japanese empire, in his newspaper *Jiji Shinpo*.

In contrast to the mythical collaboration with the Choshu Five, Glover was central to the defection of another important early group of ryugakusei, the Satsuma Nineteen, in 1865, via William Keswick in Hong Kong. His increasingly close friend Godai had understood the need for a mission since Kagoshima, and Glover had spent some of 1864 thinking this over and planning a schedule. Many of the Satsuma Nineteen students came from the feeder institution which Godai and other leading Satsuma samurai had set up in July 1864, Kaiseijo College, teaching science, languages and military discipline. The aim of the college was to turn out young men with leadership potential and heads for logistics, and ambitions to study abroad, in numbers pointedly greater than those of Choshu.

At the edge of Europe the first Satsuma visitors experienced a conversion of a different order than they had had after watching the Battle of Kagoshima. Godai claimed that all the latent Europhobic joi of his party evaporated as soon as they reached the continent:

[m]ore than half of our number had been leading instigators of anti-foreign sentiment, but when they stepped ashore at Malta in the Mediterranean and saw for the first time the enlightened progress and the mighty power of Europe they awoke at once.

The Satsuma Nineteen were met by Glover's colleagues in Southampton on 21 June 1865. After a night in the Queen's Hotel, they moved to lodgings in Bayswater, an area of London which, almost exactly a century later, would become known for a generation of Caribbean immigrants. The youngest and most celebrated of the group, Nagasawa Kanae, too young to enter London University, was sent to the Glover family home of Braehead, and Choshu and Tosa would follow. The young Nagasawa, freezing, swordless, and unused to stodgy food, nevertheless adapted quickly, communicating with the remaining Glover family in rapidly improving English, and is one of the real all-round pioneers of this story:

> As he was still in his early teens, Nagasawa spent his time in Aberdeen staying at Braehead House, the Glover family home, and the sixteen-year-old Mori [Arinori] may also have lodged there. The other students, however, found accommodation in rented housing. After initially staying near the city centre in the home of a bootmaker called John Burnett at 85 Hutcheon Street, for example, Nomura [Fumio], Ishimaru [Torogoro] and Mawatari [Hachiro] were found separate houses further away in Old Aberdeen. Not only were these closer to Braehead House, but they were chosen, so their tutor explained, because it was quiet there and conducive to their studies.

Extraordinarily for someone who was not a native English speaker, according to the *Aberdeen Free Press*, Nagasawa was top of his class at the Gym for Latin, English Grammar and Reading, and Geography in 1866 and 1868, and top for Arithmetic, Dictation and Writing, and Grammar in 1869. He is known to have had problems controlling his temper in Aberdeen: he was the victim of various forms of teasing and couldn't help a typically samurai reaction. Being the youngest, the baiting seems to have affected him more than any other of the Satsuma Nineteen. At least once he got into a serious fight with local boys: Alex McKay has recounted the story, dramatised by Alan Spence, of how Nagasawa once used the gift of a pocket watch from the Glovers to strike another boy – an ironic use for this symbol of British gentlemanliness where his sword had had to be offered up to the modern world. Later undergoing a total westernisation and a conversion to the Christian sect The Brotherhood of New Life, he followed the preacher Thomas Lake Harris to Santa Rosa, California, where he founded a winery and led the local chapter of the Brotherhood until his death in 1932.

But, while Nagasawa was in Aberdeen on 30 August 1865, the *Owari*, a ship built for the bakufu, was launched, and the naming ceremony was performed by Mary Glover in front of a number of bakufu officials. There is no easy way to explain the conflict of interests in the Glovers' looking after a rebel boy while sponsoring his mortal enemies. Glover was, in absentia, while displaying the civility and hospitality which marked him out as a clan confidant, still hedging his economic bets, as he had in 1861.

His thinking changed when the hapless Consul Rutherford Alcock retired in July 1865, making way for Harry Parkes, who had begun his career as a respected Chinese interpreter and who recognised Glover's importance to the internecine struggle. Like Satow, Parkes saw that the Foreign Office's stance of only recognising the power of the bakufu was inadequate for a developing national situation in which the rebels were the ones looking outwards. Under the influence of Glover and Satow, Parkes was less closed to the Satsuma cause. The clan had to restructure from 1863 and was becoming markedly Europhile.

As Glover's arms business grew and the clans rearmed, Godai kept him informed about Satsuma affairs and Glover became a cipher for Parkes. Glover now had the confidence of prominent members of both main clans. At New Year 1866 the seemingly impossible was suggested, and talks outlining a Saccho alliance were held in secret in Kyoto. The talks were attended by the key diplomatic forces behind Restoration – Kido Takayoshi from Choshu and Sakamoto Ryoma from Satsuma – and ended, extraordinarily, in success. Where the story becomes interesting is that it is probable that Glover knew about the Saccho alliance, signed on 7 March, before he arranged for a key meeting between Harry Parkes and Shimazu Saburo, 'Prince of Satsuma', in clan homeland in Kagoshima. Glover himself certainly claimed to know about the nascent agreement and to have helped Foreign Office officials to Kyushu to attend. If so, he was quite deliberately drawing British sympathies towards a combined rebel front and giving the wobbling bakufu its last big push.

This early piece of inside-track diplomacy, which brought together the combined clans and the British Foreign Office, was described by Glover in his 1910 interview as 'the best thing I ever did'. The degree of his influence is debatable, but he was very thorough in making arrangements for Parkes and other dignitaries including Admiral King to leave Edo (Tokyo) for Satsuma territory. King stayed with Glover at Ipponmatsu, listening to Glover in the bay arm of the house lobby for freedom of trade via a new

pan-rebel government. Meanwhile, further south in Kagoshima, Parkes was
being wooed by the Satsuma daimyo with shows of opulence. Since Glover
probably knew about the Saccho alliance and Parkes probably didn't, it
looks like Glover calculated that if Shimazu persuaded Parkes to his side,
the bakufu would be left isolated. Their only allies would be the French,
who would be unlikely to intervene to prop up the old government. After
a night in Kagoshima, Parkes realised that Glover had had influence over
the clans from as early as the 1863 battle. When the two got together again,
Glover felt that he had proved a point. Parkes was still wavering, but had
been eased towards Saccho support by Glover's pitch. By the summer of
1866 Parkes's support for Satsuma, like Satow's, could be read in the press.
In his last interview Glover described Parkes's guarded favour for Glover's
argument (and here I follow Alex McKay's translation):

> At about one o' clock, when supper was finished, everyone left except
> Parkes and me. Parkes said, 'For Japan's future, I've got to help the
> shogun.'
>   I told him, 'The future of Japan is already in the hands of the
> southern daimyo. Japan's future depends on them'.
>   Parkes didn't agree with me. We talked until dawn. He couldn't
> decide whether he should support the shogun or Satsuma and Choshu.

However, the idea of an Anglo-Saccho agreement as a fait accompli for
Glover over Foreign Office stagnation may not be so clear-cut. A circular
from the Foreign Office almost immediately before Parkes left for the Kyushu
summit renewed the British government's state of neutrality, and as a loyal
civil servant without any strong political views and nothing to gain by going
against the Foreign Office, Parkes would have been reluctant not to toe this
line. Besides which, relations between Glover and Parkes were thorny. Parkes
is known to have taken a dim view of Glover's business activities in general:
looking back three years later in a letter to Lord Stanley he described Glover's
arms dealing as an 'unhealthy feature of Japanese trade'.

Glover felt that his selling the Saccho alliance was a coup, but there are
also indications that his mid 1860s career path saw him significantly ostracised
by both his own government and Jardine Matheson, who tried as far as
possible not to acknowledge arms sales. Still, having risen under the tutelage
of Mackenzie, Glover had learned to put up with a degree of ostracism.
And we will never really know whether the diplomacy of 1866, certainly

arranged and brokered by Glover, was decisive in preparing for the Meiji Restoration by convincing Parkes to support a clan alliance. If it was, it certainly was the most significant single act of Glover's career, as he later claimed, and one of the founding moments of modern Japan. That King subjected himself to Glover's hospitality and propaganda in Ipponmatsu, and that members of the Legation later commended Glover's skilful management of the Parkes visit, suggests that Glover provided at least a strong impetus.

Yet in the Saccho rivalry, Glover still felt more sympathetic towards Satsuma than Choshu. The memories of the nights of 1862 and 1863 locked up in William Alt's house were not easy to extinguish. Choshu's Ito would never quite forgive Glover for this early favouritism. It was not the Choshu Five but the Satsuma Nineteen, young men selected and organised by Godai, who had been Glover's first vital student-smuggling mission, though there would be many others afterwards from Choshu once the bakufu had weakened and the clan had become more Euro-friendly. From the time of the Satsuma Nineteen, ryugakusei of many clans were encouraged to go to Glover's home town, and for a while there was a significant Kyushu–Aberdeen diaspora:

> Glover certainly orchestrated the escape of the second Choshu party ... at Shimonoseki in 1865. He was also behind the escape of Ishimaru, Mawatari and Nomura from Nagasaki later that year, and even promised to cover the Hizen [clan] students' travel expenses. A few months later, he was again involved in Kondo Chojiro's fatal attempt to leave Japan. As a result of his activities, Glover's home town of Aberdeen became a regular destination for illegal travellers. By early 1866, there were five Japanese students staying in the city, compared with nine in London, and one in Glasgow.

The Hizen students who arrived on 26 March 1866 in particular achieved fame in Aberdeen – and were perhaps of even more public interest than Glover himself when he returned a year later. However, Glover would later bare his economic teeth by turning on some of his students, quickly recalling loans which he had apparently made in a spirit of open-ended friendship. But there is every indication that he was seen as a connector and benefactor by many of the students he took into his care from the time of the Satsuma Nineteen. As Nomura, of Aki han (in today's Hiroshima) commented, 'the arrangements made by Glover and the trouble and kindness shown by the captain on our behalf have been like that of men related by blood'.

The Choshu Five, however, remain the iconic figures of the age, as senior rebel figures leaving early and at great risk, then rising to the top two positions of power in the country. To point out that Glover was not behind the smuggling is not necessarily a criticism: he may have thought, for example, that the Five were not yet ready to go – as their belligerent behaviour on board the ship suggests. He may have watched events in Kagoshima and foreseen a bombardment of Shimonoseki, and felt that their place was there. It may also be that Glover's voice later in 1865 in dissuading Ito, by this time a close friend, from his desire to return to Britain, was a much greater service than smuggling them onto the 1863 ship, since it kept Ito in place to slip into the position of first Prime Minister after the Saccho alliance and the crumbling of the bakufu. Despite the fact that they were not his own project, the Five are almost always remembered when Glover is mentioned. The project wasn't his, but it was a British one to which he lent vocal support. Most often remembered is how they had to dress as British deck hands and lose their topknots, a story often told as one of humiliation, and a situation which provoked powerful aggressive reactions. But even more humiliating was the loss of their swords, the defining icon of the samurai. And one of the great ironies in remembering Glover as an honorary samurai is that his arms dealing eclipsed the tradition of hand-to-hand martial arts, in favour of the remote power of the gun.

SIX

The Way of the Sword

On 12 May 1868, the Choshu diarist Kido Takayoshi recorded:

In the morning I went with Ryuto to visit the Englishman [Brown and Hirota's translation] Glover; and we talked together about events of the last three years. We had a lot to say, having met after so long a time. He presented me with a pistol . . .

In the year of Restoration, of all possible choices of gift, to one of the most eminent samurai in the country's most loyalist clan, Glover offered a pistol. It is the most apt sign of his 1860s legacy imaginable.

Swordmaking is a highly evolved process and one of the most respected Japanese crafts. Each commissioned blade lies in a furnace before being hammered into shape, which tapers the edge, and is reheated and cooled, until it reaches a perfect thickness and strength. The work of experienced makers is favoured, the craft is traditionally passed down through families, and apprenticeships are measured in decades rather than years. Pre-Restoration samurai demanded perfectly tailored swords, and their blades lay against them like limbs throughout their lives. Swordfights took speed, judgement of an opponent's body weight, practised technique, and the willingness to push right through another body. They were a form of combat in which people had to be physically connected. After Kagoshima, this form of combat gave way to gunfights, where the enemy could be killed from a distance. This transition was encouraged by the mass import of the rifle, of which Glover bought thousands.

A general tendency of empire is to replace encounters based on touch with encounters based on vision. For example, when Glover was a boy, the idea of the separation of races (into three: Glover was of the white variety dealing with the yellow variety) was finding its uses in empire as a classifier of labour. The classic early account of race is the Edinburgh physiologist Robert Knox's *Races of Men* from 1850, revised in 1862, Scottish-imperial to the core, and influential during Glover's apprenticeship in China. Under the now discredited idea of race, a person's characteristics are known at first sight, removing the need for contact altogether. Anti-colonial movements have conversely often attempted to regain a sense of touch: for example, when the British empire in Trinidad illegalised percussive instruments struck with the hand – as sounding dangerously African – this gave rise to the closest the Trinidadians could get to percussion while staying within the law, steel drums.

This passage also determines the possibility of history: with physical contact, a present time is shared, since a force is felt simultaneously by two persons, while with vision, light takes time to cross over space, and the viewer is left to catch up. So for Japanese ryugakusei, the modern always seemed to come from overseas – as it still does today, as viewers around the world sit in front of TVs watching modern missiles hit primitive desert buildings. If history is made of shared experience, in the 1860s Japanese national history began to disappear. And cultures involved in the destruction of history are as fixated by vision as those disappearing: Glover's Britain now has less than one per cent of the world's population, and twenty per cent of the world's CCTV cameras.

Where Glover made his first fortune, despite his samurai image, was in his realisation that, following Godai's conversion after Kagoshima, and during an extraordinarily rapid conversion to the western–modern, most samurai were keen to swap the way of the sword for remote conflict. During an almost overnight change, the market was flooded with guns, and Glover was responsible for many of them. The leader of the last samurai, the last to practise bushido and persist in seeing the sword as a decisive weapon, would be wiped out less than a decade after the 1868 Restoration.

For the Glover family, the extremes of non-modern and modern warfare met in the period of only two generations. At the beginning of the family's Nagasaki story in the mid 1860s, Japan's martial resistance was based on swordsmanship, the manipulation of metal by muscle, and even the young Thomas learned something of the way of the sword after instruction from some of Ito's group in the garden at Ipponmatsu. Only eight decades later, his adopted home town was destroyed in a flash, subjected to an all-consuming light which seemed to come from nowhere. Glover made his name as a pioneer in importing rifles, gunboats and later dynamite, as witnessed enthusiastically by his son. It is a terrible irony that this process of modernisation would accelerate towards use of the supreme remote weapons in the city where he had play-fenced with Ito.

The pre-Restoration years of the mid 1860s were those when ambitious samurai most decisively laid down their swords for guns and gunships. Sugiyama Shinya calculates that 171,934 rifles were imported into Nagasaki alone between 1865 and 1868, and, in the small world of the concessions, Guraba Shokai was the most significant importer. The guns largely came through Shanghai, and the warships, which would become one of Glover's longest lasting legacies, through Aberdeen. The Aberdeen shipyard Hall Russell & Co. Ltd had been established in 1790, but only flourished in the middle of the next century, boosted by Glover business. When the clans' demand increased, the ships ordered by Glover were built by Hall Russell and mostly handled by Glover & Co. (Aberdeen) in Marischal Street, run by eldest brother Charles.

The first ship made for the Japanese in Aberdeen, handled by Glover & Co. (Aberdeen), the *Satsuma*, was launched early in 1864. The *Satsuma* made it all the way to the coast of Japan before it sank. Glover allowed himself to fall into an uncharacteristic despair in Ipponmatsu, and, in 'a day or two of despondency', the problems of Shimonoseki and the Saccho alliance seemed briefly eclipsed. It would be half a decade before the arrival of the first of the three great ships (*Ho Sho Maru*, *Jho Sho Maru* and *Wen Yu Maru*) for which he is now remembered. The *Ho Sho Maru* left Aberdeen on 4 July 1868 and arrived in Nagasaki on 24 January 1869. The huge *Jho Sho Maru*, weighing around eight times more than the *Ho Sho Maru* and costing five times as much at £46,032, was launched soon after, on 27 March 1869, and handed over to the clients, the Higo clan, on 7 April 1870. The *Aberdeen Journal* of 27 March 1869 reported the launch of the greatest of the ships as a milestone for the city:

> The launch of the vessel took place on Saturday shortly after noon, in presence of a large number of spectators. As she glided off the stocks she was gracefully named, with the usual ceremony, by Mrs. Charles T. Glover, the *Jho Sho Maru*, or *Whirlwind*. The preparations for the launch were completed under the superintendence of Mr. Main of Messrs. Alex. Hall & Co. The *Jho Sho Maru* will be commanded by Captain James, with Lieutenant Ingleback as chief officer. We understand that Messrs. Glover have secured an order for another gunboat, similar to the *Jho Sho Maru*, which has given the greatest satisfaction . . . After the launch on Saturday, Messrs. Hall entertained a large party of ladies and gentlemen to cake and wine . . . success to the *Jho*

Sho Maru was proposed, coupled with the name of Captain James, who suitably responded. Mr. James Hall then proposed, in eulogistic terms, the health of Mr. Charles T. Glover.

The *Jho Sho Maru* was the most ambitious ship ever to have been built in Aberdeen yards. By the time it left Aberdeen it had already cost the life of James Hall: while it was sitting in Aberdeen harbour, a fire broke out and Hall had a heart attack while pushing the ship free, showing the yard's desperate pride in completing the project. The *Aberdeen Journal* of 2 June 1869 reported that

> [n]o sooner had he [Hall] begun to give some orders, and while in the act of directing the water hose with his own hands, than the flames burst thro' the floor at his feet, and without word or sign, he dropped down and instantly expired.

As it turned out, this iconic ship also led to great stress for Glover, since the Higo clan, under centralised government control after the Restoration, delayed payment. But the ship remained an object of pride for the Glovers and the Aberdeen yards, and represented a change in attitude for the emerging Japanese Imperial Navy. Emperor Meiji visited the *Jho Sho Maru* in April 1871 and again in July 1872, to a 21-gun salute and the type of carnival which always accompanied him whenever he left Kyoto. Glover remembered Queen Victoria's Aberdeen visit and reflected that he had now become the centre of royal attention.

According to some accounts, Glover Brothers' business almost single-handedly revived the prestige of the Aberdeen shipyards. Others point out that Glover diverted some shipbuilding from Scotland to Japan, and yet others that the 1870s would have been a boom time for Aberdeen shipping with or without the Glovers' intervention. In any case, Glover banked on the fact that labour was cheaper in the north-east than in Glasgow. Most significantly for Japan, not only did he promote investment into new weapons, he also promoted the idea that a strong national military was central to development. Looking at British imperial success in the decades before Japan's opening, this seemed an attractive proposition and was taken up by the samurai who slid into governmental positions in the 1870s and 1880s, and who aimed to turn the age into one of expansion based on the new weaponry. From the time of the defection to England of the Choshu

Five to the height of what became known as Meiji Conservatism in the 1880s, national pride was increasingly tied to military logistics.

By time of the Restoration in January 1868, Choshu had long since passed through the frantically joi period when Ito had helped to burn down the British Legation, and had determined, like Satsuma, to reorganise its army, placing the diarist Kido Takayoshi in a brokering position. As early as 1865, influenced by what his troops had seen of foreign armies, the Choshu daimyo had taken a step away from the way of the sword by decreeing that the clan should be restructured as a western-style army on meritocratic grounds, using the latest military technology largely supplied by Glover. At the height of arms sales in October 1865, to conduct deals with Choshu, Glover disguised himself as a Satsuma samurai, his business suit replaced with a yukata and his already thinning hair tied back. Despite this comic look, Glover took his amateur espionage seriously: 'We're all here getting good experience . . . [t]here are also about thirty men here from all parts of Japan, all getting experience, and this is really a very busy place.' He may have seen this as an adventuresome piece of pantomime, but he was determined to go native to get between the clans if he had to. He was also risking treason: according to official policy, the bakufu still had British support, and Glover was by now arming against both the bakufu and the British Navy itself. Yet even while watching several years of gunrunning, British consuls had shown themselves unwilling to question him. The Foreign Office knew about but tolerated his behaviour. The young Glover recognised the slipperiness of the attitudes of the Foreign Office: on paper they were behind the bakufu, but in practice wanted little to do with what was turning into a civil war. By 1866, he realised that because of the British punitive strikes and the influence of the traders, Satsuma and Choshu were increasingly facing the bakufu together as a modern force. Nor could diplomats fail to notice the bakufu's nervousness in the face of the assembled clans: the bakufu appealed for support to the British head of state, sending 'a pointed request to the British Queen not to allow the illicit trade. The Shogun himself sent her a personal letter.'

Until 1867, Glover continued to watch his fortune rise as he rearmed the clan alliance leaders via two of the best remembered Restoration heroes, Sakamoto Ryoma and Kido Takayoshi, and organised by Ito and Inoue. Sakamoto founded a company as a flag of convenience to get around sanctions on munitions imports. He was particularly well placed to mediate, since as a member of Tosa he had numerous joi comrades, but was relatively untroubled by Saccho rivalries. As Marius Jansen says, '[i]n Nagasaki, Sakamoto's dealings were largely with foreign merchants. Of these, the most important was Thomas Glover . . .'

When Parkes softened towards the clans, Glover came to feel that his foresight into Japanese politics had been vindicated, and he began to move politically on behalf of the rebels. After the Parkes–Saccho meeting, it was clear that British diplomats mainly, if grudgingly, had come to regard Glover as an authority in dealing with samurai. However, Parkes was also under orders to threaten to remove protection for rogue traders, which he did in spring 1866. Regardless, Glover went on to sell the steamship *Union* as well as 7,300 Minie rifles through Ito and Inoue. On 22 June 1866 Parkes again halfheartedly reminded traders that anyone dealing with the rebels would lose the protection of the Foreign Office, but by this point, Nagasaki had already become a focal point for samurai from the organising southern rebel clans. Sakamoto likened 1860s Nagasaki to the most fluid times of the country: 'Nagasaki, with all these people here, is as interesting as something from the period of the warring states.'

The shrewder settlers had realised after the Saccho alliance in 1866 that amongst the clans the immediate priority was to get rid of the bakufu, and settle old scores later. Politely ignored by Queen Victoria and a Foreign Office that showed little interest in non-European domestic situations, the bakufu prepared to fall on its sword. The two clans it had been relying on to slice one another apart were now united in a common cause, and armed with guns rather than swords. There could no longer be any divide-and-rule policy. The bakufu perished under the weight of arms: with no real struggle, the revolution was more or less a velvet one, with a tinge of seppuku. As it turned out the shogun, Tokugawa Iemochi, died not long before the armed rebellion began on 10 January 1867, and the end of the bakufu era was presided over by a new shogun, Tokugawa Yoshinobu. Later that year, anticipating consistently strong arms markets when he returned to a new Japanese government, Glover took a trip home to Aberdeen, after a decade away. On 3 January 1868, in his absence, the end of the bakufu was officially declared by five han in Kyoto. In Glover's last interview, as pointed up by Alex McKay, Glover claimed that 'it wasn't simply about getting money: I believe that I was the greatest rebel of them all against Tokugawa.'

But there was an ironic outcome for Glover's Nagasaki after Restoration. In the mid 1860s, Nagasaki had been a city dependent on its frontier status, where business could take place on a semi-legal basis and weapons dealing was common. Within three years of the Reformation which standardised trade and removed the need for surreptitious deals, Hyogo (Kobe) and Osaka would both expand and sideline Nagasaki. As early as 22 July 1871, the *Nagasaki Express* was reporting that '[b]eyond having a trade in Coal and Tea, both of which articles are likely to cause few firms to remain, Nagasaki has but little business of any other description worth speaking of, so that literally the port, year by year, continues on its downward course'. While Glover was overcoming his reverse culture-shock in Aberdeen, the Japanese war economy centred on Nagasaki was in fact contracting, and military demand slowing.

Moreover, after January 1868 the rebels had to account for themselves in government rather than opposition. The transfer of power would not be entirely smooth, and the clans unevenly offloaded responsibilities onto the central government. Glover would struggle to deal with the complex power shifts and to adapt his arms and ships business to a peacetime economy. Despite these cash flow problems, his pre-Restoration arming role would be long remembered by many in the new samurai bureaucracy, who saw him as a natural connector and ally. His office became a meeting-place for high-ranking officials, and he is discussed casually as an insider. On 1 June 1868 Kido wrote:

> In the morning I went to the Glover Trading Company; and I chanced to meet Godai Saisuke [later Tomoatsu] there, as well as Joseph Heco. I talked with Glover about leasing a warship, and he assented; but we have not yet concluded the negotiations for a contract. I did make an appointment for further discussions of the matter in Naniwa [Osaka] . . .

As the clans were converted to modern warfare, facilities were built on-site for education in logistics, and there was a phase of enthusiastic training in Nagasaki in seamanship. Marcus Flowers, Nagasaki British Consul, noted in 1868 that

> so anxious are they to learn that there is not a single steamer that enters the harbour but they are sure to visit and take minute copies of everything they see, and such rapid progress have they made with regard to machinery, that they are able to work all the steamers they have recently purchased themselves.

After Restoration, Godai, Ito and Inoue would gain important positions as reformers in Osaka, Hyogo and Nagasaki, all good news for Glover. On the other hand, after rifles had flooded the market, his days of small-arms dealing were over. The new central government would have to resist only occasional armed uprisings, or counter-revolutions, by discontented joi samurai – not a mammoth task with their new military superiority. After having made a fortune selling guns to rebels and regarding himself as 'the greatest rebel', Glover saw his weaponry pressed into service by the authorities against any remaining rebels – for example, his great ship *Ho Sho Maru* was used to put down the rebellion of Eto Shinpei in 1874.

The end of the old way of the sword was conclusively sounded with the defeat of the last samurai Saigo Takamori, a model for the film starring Tom Cruise. In 1877 Satsuma rebels led into revolt by Saigo called for an immediate invasion of Korea, a hawkish stance typical of those conservative rebel samurai of the 1870s and 1880s who feared the erosion of national pride with the new ways – a stance later embraced by Glover's allies. But Saigo's swordbearing rebels were defeated on their home turf of Kumamoto in a desultory manner without getting near the government forces (as the film shows). This would be the last uprising which the government had to exert itself to suppress, and the agents of this disarming were the politicians Glover had empowered. Where Glover is sometimes colloquially compared to Bonnie Prince Charlie, in the Saigo affair he occupied something like the opposite position: the government used his technology to disarm native rebels hanging on to seemingly archaic nationalist causes – the part played by the British authorities against Scotland in the last Jacobite defeat of 1745–46.

Despite the rapid conversion to western logistics, the newly armed Japan's desire for recognition as an imperial power would go mostly unheeded by Europe from the Restoration until well into the next century, even as it styled itself as an empire along British lines, with Inoue seeking out new colonial opportunities. The conclusion was a rejection of Japanese calls for a declaration of ethnic equality amongst the victors at Versailles in 1919, where the US used its veto to kill the proposal, by now a familiar scenario. Coming not long after Glover's death, this snub helped to create the militarism which Europe began to notice only in the 1930s. After the war, the Macarthur Constitution belatedly tried to squash Japan's national military altogether. The US-written Constitution, which still stands today, seems to reverse the arming project of Glover in its famous ninth clause, which states that Japan will never go to war for any reason. This seems like a good pacifist notion to some, but in practice turns Japan into a client state covered in military bases over which it has no authority. Deprived of their own foreign policy decisions, post-war Japanese governments have been supporters of hawkish US foreign policy, against the wishes of most citizens. The state paid $13bn towards the first bombing of Iraq in 1991, and was persuaded by George W. Bush to reinterpret its Constitution to allow participation in the 2003 attacks, to widespread public outrage. Clause nine is not a recognition of the playing out of militarisation, but a return of military control to western managers as in 1853–68.

In 1945, at the conclusion of the move from the way of the sword to the way of remote attack, Glover's son Tomisaburo walked the Nagasaki streets with the first symptoms of an unknown sickness, seeing amongst the piled dead the haunting sight of fireworks meant as makeshift funerals, often lit by children (a scene which may have some connection to Peter Greenaway's film *Drowning by Numbers*). Fireworks in Japan had been common-place since his father's experiments with dynamite, and there had been firework displays at some of the diplomatic parties at which Tomisaburo had celebrated Japanese military victories. The conclusion of the route to remote warfare indicated a melancholy return to its origins.

Today, anti-nuclear political action has a huge underground in Nagasaki, even amongst those who would, for career security, never describe themselves as political activists. On the day I was doing research in the atomic bomb museum in Nagasaki, looking through the scenes Tomisaburo had seen during his last days, the US had just started to sell nuclear technology to India – not a signatory of the non-proliferation treaty – causing speculation that North Korea and Iran would continue their own programmes. On the way to the museum I was stopped by anti-nuclear campaigners with flyers about the news. One of them introduced himself as a higaisha, a veteran of the atomic bombing. He was a well presented man in his seventies, marked with ancient weals around the neck and shoulders. It was the kind of reminder that sometimes asserts itself in the city, that most people over a certain age are carrying a memory of the bombing with them. This activist would have probably been in junior high school when a flash spun him round on his feet and waves of rubble and heat threw him onto the ground. As I left to follow his directions to the museum, he pulled me back and told me that his ancestors had been Tosa samurai.

SEVEN

On the Eve

Before he left for Aberdeen in 1867, Glover realised that the aim of the Foreign Office quiet-lifers in Japan was the continuation of settled government, whatever form it took. In a sense, he knew that the groundwork was down to traders like him, and his work ethic had prepared him for the task. The British government quietly changed their allegiance from the bakufu to the Restoration government without breaking stride. Except for times when even more free trade was demanded, this hands-off attitude had been good for business, and, in Parkes, Glover had found someone who accepted the Foreign Office's position of leaving meddling in native government to the world of commerce. A political realist, Parkes saw the Restoration coming, and after a decade of transitions, the eve of Restoration promised the transition to end them all. In a way it seems an odd time for Glover to leave Japan. He left without knowing if the old samurai powers would be able to cooperate in a new government, and what kind of living would be waiting for him when he came back.

This was also a time of modification of British imperial ambitions. The year of Restoration, 1868, coincided with Charles Dilke's influential description of a British move to cultural and linguistic, rather than territorial, expansion. Japan was never mentioned in Dilke's first edition: it was thought to be beyond the Anglophone pale, though informally it was certainly on the edge of empire. The Foreign Office had never had any designs on Japanese land, but it needed the ascendant government to contain some body answerable to the international community on Euro-friendly terms under the restored rule of the emperor – the British 'monarch-in-parliament' model. This was also exactly Glover's vision for Japan. He saw himself as a rebel, but in an entrepreneurial sense beneficial to the quiescent Foreign Office, rather than in the sense of Irish or Indian nationalist rebels, who were also making inroads around 1868. He was never a republican – quite the opposite. If anything, the top caste of samurai he supported were more like loyalist paramilitaries. A question this raises is, if we celebrate Glover's mercantile imagination, personality and willingness to take risks, don't we also have to celebrate his monarchist Britishness? This is an uncomfortable question if we insist on seeing Glover as a specifically Scottish hero. In any case, his movements of 1867 show that, as he boarded the ship back to Aberdeen, he was thinking about Restoration in something like the following ways.

Britain was fixated on its imperial rival: the days of the Seven Years' War and the Napoleonic Wars were over, but the whole of the nineteenth century saw continued scuffles between Britain and France over territories in almost every part of the globe. The bakufu looked towards France for support, and French traders dealt almost exclusively with the bakufu until 1865, when the amateur Japanologist Charles de Montblanc started to court Satsuma. The key moment in Montblanc's attempts to outpace Glover came at the Paris Exhibition of 1867, which promised a showcase for Japanese culture at the very moment bakufu power was breaking down. After making extravagant diplomatic overtures to Satsuma, Montblanc had been commissioned to represent the clan at the Exhibition, to the anger of the shogunate, which thought it could rely on the French. Towards the end of 1865 the bakufu had become concerned that Montblanc was arranging to represent the clan under the non-Japanese rubric of Kingdom of the Ryukyus (Okinawa), claiming the pro-rebel high ground. When shogunate officials turned up in Paris in April 1867, Montblanc had indeed arranged for Satsuma to be represented as the Ryukyus, and shogunate representatives were left, thousands of miles from home, with no recourse but to complain to Napoleon III that the legitimate nation was not being represented. And, as Alex McKay puts it:

> Montblanc went further. He had a special decoration designed which featured a white cross in a circle superimposed on a red five-pointed star. Napoleon III and other civilian and military dignitaries attending the Exhibition were awarded this honour, giving Satsuma the image of a sovereign state and no doubt further irritating the shogunate. The Count [Montblanc] at this stage was very well regarded by Satsuma.
>
> He took full advantage of his new status. A credit for 400,000 francs was opened for him to enable the purchase of arms and the dispatch of naval officers to help Satsuma set up its own navy. These events, certainly, when he learned of them, would have greatly disturbed Tom Glover – up to this point *he* had been the only European trusted by Satsuma in this way but was being beaten at his own game.

Montblanc's opportunism backfired when the pro-shogun minister Leon Roches had to answer to the Japanese government for Montblanc's behaviour, and was forced to denounce the maverick and have him banned from Satsuma territory, apparently with the support of other leading Satsuma figures friendly to Glover. Nevertheless Glover's monopoly on representation of the rebel clans had been threatened, and there was a brief competition for the clans' attention between Glover, with Parkes and Satow behind him, and Montblanc, with lukewarm gestures from the French government. But the French on this occasion again looked like they were in another losing imperial battle.

Montblanc's and Glover's attempts to foil one another are described in carefully researched detail by McKay as a story of personal rivalry, but both figures were also aware that they were representatives of their own nations. Glover would later write that the scramble for access to the clans had been for 'the grace of her Majesty'. We should take this with a pinch of free trade salt, but the cultural supremacy of Britain over France was primary to all loyalist pioneers. As Ian Nish says, 'Britain was . . . eager to take a share in the modernisation of Japan's military institutions for reasons of international rivalry, if for no other.' Glover understood in this sense that he was a kind of untrained ambassador, and that in business he would be given a degree of licence by the British government. Meanwhile Britain was winning hearts and minds through the ryugakusei: the Choshu Five had favoured England as a destination over any other country including France, even at the expense of foregoing Oxbridge, which had rejected them on sectarian grounds.

Implicit in the Victorian cultural imperialism absorbed by Glover was the idea of the 'free-born Saxon', an emotional differentiation of the British empire from the French. The free-born Saxon, unlike his (sic) Norman master, didn't need laws because he had an inbuilt sense of decency. He didn't have to cite rules over local disputes, he didn't need a bill of rights or even a formal constitution, and he acted on instincts of fairness. For the free-born Saxon, there were no definite guidelines, only common assumptions, and these impulses remain today in arguments against writing a British constitution. To most samurai rebels, this conservatism made the British tradition highly attractive, since it allowed them to maintain neo-caste rules after Restoration via an unexamined ethnic identity assumed by all. Glover, of course, was by no means a Saxon, but in a gentlemanly sense he identified himself as such when he went to work in the British informal empire. His measure was fair play, not law. He rarely consulted contracts and judged his partners as to whether they were 'decent men' (otokomae).

During his more defensive moments, Glover may even have felt that since modern Japan represented a test case for western policy, Britain was behind a deliberate regime change, conducted under the guise of business and using traders like himself at its sharp end. Later in life he would have dealings with British and Japanese intelligence about which we will only ever know a limited amount. Now he was already perceiving the government's tendency to organise from the top down. From the mid 1860s he was testy with amateur Japanologists, with whom he had, as one acquaintance recalled, 'less patience than one might have with a wayward pet'. Early on he assumed semi-diplomatic powers, which earned him informal warnings from the Foreign Office throughout the 1860s. But the government supported Jardine Matheson much as it did the East India Company, and Jardine Matheson could be relied on to remake the country in a new form if need be, assuming that it was backed by the British military. Glover may have wondered at times if he was a pawn in a Foreign Office modernisation of the governments of the Far East. Only very occasionally was his behaviour reprimanded by the Foreign Office, and the most notable warning concerned his mistreatment of native workers, which was itself perfectly samurai-like behaviour. He had realised that the habit of shouting at underlings was even more natural in the Japanese caste system than it was in the British Navy. If the Foreign Office really did mastermind a regime change, then at some point in the mid 1860s, even before the Parkes–Saccho summit in Kagoshima, it must have realised that the vacuum left to the clans after sakoku was ripe for a European-style ethnic pride, creating a 'catch-up' empire in cultural debt to Britain. In this sense, Glover certainly sometimes felt he was grooming ryugakusei to act as native representatives of British interests. Jardine Matheson agents' tendency to push situations beyond current foreign policy may have been covertly viewed by diplomats as a testing ground for government policy.

What remains most pronounced in Glover's activities of the 1860s is the nature of his modernising mission. In particular, the political classes of European powers exported the idea that an expansive imperialism was a product of any healthy civilisation. Glover's education at the Gym, his monarchist upbringing, and his corporate training, had all taught him to equate the imperial with the advanced. It is no coincidence that this era of change also saw a Japanese love of the paraphernalia of British imperialism. There were two Japanese translations of *Robinson Crusoe* just before the Restoration.

This best known work by the most significant pamphleteer for British Union, Daniel Defoe, was based on the experiences of the Scottish imperial adventurer Alexander Selkirk and encouraged the qualities that would serve Scots best in empire – self-reliance, inventiveness, the Protestant work ethic, and faith in Providence. These were precisely the qualities which Glover took to Japan, and Crusoe's tale of imperial adventure arrived just as the country slipped under the influence of British politicians and Scottish merchants. Progressive samurai in this sense accepted imperialism as a kind of pyramid selling via Scots who had already bought in during the Scottish Enlightenment, where Protestantism, overseas investment, and Good English were ascendant. The Meiji intellectual Soseki Natsume, a novelist known to every schoolchild and the first Japanese university lecturer in Japanese literature, wrote, as he stood in itchy tweeds in Pitlochry, that the vulgar study of English could only damage Japan by corroding native morals. He returned to Standard English-based London, then Japan, and his point was reflected in the 1890 Imperial Edict on Education: Japanese education should retain the idea of Good English and the strong canon of exemplars that Britain had developed at the height of its imperial success. Even today belief in a single correct grammar remains strong in Japan, even though this ideal has broken down in Britain itself. Glover wasn't that interested in language – or, for that matter, education – but he saw that Japan was culturally preparing itself for empire, and wanted to make sure it followed the British model rather than the French, which meant an acceptance of the Protestant–Anglophone–enterprise model. Japanese imperialism would now take on a quasi-British role in extending a protective umbrella over recovering neighbouring countries which had also been affected by unfair trade agreements. As soon as 1875, Japan was making a land agreement with another major European power, Russia. The conquests of Formosa (Taiwan) and Korea were seen as important for both national self-image and for the progressive mindset of the region. The Glovers encouraged this kind of expansion vigorously, at least till the start of the twentieth century. It required the import of arms and technology whether or not there was a war on at any given time, and turned arms dealing into a job for life.

No single one of these interpretations of Restoration was overwhelming in Glover's mind. He was mostly too busy making money for any such reflection, but they remained central to his behaviour. The rivalry between Britain and France certainly did affect world events in the mid-nineteenth century, and one of Glover's closest rivals, Montblanc, certainly was a supporter of the bakufu until he discerned its downfall. Obstructing French plans was definitely an ongoing motive for the British Foreign Office, and the young British merchants perceived this rivalry. Whether the British government had the foresight to consciously stage-manage a regime change is more doubtful, but Glover was constantly surprised throughout the 1860s that the Foreign Office didn't do more to curtail his political activities. That Glover was proud to offer Japan the chance to develop a new imperialism is undoubted: mid-Victorian Britain did see empire as a normal stage of development. And it seemed that Glover was right to return to Aberdeen in 1867 with peace of mind, since he appeared to have the stable political environment he wanted. But all was far from well.

EIGHT

The Slippery Slope

By the first month of 1868 Glover's rebel friends were in government. But as soon as daimyo power passed to the post-Restoration government, a number of clans defaulted on arms payments, creating cash flow problems. Investing in the clans, Glover was not quite putting his soul over his business sense – he'd simply got more than he bargained for when the government started controlling finances previously under clan control. Three years before, this might not have worried him, but by the time he took his 1867 trip back to Aberdeen, he was already seriously in debt.

During the Aberdeen trip, he reflected on an era of spectacular political success and recognised that he had fallen foul of the short-termism of most young headstrong traders. A sense of financial foreboding was one of the reasons he went home. By the time he left, Guraba Shokai already had debts of over $150,000. Glover wavered but determined to stay in the new Japan, perceiving his centrality to the new government and realising that he couldn't run from his financial responsibilities. But even as he vacationed in Aberdeen, he was beginning to understand that it would be increasingly difficult to manoeuvre amongst mounting shortfalls.

Before Glover left for Aberdeen he could still have paid off all his debts by selling his real estate, which would have saved him a lot of heartache over the coming years. Instead, when he returned to Japan in January 1868 he consolidated his property in Kyushu, as well as building a portfolio in the expanding areas of Yokohama and Hyogo. At the same time, having come to terms with a peacetime economy, he tried to reinvent himself as an industrialist. Assessing his previous low-return investments and the scale of his own debts, he felt that he needed a more aggressive strategy. Normally a careful researcher, he came to see the coal mine on the island of Takashima as a potential saviour. But the transition from arms dealer to industrialist, saddled with clan defaults, an excess of unsold weapons, and the possibility of a risky mining investment, would lead him into a series of uncharacteristic misjudgements.

The political intriguing of the pre-Restoration years had proved too much for brother James who had quit Guraba Shokai on New Year's Eve 1864 and gone home to form Glover Brothers (Aberdeen) Shipbrokers Ltd with the eldest Glover brother Charles. James married Mary Donnell on 7 September 1865 and settled in Aberdeen. Meanwhile, Kenneth Mackenzie had returned from China in 1867 to a position with Guraba Shokai just before Glover's own Aberdeen trip, this time working for his former protege. Mackenzie was both a great emotional support for Glover and a terrible influence on his accounting scruples. When Glover got back to Nagasaki in January 1868 they would set up the old partnership, over $220,000 in the red. In Aberdeen Glover had been concerned enough about his over-investment in arms and real estate to involve his family, who took out a loan on the strength of his apparent success. His return was in many ways glorious but one of its aims was to get help and advice. The strain of his debt spread out across the family and may have contributed to the ill health of Alex, from whom Thomas would continue to borrow heavily.

Even before he hit on the idea of the mine, Glover had been fishing in his restless way for more sustainable industrial enterprises. He netted one well-known red herring in 1865: he is sometimes credited with being the father of the Japanese railways – as a headline in the *Evening Express* of 5 February 1969 has it, 'An Aberdonian founded Japan's railways!' The railway itself was less deserving of an exclamation mark, if still indicative of a powerful mercantile imagination. In 1865 Glover imported the first steam locomotive, the *Lord Wellington*, nicknamed the *Iron Duke*, which had already been shown at the Shanghai Exposition. Glover brought the *Iron Duke* to Japan and successfully ran it on a stretch of narrow-gauge track laid on the harbour beneath his house. This mini-exhibition was carried out in an experimental spirit that never expected any real financial gain, but showed to all potential collaborators an eye for a long-term industrial project. The locomotive was transported to Yokohama, where it was test-run on a tiny track as an amusement. It was watched by some of those who would set up the country's first working railway from Tokyo to Yokohama. By this time, Glover's north-east Scottish acquaintance Richard Brunton – himself born into a coastguard's family in 1841 in Muchalls, just north of Stonehaven, and known to the Glover family through the service – had already become one of the first engineers to do a feasibility study of a Toyoko (Tokyo–Yokohama) railway, which he presented to the emperor in March 1869. After this, Brunton established a telegraph line between Kanto and Kansai in 1870, then started on extensive city planning for Yokohama, finally completing an Ordinance Survey map of the country in 1876. A part of the Toyoko railway Brunton helped to design was working by 1872, and in this sense Japanese rail does indeed have strong roots in the maritime entrepreneurism of north-east Scotland. Less often noted in Glover lore, though, is that Hizen samurai had already borrowed the technology of a post-Perry American party as early as the end of the 1850s to build two working-model steam engines themselves. Hizen samurai founded Japan's railways!

Only when the Restoration was all but assured did Glover return to Scotland, and simple homesickness and economic worry were the two main reasons behind the trip. In addition, on 3 February 1867 Emperor Komei had died, to be replaced by Emperor Meiji, who was both liable to be obeyed by the nascent government and was too young to have been inspired by the ultra-joi generation of hardline ronin Yoshida Shoin of central Honshu and Ii Naosuke of Hakone, and this more stable environment seemed safe enough to leave. There was also a practical objective: by the time of the new emperor's coronation Glover had become engaged with the Satsuma daimyo in negotiations concerning the excavation of land for a shipping project which he felt called for a trip to the Aberdeen yards. This was the construction of a slipway to be taken to Nagasaki in bits and assembled on-site, in the same way as had the patent dock been taken from Aberdeen to Fraserburgh during Glover's infancy. The slipway would eventually allow the Japanese Imperial Navy to build and repair its own ships, and would end its reliance on foreign-built vessels. In Aberdeen Glover contacted Alexander Hall & Sons, the shipyard with whom the family had long collaborated, and negotiated its construction.

His arrival in July 1867 was the first time he had been on British soil for ten years. He had undertaken the journey with brother Alex and his wife Ann. The journey was fraught, and the couple had broken up by the time they reached Scotland. Thomas was welcomed warmly back to Braehead, having sent exotic visitors to the house over the decade. He had also made something of himself in trade – though his return wasn't big news in the Aberdeen press. His family listened to his business projects eagerly, and perhaps too optimistically. The visit wasn't entirely happy: as well as the financial worries dawning on Thomas, in September the newly married James died unexpectedly, promising a sombre autumn. The split of Ann and Thomas's soulmate Alex also cast an ugly shadow, with its hint of possible extramarital activity. Ann had given birth to still-born twins on Christmas

Day 1866, and since she and Alex had only married on 1 June, she was probably a couple of months pregnant when they made their decision to stay together. If their marriage was one of convenience, it isn't surprising that it didn't last in a society in which marriages of convenience were routinely broken.

Thomas's return to Nagasaki, this time with youngest brother Alfred, came at exactly the time of the organising of the new Meiji government. After a characteristically short break to recover from the trip, on 27 January 1868 he wrote to William Keswick of Jardine Matheson Hong Kong to thank him for keeping his account open in his absence, and got back to work. But Glover and Mackenzie soon realised that an excess of weapons, debts left by the old company, and the ceding of power by the daimyo, had all resulted in financial problems beyond their expectations. As the bakufu had evaporated, there had been a rapid dip in the value of Enfield rifles, of which Glover had bought several thousand too many, even allowing for the fact that Tosa had taken 5,000 in 1867. He realised that the days of arms yielding huge profits were gone, but he lacked the capital to move into manufacturing. There was no question of a return to small trading in the 'big three': by the late 1860s, Chinese traders had taken over the majority of the foreign markets. So at the end of 1868 he decided to put his energies into mining speculation. The Kosuge Slipway, commissioned in Aberdeen after the model of the Fraserburgh patent dock, would be a great success: the real slippery slope was the mine.

The slipway would turn out to be one of Glover's greatest works. He set aside $40,000 to refurbish an area of the dock for ship repairs and building, and the construction of a unit to house it, and work started on 19 January 1869 by Alexander Hall. The slipway was taken in sections to Nagasaki on the *Ellen Black*, captained by an old friend of Glover's, John Henderson. At 110 feet long and 24 feet four inches wide, the slipway could handle the repair of ships of up to 1,200 tons. Because of its appearance, it became popularly known as the Soroban Dock, the soroban being a Chinese arithmetic tool with beaded wires on a ridged background, usually translated as 'Japanese abacus'. It would soon be used by another Scottish shipbuilder, William Blaikie, who had manufactured some of the first steamers made in Japan. Its potential was appreciated by Glover's old clan friends, and later that year it was bought by the Meiji government for $230,000. Although this represented a useful profit for the debt-ridden Glover, it was also, more than any of the great ships, the most important investment in Glover goods the

Japanese government made, since it marked a change from buying foreign ships to domestic manufacture.

The slipway would later become a cornerstone of the policy of the new zaibatsu (semi-national company) Mitsubishi, as well as the Japanese Imperial Navy. Although the three great ships loom large in the story of Glover's life, his growing hope for the new state is shown in the way he saw the slipway as a priority, recognising its long-term potential in making Japan more self-sufficient. Although the Aberdeen visit was partly intended as a chance to spend time with his family after a long absence, he was often seen at the shipyard concerned about the project's completion. The Nagasaki version of the Stevensons' Fraserburgh dock was sited in Iwasedori-ku and its remnants can still be seen from the roads leading down from Glover Garden. Worryingly, around the time of Restoration, the tendency within the nascent government had been to reject collaboration with foreign speculators: attempts at harbour construction for Satsuma had merely resulted in the clan's starting work without foreign help in March 1867. However, Satsuma had abandoned any hope of mine development without outside expertise, and Glover's more memorable legacy would be Takashima. Already known as a hard worker, in the mine he would see more work than he had imagined possible, as well as a series of accounting accidents that would finish off his hairline.

By the beginning of 1869 Glover was beginning to feel forgotten by a government determined to demonstrate its independence. 'All is going extremely well in the clans,' he writes, 'but I can now only watch [many of their] activities.' Although he is sometimes seen as having been manipulated during the set-up of the mine, in this precarious financial situation Glover took a new-found toughness into the contractual negotiations. He opened with a series of outrageous offers, apparently waiting for Hizen to get tired, guillotine negotiations, and sign at somewhere near a middle ground. The contract was subject to various initial revisions in which Glover tried, amongst other things, to get Satsuma to bankroll the project without limit. For the negotiation period Glover remained uncharacteristically silent, in a small Satsuma meeting room in which there was barely enough space for himself, Satsuma's Matsubayashi Genzo, and two interpreters. The stony atmosphere was broken only by the sliding of the door when tea was brought in by a servant, who shuffled out backwards on her knees.

Glover still didn't have enough Japanese to negotiate on his own, and Matsubayashi had to field his demands through the interpreter Joseph Heco, a figure known amongst the foreign community for his reliability and easy-going nature. This time Heco was under a heavy responsibility: Glover was nervous going into the negotiations, and though he was usually satisfied with second-hand explanations of the contracts he signed, his reliance on trust was wearing thin. As the son of a Choshu samurai later wrote: 'In the early days dealing with foreigners the paperwork was merely ornamentation. After Meiji 0 [1868] things changed, and both sides became much more careful about what they wrote.' The land contract for the mine was eventually ratified by Matsubayashi under some pressure and in legally dubious circumstances, without proper witnesses.

The first agreement ran something like this: capital had to be found by Glover for mining equipment and for an unconditional default of $43,750 which Hizen already owed him. He would pay the clan royalties irrespective of yield, a painful clause for him, and one which had held up negotiations. Through his own company he had to borrow about another $150,000 as investment capital to get mine construction started. In adding these sums to his existing debt, he was gambling on a hunch that the mine would yield in time. And his other assets were not performing well: in particular, his substantial Nagasaki real estate plummeted in value as the action moved east in the new national order. He agreed to lease the mining land for seven and a half years, which suggests that he had decided to make Nagasaki his long-term home. This decision may also have been influenced by a recent introduction to a new girlfriend by Godai, one with whom he would not be able to spend time for a while to come, but would later marry. Edward Harrison recommended an S. Millership, who became the mine manager. In May 1869 Glover followed a trusted pattern and brought in additional expertise from Britain. At the start he knew little about the mining business as he would learn to his cost. His team came up with a forecast of coal production which he allowed to bind his financial behaviour for the coming years, with a characteristic sense of enthusiasm and an uncharacteristic lack of foresight. The forecast said that the mine would produce an average of 200 to 500 tons a day, yielding a profit of at least $90,000 a year, which would put the project into the black in two years. This would prove to be wildly inaccurate.

At first, Glover felt vindicated when Takashima coal was tested at sea on 8 December 1869. The quality was higher than expected – Sugiyama Shinya points out that its bituminous quality made it 25 percent more efficient than British coal – and it was expected to raise a high price. At a burning rate of 35 tons per day, it could produce speeds of 11 knots. Glover had also reckoned that, using low-cost native labour, Takashima coal would be very cheap to produce: it was projected to cost $2 per ton to extract, and would be sold at $4.50 per ton. As soon as the project was started, he aggressively marketed the coal in the press as higher quality than Welsh or 'Northern' coal (a loaded adjective: there is nothing in the newspaper advertising to suggest whether Northern means the north of England or the north of Britain). The most effective notice was in the *Nagasaki Express*:

Takashima Colliery

THE undersigned are prepared to supply Ships or Steamers with COALS from the *Takasima Colliery* – (8 *foot seam*) – in quantities as required.

Present price $4.50 per Ton, free on board.

GLOVER & Co.

This advertisement helped to attract a standing order of 1,000 tons per month from P. & O., and the navies of large powers including the US and Russia also became sometime customers. The orders were good for business, but Glover realised that a mine working to a steady and high demand would require steady and high investment, and this fact persuaded him to risk the anger of the samurai he had tried to outstare during negotiations in 1869, by postponing the royalties due to Hizen.

Driven by the energy of the first settlers, for whom investment always seemed to lead to profit, Glover ploughed money into the mine. The work-force at Takashima became huge: at its height it expanded to other islands including Nanoshima and Sakurajima, and there were 5,000 workers in all, including about 4,000 in various sections of the mine, and 800 on the mainland transporting coal into the city more or less hand-to-hand. This was hardly a model of industrial reform, but it did show a willingness to work with the barest improvised methods. Millership had the miners build a skeleton structure to work within, from which they proceeded sideways, using steam engines for the extraction of coal and exhaust gases; and a rail was completed towards the end of the year. Unlike Britain, which had already had to learn from a history of mining disasters, there wasn't any

serious safety plan for Takashima. And profits hinged on the fact that wages
were much lower.

The only accounts of worker unrest that remain from the period of
Glover's ownership consist of scribbled notes on diminished production –
miners were not provided with a suggestion box. But there are hints from
observers about the mine's management, which was 'of the strictest – [miners]
emerged from a day spent underground with scarcely enough money to feed
their families, and too often too little coal'. Miners worked eight-hour shifts
for twenty days a month in dangerously dusty shafts, and because of the
heat they were usually completely naked. And, as Olive Checkland has
noted, they were often forced to buy work necessities at inflated prices – a
common ploy of British industry. Glover was not the toughest manager
Takashima would have, but even during the first few months of production,
as one commentator has put it, 'the mine seemed constantly on the verge
of industrial dispute'. The workers' unease didn't help Glover's state of
mind, as he struggled with increasing debt. Having found the big project
he had been looking for, he was overworked, overstretched, prone to feelings
of guilt over working conditions, and suddenly isolated. Although he had
semi-formal friendships with the likes of Harrison and Mackenzie, his only
intimate relationships were with yujo.

Jardine Matheson were from the outset disappointed at Glover's financial
control of the mine, and said as much in a letter dated 18 June 1869. They
did however agree to fund him to the extent of another $42,000 when he
confidently presented the original forecasts. In the same month he added
lot 84 to his real estate portfolio – though ominously brother Charles paid
for this. Later in June, he asked James Whittall of Jardine Matheson Yokohama
for 'between $70,000 and $80,000'. As soon as autumn, he was pressing
Whittle for yet another $30,000 to increase coal production by the end of
the year. His responsibilities were nearing half a million dollars, and still
there was no sign of the big seam of coal.

The first phase of the mine was completed by the end of 1869. When
he looked across the harbour to the island, Glover saw a Dickensian
landscape on the idyllic islands through which he had entered the city a
decade ago. But he was steadfast in his Victorian belief in industrialisation
as a cure for social problems. The miners were not so enthusiastic.
Takashima was, in a description that recalls *Hard Times*, 'bathed in the
white steam of machines and exhaust pipes, the noise of steam engines and
picks'. The island 'smelled of oily coal and was peopled by near-naked

workers, exhausted by the atmosphere underground and squeezing into claustrophobic seams'.

It was during the winter of 1869–70 that, lacking the leverage over the former rebels who were now in government, and also lacking any proper personal relationships, Glover's nous completely deserted him. His first major financial problems were triggered by clan defaults over payments for the *Jho Sho Maru* and a surplus of guns, but, as time went on, his own over-investment in the mine became a vicious circle. As viable amounts of coal failed to appear, he was forced to buy time with Jardine Matheson through a loan of $45,000, with the low-interest Netherlands Trading Society on 26 November 1869. Since the NTS were a semi-nationalised Dutch company in the style of Jardine Matheson, this act seriously contravened British trading protocol, and Glover realised that he had cultivated a habit of dissimulation in his business as well as his personal life. Double-dealing with the employer who had given him his first break played on his mind, and he fell into a spiral of overwork, anxiety and solitude. With Mackenzie and with the Satsuma leaders, he had bent the rules of trade, but this was the first time he had actively misrepresented himself to the organisation from which he had taken his trade philosophy.

The extent of over-investment during the mine period of 1869–70 will always remain unknown, since the only records, Guraba Shokai's own ledgers, show a degree of creative accounting. Later, outside auditors would admit to having to leave wide margins of error. As time went on Glover realised that his real estate investments of the past couple of years should have been used to prevent over-borrowing for the mine. But he pushed east, and by 29 May 1869 he had invested heavily in land in Hyogo, finding it hard to forget the excitement of moving into new markets with Mackenzie. In the midwinter of 1870, the decision was coming back to haunt him. By this time he was no longer able to borrow from a single source. This meant that he was forced into borrowing numerous small sums from different backers, and was unable to consolidate his debt. His willingness to accept payment in kind would prove to be another disaster, when Hizen's rice payment, which they claimed to be worth $360,000, turned out to be far from the mark. Not only was this against trade laws, it was a crushing shortfall.

Although his financial position was making him increasingly anxious, Glover never lost faith in his mining vision. In this he was justified – the mine was a good investment, but it was disastrously financed. He realised that, as well as being too short-termist, he had given himself a false sense of confidence because of the part he had played in the rebel heroics of the 1860s, and clan representatives, now the central government, became less frequent visitors at Ipponmatsu. One account suggests that this change of status was reflected in his body language – where before he had stood broad-shouldered and strode quickly, supervising various tasks on-site, he was now more often to be found hunched over his desk in the small colliery office. He was assumed to have gone inside because of the cold – but the office was no warmer than the mine. He saw his standing with some clans erode when Isahaya (of today's Nagasaki-ken) failed to make their payment on the Glover-brokered ship *Argos*, and the situation worsened with Higo's unreliable financing of the *Jho Sho Maru* – a problem of a larger scale altogether. Meanwhile, Hizen's royalties on coal extraction had to be paid, whether or not the mine was producing on schedule, and the payment rates were not always favourable – Glover's forex profits seemed a distant memory as he found himself victim to fluctuating currency rates.

Despite the financial crises, there was a pride in the three great ships built in Aberdeen and sold to the clans in government. The giant *Jho Sho Maru* soon became part of Aberdeen and Nagasaki shipping folklore. It was a 1,000-horsepower vessel, huge by the standards of the time, measuring 46 feet in length, and capable of a speed of ten knots. It left Galway on 1 August 1869 with Alex on board. Captain James Jones, recommended by Alexander Hall in Aberdeen and employed by Higo, travelled around the west of Ireland and around South Africa, rather than through the Suez Canal opening just at that time. The ship had become notorious before it even left Aberdeen: during its conception the *Jho Sho Maru* had aroused the suspicion of the Admiralty, since it was intended for the use of a clan who were then still officially terrorists. But its arrival signified a concrete achievement for Glover, in the midst of his growing financial despair.

Even so, Higo agreed to pay only 50,000 of 80,000 ryo they owed as down payment for the ship. Jardine Matheson's Whittall was now also asking for repayments – though Whittle's faith in the profitability of Takashima made him hold off longer than other creditors might have. Soon, the British Consul joined the NTS's F.P. Tombrink in expressing concern. Glover used the *Jho Sho Maru* as collateral for a £20,000 loan from the City of Glasgow Bank, originally taken out by his family while he was in Aberdeen. The ship was also remortgaged for a NTS loan, raising the stakes, since the NTS was on-site and could manipulate Glover's concern at the prospect of their blocking Higo's receipt of the ship. As the coldest months of winter came, the stress began to show: Glover took to berating his manager, who often threatened to leave, as well as obsessing over mine equipment. He knew that one big seam would end his troubles, but during his ownership the big seam never appeared.

Higo were aware of Glover's anxiety and, now in government, in a powerful negotiating position. Although they had participated in the arms frenzy of the early 1860s, Glover had no strong allies in this clan, and some may have resented his Satsuma favouritism. They began to operate on the border between firmness and bloody-mindedness, bringing up quibbles over both the armaments and, more exasperatingly, the ship's overall length. Glover recognised the question of length as a delaying tactic and refused to rise to the bait, but took seriously the demand to increase the number of guns from eight to ten. Again he went to the NTS, and used the upgrades as a reason to borrow $60,000 – even though the guns needed to meet the new Higo specifications would cost only a maximum of $10,000 each. The remaining $40,000 was silently swallowed by the mine. This time, having run out of firm collateral, he put up a share of the mine itself. He was quickly running out of options: to stay afloat from day to day, he was mortgaging the very projects around which his life in Japan revolved. He looked out at his workforce through the dusty windows of the colliery office, and felt the mood of reckless speculation of his youth coming to a close.

By the time it had become obvious that Higo were going to delay payment of the full price of the *Jho Sho Maru*, Glover found himself due to make an interest payment of $48,611 to the NTS. Perhaps the Dutch, like elements within Jardine Matheson, could be delayed by positive mine forecasts: Glover began to make a show of increasing mine production, building a besso – a small residence – on the island, facing back towards Nagasaki city, where he would sleep in rough and initially freezing conditions. During the most fraught times of the winter and spring, he would live in the besso for weeks on end, woken by the cold before dawn and working into the night. The small boats taking the coal to the city were pulled by tugs which made an almost unbearable noise. Every morning brought the roar of engines, smoke and a sense of his own imprisonment.

Another disaster befell the accounts on 12 January 1870, when the steamer *England*, perhaps aware of the unreliability of supply, dropped the price it was willing to pay for Takashima coal. As well as being a direct financial blow, this also focused the attention of Jardine Matheson, who expressed further concern about Glover's ability to manage his debt. Again he charmed them, referring back to the original forecast, but from January he felt the company's gaze on him almost constantly. Whittall, showing great loyalty, assured the company that the security for the capital investment in the mine was sound for yet another $100,000. The mine did reach 50–70 tons per day at points during that month, and things seemed to be looking up, but this was still far from the original estimate of 200–500 tons.

Glover meanwhile had to go to the Shanghai arms market to buy the extra equipment demanded by Higo for the *Jho Sho Maru*. Although he should have been trying to avoid his creditors, in his distraction he bought two 64-pound guns from a Captain Forbes, a trader with whom he had already had dealings, and to whom he still owed $34,000 from a deal two years previously. This transaction flagged up another old debt. The arms Glover bought on 29 February 1870 cost $16,499, and Forbes was now after him for over $50,000.

Nor did Whittall's optimism over the medium-term viability of the mine, upon which the abeyance of Jardine Matheson depended, prove to be well founded: although there would be a small rise to 1,746 tons in April 1870 and to 1,880 tons in May, in June this would return to 785 tons, due to a leak and labour disputes. During the vital winter months, production remained in triple figures. On only one day during the whole period was the mine producing at the forecast rate. Miner–management relations were made worse by the fact that Glover felt forced to make job cuts and to cut the wages of those left. While his reputation was still high amongst some of Nagasaki's Anglophile samurai, it was low amongst the city's emerging industrial workforce. There were no Japanese managers at all.

By spring 1870 there was no denying that Glover was in a serious debt spiral. As he had feared, he didn't get the agreed price for the fully equipped *Jho Sho Maru* and immediately went back to Jardine Matheson Shanghai for another $30,000. Beginning to show signs of serious agitation, he spilled out various personal reasons for the Shanghai loan, including the ill-health of his brother Alex. This latest loan was of a minor amount, but its collateral was the remaining quarter share of the mine – the other three quarters were already security – meaning that his entire project was now remortgaged. His great industrial venture was no longer his own – and he still had to find a way to service the loans.

Higo didn't know that their ship had been remortgaged: they had been expecting to use it by mid March 1870, whereas in reality it could be repossessed at any time. Glover was buckling under the weight of the deception: on 3 March 1870 he wrote, 'I find it no easy matter to keep going.' Twelve days later, in a letter to Johnson of Jardine Matheson Shanghai, he seemed even lower, realising that his financial position was affecting his family and that he could rely less on the old clans:

> I am in a hole . . . about this payment as I find the corn [rice] which Higo intends to pay in will from the depreciated state of our currency . . . the balance less [sic] by some $15,000 less than I expected . . . If the Bank will not discount this paper and I cannot use it as a payment on the £20,000 I am in a complete fix and know not what I can do . . . Everything goes well with the Mine and all I require is time.

But time was what Glover no longer had. In desperation he tried to get rid of the mine altogether, once trying to float shares in Yokohama, finding too few takers for his $370,000 of stock, and once trying to sell it to the Meiji government, who politely refused. In mid March Johnson at Jardine Matheson Shanghai asked Whittall for a credit check, and on the 13th he found out that the mine had been used as collateral for the NTS loan, realised that he'd been lied to about Glover's dealings with foreign creditors, and began to unravel the story. Ironically, given Glover's personability, Whittall's anger was more damaging than any single financial miscalculation: it resulted in a letter to Johnson which joined up all the threads Glover had been trying to keep apart. Two days later, H.C. McLean was sent to Nagasaki to deliver a strong demand for repayment to Jardine Matheson. Glover found that Johnson had gone cold and realised what had happened. His creditors were comparing notes like hidden mistresses. Whittall turned up on 23 March to do a full audit, in a frosty atmosphere. A final attempt to pay off Jardine Matheson loans with NTS money failed, and, as he looked at the *Jho Sho Maru* unusable in the harbour, Glover felt disaster nearing. Higo brought him some cash on 7 April, knowing that this was too late to make any difference. Jardine Matheson went ahead with a total audit, including the ships and all of Glover's real estate. One of the greatest disappointments for them was that the mine was still lacking equipment, the reason given for so much of the borrowing.

And yet Glover still had the media on his side. His friends in the local press remembered the panicked nights of 1862 and talked up his persistence. One of his great talents was using media spin, and the press continued against all indications to claim that Takashima was on the verge of success. A report, resembling an advertorial, in the *Nagasaki Express* of 23 April 1870, claimed that production was about to reach 400 tons per day (a quota it never neared), that the new samurai bureaucracy were in awe, and that Glover's personal energy was drawing Japanese engineering up to British standards:

> Much has been done by Messrs. Glover and Co. towards getting the Colliery in full working order. A substantial tramway has been laid from the pit's mouth to the sea, and a fine pier is in the course of construction, which will shortly be finished.
>
> As yet the yield of the mine is comparatively small, being only about 150 tons per day, but improvements are being carried out as quickly as possible, whereby the yield will be increased to at least 400 tons a day.
> . . .
> The brother of the Prince of Higo paid a visit to the mine on the 12th instant, and explored it thoroughly. He expressed himself very much pleased with all he saw, and paid a well merited compliment to Mr. T.B. Glover for his energy and perseverance; and further, expressed his regret that his countrymen had not adopted the European system of mining, years before.

This was cold comfort to Glover making his final move on 11 May, as the island was covered with sooty cherry leaves. In a new contract with the NTS his collateral became the future profits on the mine valued at their original projection, to be repaid at 15 percent annual interest by the end of January 1873. Living in a hut on an island bathed in modern pollution, and sleeping on tons of unextracted coal and dirty pink leaves, he settled in for a summer of back-pedalling. He was now mortgaged to the extent of future profits which everyone except the most spin-happy readers of the *Nagasaki Express* knew would never be realised. The NTS had constant and immediate power of foreclosure, and therefore virtual control of the mine.

Glover's career as a magnate of heavy industry had been short and would be copied by others, but for him it was over. The NTS were now de facto mine managers, and not even the most creative proposals of collateral could raise any more credit. Although he knew there was coal there, he also knew that he would never have the time or financial control to keep the mine as his own. As a consolation, the last of the three great ships of the era commissioned by the Glovers, the *Wen Yu Maru*, was sold to Choshu on 19 July. Even the ship, though, was ill-starred: it would be the only one of the great three which wouldn't survive to see active service in later imperial wars. But its arrival was met with as much press notice as the other two, and Glover knew that even as the mine was going down, he would be remembered for the ships. On 23 July the *Nagasaki Express* reported the ship's progress:

> The British Steamer *Wen-Yo-Maru*, Capt. John Gibson, left Aberdeen on the 5th March, under sail, arrived at Plymouth on the 10th, at 2.30 P.M., left at 5.30 P.M. the same day. Had fine weather to the Equator which was crossed . . . reached Cape of Good Hope on the 8th of May . . . rounded Saint Paul Island on the 29th May and had moderate breezes to Anjer where she arrived on the 17th June; from Anjer had light S.W. winds, arrived in port on the 19th instant at 2.30 P.M.

This time, the buyers, Choshu, gave Glover fewer financial problems than Higo – as might be expected, given his personal friendships and Choshu's financial power in the new Meiji government. He received substantial funds of $145,000, plus another payment of $35,000 from Higo. By this time, though, the money was no longer his to receive.

While the new *Wen Yu Maru* was being admired, Baldwin declared his intention to foreclose. Forbes followed on 30 July, and various other creditors took legal advice. On 26 August 1870, a Jardine Matheson report criticised the short-termist way the mine had been managed, saying, in stark contrast to the press, that '[t]he present workings are laid out without any system or view to facilitate future work'. The company severed its links, and Glover gave up, with some relief, temporarily leaving the running of the business to Henry Gribble and J.J. Fisher. He was informed that he would have to close down the business by 16 September.

The problem for the many smaller creditors now was that most of Glover's worth was already mortgaged to the NTS, and they had little influence over the finances of the Dutch giant. The NTS had astutely realised that the mine equipment was worth more working than not: long before the bankruptcy hearing, they had had an eye on the mine's evident potential and Glover's management. Even before bankruptcy, Glover watched the NTS draw up plans for further mine expansion which would turn him from owner to tenured employee. Unlike the smaller, cash-strapped creditors, the NTS were able to view his distress as their own potential investment, as they took over the mine. Their only task was to persuade the other creditors that liquidating the mine was not the best way to recoup their money. Of course, in banking on the mine the NTS were poaching Glover's consultants' research: the project had become a lesson in how industrial instinct could collapse under over-investment.

A bankruptcy hearing consisting of a double meeting of Glover's creditors in the British Consulate in Nagasaki was convened on 16 September, lasting till the eleventh anniversary of his entry into Nagasaki on the 19th. The hearing was sobering: Glover struggled to look dignified under the gazes of creditors he had tried for months to keep apart. He also had to physically support the now frail and almost sightless Mackenzie, whose influence had shown both in Glover's rise and in his casual attitude to accounting. The two came together in defeat as they had in success eleven years before.

The simple part of the court action was the production of an enormous list of creditors and an estimate of Guraba Shokai's assets, with three caveats. Firstly, the effect that insider trading with Glover Brothers (Aberdeen) had had on Guraba Shokai's value was difficult to determine. Secondly, accounting irregularities arising from an informal relationship with Dow & Co. in Shanghai had caused around as much as $300,000 worth of fuzziness. Thirdly and most sweepingly, the books were full of gaps which could never quite be explained. This last would be the most damaging to Glover's professional credibility.

The accounts of creditors during the hearing unfolded the story of how Guraba Shokai had lost control. Intended as an investment, Takashima had become massively over-mortgaged. The company had debts totalling $681, 570 – 19 per cent of which was owed to his brothers' own company in Aberdeen. So exhaustively had assets been stripped that there was only around $1,000 left in liquid form. 'How on earth,' the court asked, 'did he spend this amount of creditors' money?'

The answer to this question was not in the absolute amount of spending, but in his holding onto the entrepreneurial enthusiasm of the turn of the 1860s long after the bubble had burst. Industry, he now saw, unlike foreign exchange or commodities trading, demanded long-term financial planning. And yet he felt that things could have been much worse. As it was, he was able to stay on at Takashima as manager and realise its potential, which, despite a feeling of submerged despair, was something of a moral victory. Although the profits wouldn't accrue to him personally, his industrial instincts would be seen to be vindicated. Asked in court if he was willing to cooperate in continuing to run the mine for his creditors, he became a model of humility: 'I apologise for the great inconvenience I have caused everyone . . . if the court will allow me I am fully willing to work towards the plan [involving keeping the mine going] to compensate the [Netherlands] Trading Company.'

The next month the *Nagasaki Express* carried the official notice:

NOTIFICATION

The Bankruptcy Act 1870
In her Britannic Majesty's Court, at Nagasaki
In the matter of a special resolution for Liquidation by arrangement of the affairs of Thomas Blake Glover and Kenneth Ross Mackenzie, trading at Nagasaki and elsewhere in the Kingdom of Japan under the style of Firm of Glover and Company.

This is to notify that F.P. Tombrink, Esq., of Nagasaki has been appointed and is hereby declared to be Trustee under this Liquidation by arrangement. Messrs. Julius Adrian, & Howard Church and William Robertson are appointed a Committee of Inspection. Given under my hand and the Seal of the Court this 19th day of October 1870.
A.A: Annesley,
H.B.M.'s Acting Consul
26th October 1870

The NTS still had to deal with the smaller creditors, with their more pressing cash flow concerns. But the Dutch put their case well, promising 'greater and more speedy' remuneration if Glover was allowed to continue working the mine for creditor benefit. They presented the assembled minnows with two alternatives, of estimating the company's total worth at either $594,150, including money tied up in the mine, or at $322,340 excluding the mine. Showing a flair for lawyerly rhetoric, F.P. Tombrink portrayed the second option as superficially more attractive, before appealing to the smaller creditors' business sense in showing that more compensation could be wrung out of Glover in the long term if the mine were to be kept running.

Mining was, after all, the only use for mining equipment. There was almost certainly coal there, and Glover was the only person with the experience and passion to see it through.

On 21 September the loyal *Nagasaki Shipping List* vouched for Glover's willingness to put every effort into the mine, despite the change in ownership:

> . . . while the NETHERLANDS TRADING SOCIETY is to carry on the working of the Takasima Coal Mine . . . we trust yet to see the fond hopes of Messrs. Glover & Co. realized, that all their Creditors will eventually be paid up in full. We omitted to notice in our former report that at the public meeting held at the Consulate, Mr. T.B. GLOVER, enthusiastic to the last, had voluntarily offered his service *gratis* to superintend the practical working of the mine, he himself has thus apparently small doubt of ultimate success.
>
> Under the able direction of the Netherlands Trading Society, coupled with the active management of Mr. Glover we doubt not the Takashima Mine will yet come to the front, but the scheme is no child's-play and calls for the most strenuous efforts on its behalf before it can struggle into freedom.

The same reporter, having noted the difficulties ahead for Glover, posted his faith in his success by stressing not only the quality of the coal and of the scheme, but also the personality of the entrepreneur who had spotted its potential:

> the Takashima vein is of undoubted superiority, it is literally the *West Hartley* of Japan; and must ever command a ruling position in the market. There are Seamen in this port who have tested its virtues, and are wont to extol it in most high-flown language, as far exceeding any English coal that finds its way to these parts . . .
> . . .
> we would supplement these remarks by wishing every success to the undertaking, fortune favours the brave, let the motto of the Mine henceforth be *Nil Desperandum*.

The NTS paid Glover a salary of $200 a month – a lowly amount for a self-styled magnate, but more than the *Nagasaki Shipping List*'s 'gratis', and he didn't complain. His spirits even seemed to rise, and he often stayed in the island's besso, looking forward to the big seam, even though it wouldn't make money for him. His old work ethic caught the attention of Iwasaki Yataro, founder of Mitsubishi in 1873, and this relationship would be of more benefit than would have been any direct profits from the mine. And as it turned out the loss of ownership offered Glover various freedoms in the running of the mine, not all of them to the benefit of its workers: he was able, for example, to increase his profits by downsizing staff without the patrician guilt of an owner. He was still, though, saintly in comparison to the mine's next boss, the Tosa samurai Goto Shinpei, whose attitude was that '[t]hese miners are not people to be looked at in the same light as ordinary mankind, as they are animals like beasts or birds which begin to seek for food and drink when they feel hungry or thirsty and know today but not tomorrow'. Goto's description bears a strong resemblance to the way European colonisers saw natives as nobles sauvages whose saving grace was that they had no conception of future or past. Glover's NTS handlers were similarly patronising:

[w]ith a little good management they will do a good deal, but it must be born [sic] in mind that in Japan . . . the people are attached to their customs and habits, which must not be interfered with. Anyone who would attempt to introduce suddenly Western ideas and manners would meet with great difficulties, whereas a little sympathy and indulgence would far better promote the object in view.

Despite the NTS's conviction of their naivety, the miners began to organise. Fortunately for Glover, protests were only really virulent in 1872 and 1873, after he had given up management. More importantly, he was also now able to turn from his despair of summer 1870 to a personal life. Naito Hatsuho suggests that bankruptcy may have brought him a sense of shame which distanced him from his family in Scotland. This would certainly explain his absence from the country after 1867. But he had also been waiting to turn to a family of his own.

Glover had probably known his fiancée Tsuru since January 1869, but had been prevented from marriage since then by financial problems. Still, during this period of engagement, he managed to father a child, his son Shinsaburo, to another yujo, Kaga Maki. His marriage ceremony to Tsuru – not his first, but his first to take on an air of formality with reliable witnesses – was as serious as a marriage of convenience could be. When they were introduced, he sat stiffly opposite his wife-to-be in a small tatami room, firstly in the company of an intermediary, then alone. Tsuru was still an adolescent and had little to say, and Glover's small talk was notoriously wooden. Nor did it help that they didn't share a language. But a degree of awkwardness is expected in arranged marriages and didn't get in the way of the agreement. The intermediary returned after an interval judged not to let the atmosphere become too heavy, and the bond was sealed. The marriage remained paralegal – it was really a recognition of Tsuru's tenure as yujo to live with Glover in the kyoryuchi. The only register which would link the two would come after the birth of their own child in 1876.

Tsuru, according to Naito, had probably been found by Godai to suit Glover's tastes. When they met she was 17, with soft features and a broad face. Even at this age, she was already a mother of one. She had been born in Shinbashi, Osaka, then adopted, and moved away from her husband after divorce. Tsuru was a shadowy figure both before she entered the Glover household and, significantly, after the birth of their daughter, when she disappeared indoors – a move usually described as 'typically Japanese'. Since Glover had a ship named *Otsuru* in 1869, it's likely that he had made a decision about marriage by this time, and was sitting out his financial problems. Even after bankruptcy, Tsuru didn't join her husband until he had weathered the worst of the financial storm, and she remained in Osaka till then. Her presence became a major incentive for Glover to clear his debts.

This turn from business overload to the promise of a family life in 1870 was a source of relief even in the midst of apparent failure. Throughout his life in Nagasaki Glover wavered back and forth, usually forth, from a Christian position of monogamy, but his marriage to Tsuru was a real one in the sense of family-building, a long one by today's standards. He referred to her in public as 'my wife', and the press called her 'Mrs Glover' or 'Lady Glover' – not typical for marriages of convenience. Much later in life a sense of repentance gnawed at him as he recalled the number of women he had bought, declared and undeclared. He attended the berating sessions of George Smith, who was writing as early as Glover's wildest days in the *Nagasaki Shipping List* on 17 July 1861 that 'sad indeed are the temptations to which young Englishmen are exposed who take up their residence at Nagasaki, Kanagawa and Yokohama'. Moving from one girl to the next was initially irresistible, and all too soon emotionally exhausting. In his marriage to Tsuru, Glover felt that he had found something much more fulfilling. There would be other women, and quite possibly other, less formal marriages of convenience, but his days of all-out sexual entrepreneurism were over, and he made his family-minded intentions clear to the wider community.

By this time it was almost a decade since he had fathered his first son in Japan. Umekichi (a name transliterated as plum – luck) had been born to another yujo, Hiranaga Sono, with whom he had undertaken a marriage of convenience in September 1860. Umekichi was born on 4 September 1862, but he was premature and didn't survive beyond four months. Glover did register his name on Umekichi's birth certificate, but not his nationality. The baby that was, as far as we know, his second son, Shinsaburo, later Tomisaburo, was born to Kaga Maki, just as he was readying to settle with Tsuru, and this child was healthy. Glover had minimal contact with Hiranaga and Kaga, and was scarcely in touch at all until, after the birth of his daughter with Tsuru, he discovered that he and Tsuru couldn't have any more children. In need of an heir, he decided to find Maki and adopt Shinsaburo, not to the exaltation of the biological mother. Thanks to Glover's friends in local government who controlled the family koseki (records), Tsuru became the baby's mother, and until recently most assumed she was the biological parent. At some point later, probably in 1888, Glover and Tsuru officially changed the boy's name from Shinsaburo to Tomisaburo.

In September 1870 Glover looked back at the slippery slope of the mine from his bing on the island, and wondered at the disaster. Perhaps he had put too much trust in his friends in Choshu, Hizen, Higo and Isahaya, which sat uneasily with their new political status. Not even Satsuma, Glover's comrades during the Satsuei war, seemed very willing to help him out during 1870. Also, his enormous, but short-term, successes of the mid 1860s had inflated his faith in the early forecasts for the mine, despite all the signs to the contrary. He had envisaged himself as a great industrial leader, and Japan as a pilot for mining in East Asia. There had been, most importantly, some accounting naivety, which had caused great emotional strain. One of his frequent bons mots had been 'If you can achieve a small profit, it's not difficult to achieve more: the difficulty is in achieving the small profit' – but after substantial mis-investment this needed rethinking. Then there was the failed marriage of Ann and Alex. Ann's son, Ryle Alexander, had been born on 30 November 1869, which complicated the separation. Her naming of the child after another prominent Nagasaki businessman raised questions, as did his birth so soon after the marriage. It was acceptable for relationships with yujo to people the island with Glovers – as with Shinsaburo – but for settler mothers it was a severe embarrassment.

Perhaps Glover's own earnestness about Tsuru was intended as some kind of compensation. Ironically, after bankruptcy much of the trading side of Guraba Shokai was taken over by the company run by Frederick Ringer and Ryle Holme, Ann's probable lover, without any sense of ill will. The kyoryuchi were a small world.

NINE

Mint Imperialists

M argaret Thatcher tried to keep Britain Great on the idea that if all else fails to make money, you can always make money itself. If he had been around in 1979, after entanglement with the unions and with his unshakeable faith in free trade, Glover would have become a committed Hayekian monetarist. On the other hand, if he had been around in 1979, as a busted trader in his thirties he would have been a candidate for long-term unemployment. In debt after the mine, making money by making money looked increasingly attractive, since he had no money left to make money with. He set out to get involved with the establishment of Japan's first mint.

In 1871, Japanese currency was still tied to the Mexican silver dollar at a punitive rate. Glover and Mackenzie had begun their Japanese trading careers making killings on the exchange between the ryo and the dollar. But the ryo no longer seemed a currency befitting a modern industrial nation, and Glover had noted the possibility of a new Japanese currency at least three years before. In 1868 he had realised that with Restoration the days of fluctuating rates were numbered and that an independent currency would come with unification. By the end of 1870 there was a general consternation amongst the Japanese gentry over the strength of local currency. On 16 September Kido Takayoshi recorded:

> At Ito's I happened to hear that Saigo Kichihinosuke has gone to Chikuzen on that domain's request to Satsuma to bring the counterfeiting problem of kinsatsu currency notes under control. I am not yet certain that this is true. But, if chance this kind of action has taken place, I fear for the authority of the central government. How can the integrity of the nation be maintained hereafter?

With his hard-learned lessons in finance and his acquaintances in the new Japanese government, Glover was a certainty to be around when Godai, fellow refugee at Kagoshima and the man who had probably introduced him to his wife, went ahead with the establishment of a western-style mint.

Plans for a mint had been floated around the time of Restoration, but only after things had settled down had they become more concrete. On 10 December 1870 the *Nagasaki Express* reported:

> We have great pleasure in being able to inform our readers that it is the intention of the Government to open the Imperial Mint, for the purpose of issuing the new currency, on the Japanese New Year's Day (February 19th, 1871). The Copper coinage is now being struck off, and, in the course of about a week, it is hoped that the minting of the New Dollar will be commenced. The time between this and the day of issue is but short, but . . . there is good reason to hope that when the anxiously looked for day arrives, there will be a sufficient supply of each of the new coins to meet all demands.

But long before the announcement that the mint was to open in mid February 1871 in Osaka, Glover had heard via William Keswick in Hong Kong that the mint there was closing down, and he persuaded Jardine Matheson in Yokohama to buy their machinery. Edward Whittle, Glover's eventual nemesis at Takashima, had drawn up plans for mint construction, but had pulled out when he realised the cost of the transaction. The mint was another risk, but also a potential confidence boost after losing ownership of the mine, and one backed by the government. It was never a top priority for Glover, partly because on closer inspection there was little obvious chance of quick profit, partly because he wanted to stay on the island to pay off his mine debts quickly and spend more time with his family, and partly because he would have little decision-making power over a project controlled by the new government.

At this point Glover was struggling to adapt to bankruptcy after a decade of success, and he was still tied to Takashima. At dawn he was to be seen taking a constitutional around the sooty island which would take up so much of his life. A look back across the water towards the thriving Kosuge Slipway and the ships would remain a consolation of sorts. For the first time he had no grand scheme: the mint was prestigious but low-return, and there was no simple way to get out of debt except remain at the mine and watch desultory amounts of coal being excavated. After a decade of speculation, he had become a contracted employee and felt his freedom compromised. 'There is nothing to do,' he says in May 1871, 'but to wait.' Perhaps helping to found a new national currency would restore some of his pride. He imported metals and minting machinery via the Oriental Bank in Hong Kong and, following his usual pattern, expertise from the UK. Plans for this go back as far as summer 1868, when he had started working on building up a stock of metals. On 11 July 1868, when his confidence in the mine was still high, he had written to William Keswick:

> Our Firm advises us from Osaca, date 5th inst. that all the native officials are preparing a parcel of 4,000 piculs of copper for shipment and sale on their a/c. proceeds to be placed to the cost of the Mint.
>
> One third of the above quantity will I expect be shipped by an early steamer with your firm or ours in Shanghai.

A fortnight later he had arranged for minting equipment to be placed on board one such 'early steamer':

> I have requested Mr. Groom to place the 'United Service' at your disposal for the conveyance of the plant to Hiogo and I shall be glad if you will ship by this steamer as soon as our Shanghai firm gives you notice that she is ready to take it on.
>
> [We hope to] obtain from the Japanese government the full cost of transporting the Mint from your port to Japan in addition to the cost of $80,000 . . .

But on this occasion the choice of vessel caused a gnashing of teeth amongst the staff of Guraba Shokai, as Glover accused Francis Groom of having fluffed the order:

> You cannot be more annoyed at the 'United Service' not taking on board the Mint machinery than I am as I have not only told the Japanese to expect it immediately but I myself have been waiting day by day for the arrival of the steamer.

The minting machinery certainly wasn't on the *United Service*, and it is likely that the ship it was on sank. In any case, by the time it arrived, his mine debts had become overwhelming, and the import of machinery would have to be put on hold till after 1870.

As a broker of minting machinery Glover set himself up as a link between the financiers, the frosty but still obliging Jardine Matheson, and the new

Japanese government. Jardine Matheson had long since stopped the free
flow of money to Glover by the time the mint was up and running in April
1871, but they knew of his contacts in the new government. So, even with
no initial capital, he became one of the forces behind what would become
the modern en (yen), an intermediary role for which he was eventually
congratulated by Harry Parkes.

The mint was financially trifling compared to earlier investments, but it
kept Glover in touch with the government, and he later called it 'a thing
of benefit . . . I could do in that situation'. There was also potential for
fiddles: as well as the minting machinery itself, there were profits to be made
on exchange speculation as the new currency found its feet, as well as from
the value of coin metals. Glover bought en early and waited for the currency
to appreciate, but the returns were disappointing, and in a letter to F.B.
Johnson, he claimed to have made 'not one cent profit' from the mint. He
became resentful towards Jardine Matheson, feeling that they should have
bailed him out when help was 'most needed'. He had come up against the
limits of patriotism in the face of free trade.

However, even with a patchy credit record, the mint project allowed him,
by the end of July 1871, to persuade the company to lend him another
$30,000, as well as $45,000 from the Dutch East India Company. The
Dutch soon made a demand for repayment, from the now familiar and
potentially blackmailing position of knowing that Glover understood the
consequences if Jardine Matheson found out he had been double-dealing
with two semi-national agencies. Again he found himself unable to pay the
Dutch, and again briefly in double debt, though to a far lesser extent than
during the year before. He was relatively untroubled by these five-figure
sums and knew that the mint was helping connect him to the new Executive
– though not, apparently, that the mine was endearing him to what would
become Japan's biggest company.

As with investment in the mine, investment in the mint was sometimes
used as a flag of convenience for general borrowing, as Glover tried to
reduce his time on the island. In the familiar way, he overpriced the minting
machinery '$75,000 to $80,000', intending to put the profits towards clearing his own Takashima debts. Even though he no longer owned the mine,
he was still funding its debts from the margins of other deals. On 24 July
Kenneth Mackenzie sold the minting machinery for $60,000 plus $5,400
transaction fees.

The investments in currency and metal never yielded much. But Glover was right in his seeing that the mint site of Kansai (the mid Honshu triangle of Kyoto–Hyogo–Osaka) would become a major economic hub – which partly explains why he had been keen to buy real estate there when Takashima should have indicated that he couldn't afford it. Hyogo had been opened up by a shipping route to Osaka in May, and Kansai's urban centre had by now become much bigger than Nagasaki. Ironically, since it saw the end of surreptitious dealing, the Meiji Restoration had been a deathknell for Nagasaki as a major cultural centre, and the city wouldn't recover until the 1890s.

With the mint management in the hands of the new government, Glover accepted his share of reflected glory and very modest profits, and turned his attention back to the mine. He may have hoped that a move to finance would help his cash flow problems, through a wobble in the new currency or insider information. No such information came. He was also now without some of his most important colleagues: by the end of 1868, during the beginning of the Takashima crisis, his key collaborators had begun to doubt his judgement, and Edward Harrison, Ryle Holme and Francis Groom had all declined to renew their contracts, leaving him adrift in the Nagasaki business world and alone on the island except for his brothers, who frequently visited to lend moral support.

In formal government, things were looking up: in 1871, Ito Hirobumi was made Minister for Public Works, which meant that Glover was under his old friend's authority in his capacity as manager of the mine. He was again answerable to someone who could ensure his promotion in the world, and this brought him some relief as he continued his dawn-till-dusk shifts till his debt was paid. The NTS retained ownership of the mine until 1874, but even after Glover relinquished management, the quality of the coal remained close to his heart, and at times he became slightly paranoid of corporate espionage. As soon as 14 December 1870 he felt strongly enough about imitations to take out a press advertisement:

To prevent inferior descriptions of Japanese Coal being sold as *Takasima*, the proprietors of this Colliery beg to notify that for the future no Coal will be sold without a certificate.

By the summer of 1872, the second shaft of the mine was at last producing amounts of coal which were somewhere near the initial projection. Things seem to have gone right at the mine soon after Glover left and the pressure to produce subsided. He managed to pay off three quarters of his debt within two years of bankruptcy, sooner than the NTS had demanded. More good news was to come at the end of 1872, when the Meiji government demanded that daimyo surrender their land to the national authorities, and the Hizen stake in the mine passed to the Mining Department of the Ministry for Public Works, run by Ito. Glover still owed Hizen royalties, but these in turn were payable to the government, and the connection with Ito forged over flasks of sake in the mid 1860s would go a long way towards clearing both his debt and his name.

By the turn of 1873, Godai was Glover's minting contact and Ito his mining contact, and Glover again felt connected to the strings of power. He maintained his regime of rising at dawn amidst the pollution of the mine and watching the work or sitting in his small office going over the figures. Meanwhile, Hizen rebels who resented what they saw as their land rights being moved east to the new government attempted a rebellion. During one riot stemming from old inter-samurai rivalries, British overseers killed several mine strikers and wounded more. Glover watched his countrymen's (and they were likely as not Scots) behaviour with a mixture of laissez-faire stoicism and horror, writing to Keswick that the quashing of the uprising had been 'barbarous'. Nevertheless he continued to drag coal from the island and do very little else, mostly separated from his new wife, and was rewarded by the project's getting back into the black sometime during the autumn in 1873. It was not the phantom profits of the mint but these Herculean efforts in working off his mine debts which would attract the single most important business relationship of his life, that with Mitsubishi.

Alex stayed in Nagasaki until Thomas had paid off his debts, as did, more sporadically, Alfred. In January 1874 the Japanese government bought the mine from the NTS for $400,000 plus a possible kickback to Glover. Later it would go to Mitsubishi, to Glover's even greater benefit. After a few months of government control, Goto Shojiro took ownership in September 1874, provoking worker unrest beyond the scale of anything during Glover's day. By this stage Glover was glad he had relinquished management: after Goto took over the mine, various financial disasters befell it, and his rule was thoroughly despised. In the spring of 1874, Glover was at last able to enjoy his freedom, as well as his still fairly new marriage, relaxing in Ipponmatsu living on savings from his gratis wages, then escaping the heat in the mountains in summer, writing to Jardine Matheson that 'it is very great to be relieved' of the burden of management.

Ito was pleased with his friend's job, since at the end of the year Glover's initial projections came to fruition and production doubled almost overnight. This, however, startled Goto, who struggled to sell the surfeit of coal. Inexplicably, he panicked and fled to Tokyo early in 1875, and for a year the mine produced next to nothing. As well as being an absentee landlord and annoying the government, Goto had become an object of hatred amongst the miners. Within a year of his takeover the working month had increased to 26 days of eight-hour shifts, where at the time of Glover's bankruptcy it had already seemed steep at 20 days. Safety was virtually ignored: the mine's pumps were ageing without reinvestment or apparent interest on the part of the new manager. In 1875, firedamp was discovered. Even so, much of the foreign community breezily assumed that the native workers were too proud, or brutish, to take safety seriously: for the *Nagasaki Express*, during the 1875 safety lapses, the 'burning to death of one man . . . was not sufficient to awaken any keen feelings of the danger to which they are subjected'. If this was true, by December of that year they were wide awake: an explosion caused by the preventable incursion of sea water killed 44, injured 24, and left 5 missing. Watching blackened bodies being dragged up to the mine's surface, Glover also felt a dark sense of relief that the lack of funding had not been down to him. His name as industrialist visionary was assured, after a fashion, and although he had created all sorts of accidents waiting to happen, Japan's first major industrial disaster couldn't be put down to him. The mine was up and running again by March of the next year, but Goto, an unreconstructed samurai, continued to show so little consideration for his workers that in the ensuing two years the unrest escalated, culminating in an all-out revolt in July 1878.

Glover later went some way towards making peace with the miners by helping wrest control from Goto into the hands of Iwasaki Yataro, also Tosa, and the head of Mitsubishi, which was rapidly expanding as a shipping line with government support, in part because of troop-carrying to Formosa. Mitsubishi officially took over the mine on 30 March 1881, and the deal is reckoned to have cost one and a half million dollars. As well as developing the mine, Mitsubishi were building on the earlier work of the Glovers to become a major shipbuilding concern, and Iwasaki, who had been watching Glover, would replace Ito as his most helpful comrade in economics and politics from the mid 1870s. Mitsubishi's growth was explosive, and in 1884 the company took control of the Nagasaki shipyard, becoming outright owners in 1887. The next year they lost their shipping monopoly, but had already diversified too much and become too important to the government for this to do them much damage. Glover certainly didn't found Mitsubishi, as is sometimes written, but he became a conduit for imported ideas to help the company grow. He would later, at Iwasaki's request, go back to manage the mine, no longer under the same terrible circumstances. Under the NTS he had been stuck in his besso till 1873, but with Mitsubishi he returned in much more comfortable conditions, with increased productivity, and with bridges with the Nagasaki foreigners largely rebuilt. Finally Takashima was closed in 1886, leaving a ghost town with abandoned mining machinery, which was later turned into a small museum.

After leaving the mine at the end of 1873, and with the consolation of having had a hand in the mint and recovering his standing with the government, Glover reconsidered his career position. He had moved from trader to industrialist via dabbling financier engaged in actually making money, and it had all been far from how he had hoped. He was no longer in debt, but neither was he anything like wealthy, and after Takashima, he was in no hurry to throw himself into one big business project again. His daughter Hana was born in 1876 to Tsuru and, on finding that Tsuru was unlikely to have any more children, the couple moved to recover his son from Sono Maki. He had become a middling businessmen with a wife and two kids, relieved but slightly empty. Much of the time when he was trying to develop the mine had been spent telling outright lies, alienating much of the foreign trading community. From the mid 1870s he set about re-establishing his relationships with foreign businessmen, the more sympathetic of whom recognised him as a fellow trader who had overstretched but refused to flee. With the loss of Harrison, Holme and Groom, the old team had broken up, and it would be a struggle to regain the trust of the foreign traders who remained in the city. He had, after all, spent three years stuck on an island. The new government was very usefully on his side, but the Japanese trading community was harder to gauge – until he realised how much he was favoured by Iwasaki.

His real break came in the year of Hana's birth, when Iwasaki offered him the chance to give up his entrepreneurial and industrial urges and to take a regular salaried position. Mitsubishi would buy the mine and other, more successful, projects. By now, not only had his debt been cleared, his messy, seven-year lease with Hizen was coming to an end, and he was completely free. Iwasaki, having studied Glover's behaviour at Takashima, invited him to come to Tokyo permanently to work as an adviser for Mitsubishi. Glover wanted to take the chance, but to do so, he would have to leave his base of Nagasaki behind.

Thomas Blake Glover (1838–1911).

Right. Brochure for Ipponmatsu, Thomas Blake Glover's house in Nagasaki – a brochure provided by the city authorities.

NAGASAKI
GLOVER GARDEN

Below. The plaque at Glover Garden in Nagasaki, showing marks where the first line has been altered.

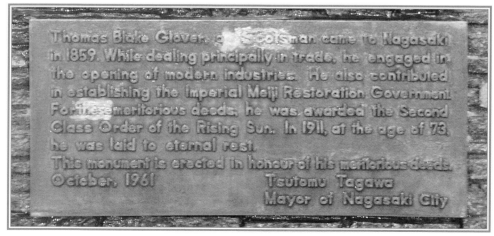

Thomas Blake Glover, a Scotsman came to Nagasaki in 1859. While dealing principally in trade, he engaged in the opening of modern industries. He also contributed in establishing the Imperial Meiji Restoration Government. For these meritorious deeds, he was awarded the Second Class Order of the Rising Sun. In 1911, at the age of 73, he was laid to eternal rest.
This monument is erected in honour of his meritorious deeds.
October, 1961   Tsutomu Tagawa
                                 Mayor of Nagasaki City

Thomas Blake Glover's parents,
Thomas Berry and Mary, in 1875.

1. Main House
2. "Govie's" Room
3. Wing
4. Dining Hall
5. Big Hall
6. Play Room
7. Tutor's Room
8. Little Hall
9. Wooden Class Room
10. Engineering Class Room
11. Large Class Room & Vestibule
12. South Class Room

An illustration of Chanonry House School, the Gym, in Old Aberdeen, where Glover was educated. Today the building lies within the campus of the University of Aberdeen.

Tsuru Glover (1850–99), married to Thomas Blake from 1870.

Takashima island

Takashima mine from the inside, as the mine framework is constructed. Glover worked here full-time from 1869 to 1873, staying as manager after bankruptcy in 1873. He returned often until 1886.

Ho Sho Maru in Japan, completed in Aberdeen in 1868, delivered the next year, and brokered by Thomas Blake Glover in Nagasaki and his brothers in Aberdeen.

Jo Sho Maru in Victoria Dock, Aberdeen, in 1869, brokered by the Glover brothers. It was delivered in Nagasaki the following year and remained the biggest ship in the navy during the era.

The Glover family at the turn of the 20th century. Back row from left: Tomisaburo, Alfred, Thomas. Front row: Martha, Hana, Waka.

Right. Thomas Blake trout fishing at Nikko.

Below. Tomisaburo visiting his family in Fochabers, Aberdeenshire, 1903.

Mitsubishi offices in Marunouchi, central Tokyo, then the main business district and today one of the most well known commercial areas.

Kirin beer bottle label, 1889, designed by Thomas Blake Glover's daughter Hana. Kirin grew from Glover's Japan Brewery Company and was later taken over by Mitsubishi.

Tomisaburo and his wife Waka on vacation in the mountains.

At the turn of the 20th century Glover often participated in this kind of fancy-dress ball, which demonstrates late Meiji period attempts to integrate the Japanese empire.

TEN

Another View of Samurai

The anti-bakufu samurai leaders who were supported into Restoration by Glover were rebels and revolutionaries. But depending on context, rebellion and revolution can connote anything from human rights protest to corporate regime change. Glover helped Japan forward into the Meiji Restoration. Is forward here free trade or a new age of justice and equality? The word slides between the two with confusing ease. For Glover, which way was forward?

Perhaps the best way of describing the 1868 Japanese Restoration of the Emperor is as a turning of the established caste system into a class system. For Victorians, forward came largely from progress through social class, exemplified, in continental form, by the French Revolution, when a hereditary elite had their privileges taken away by an aspiring middle class. This understanding of forward in turn came from ideas of universal civilisation during the Enlightenment, which had Aberdeen as one of its centres – sometimes obscured by concentration on Edinburgh. The atmosphere in which the Glovers grew up in the mid nineteenth century was still that of the Aberdeen Enlightenment. Correspondingly, after 1868, many of Glover's Japanese allies set up discussion groups on Enlightenment politics. He felt that the new Japanese political system was moving towards the kind of class meritocracy which he, a hard-working boy from an improving family, could believe in. In this sense he was a revolutionary.

In Japan today it is often said that everyone is roughly of the same class. This comes in part from an assumption, these days imported from the US, that class is about the same as wealth. Glover never thought in these terms: as his management of Takashima shows, he understood the stark divisions of industrialisation and aimed to use them. In Britain money stayed roughly in the same families, but social class allowed for the ideals of self-improvers like himself, the progress of Great Men described a few years before by fellow Scot Thomas Carlyle. For these Victorians, hard work always promised the chance of advance. In practice of course, the possibility of advance was carefully managed. Similarly, after 1868 samurai remained in most of the top positions of power. Some were worried about the idea that their authority could be challenged by class mobility, but the emerging divisions after Restoration corresponded almost exactly to those between samurai and lower castes, and Glover encouraged his samurai friends into new positions of power. In terms of absolute equality, the Restoration showed little sense of rebellion.

The Japanese classless society myth also fits well with the idea that bushido, the samurai code, disdained anything as base as personal gain. This is misleading: bushido was, in our terms, amoral, and saw advancement as an end in itself. And the ambitions of individual samurai were the primary factor of political development in the 1870s and 1880s. The main question for samurai and daimyo since the 1860s hadn't been whether power was going to change hands – they knew it was, at some point – but how it was going to change, and how much power each individual would have in a new regime. As Marius Jansen has shown, during the mid 1870s samurai were most interested in the maintenance of hereditary privilege, tenured stipends, and the establishment of shigakko, military-religious schools, to be drawn on in the expansion of Japan's new modernity abroad, with the Korean peninsula their primary target.

For aspiring samurai, now becoming middle-class citizens, Glover's idea of forward arrived at just the right time. Rebel samurai, and even bakufu samurai of a modernising mindset, had been aiming to educate themselves in foreign politics for a decade before Glover's arrival, in the tradition of Yoshida Shoin and Ii Naosuke. Yoshida had in turn been taught by Sakuma Shozan, whose 'Eastern morality, Western technique' was a marriage of classical Chinese ethics and western science. These samurai went to great lengths to get at the logistics of the outsiders, and Yoshida was ambitious enough to try to stow away on the ship of Commander Perry himself in 1854. When this failed he returned to inspire, in the few years before his death, the generation from which early Meiji politicians, including Glover's ally Ito Hirobumi, would emerge.

Samurai 'classical Chinese ethics' is a mixture of Confucianism and court loyalism. Classical Confucian thinking demanded respect for roles in the family and in society set down by external rules, rather than by any Buddhist self-searching. This abstract system of honour and power chimed with hopes of individual advance that a class society would bring, and, later estranged from European democracies, helps to explain why Japan was drawn to Germany. A similar Confucianism can best be seen in practice today in today's South Korea (or for that matter North Korea, where Kim Jong-Il's madcap Stalinism becomes juche, or self-reliance, through the lens of familial responsibility).

For joi samurai of the late nineteenth century, this Confucianism drove the idea of cultural self-sufficiency, and fitted well with the new imperial ideal of ethnic uniqueness. Sitting in place of European nationalism, Japanese uniqueness became a plank in the authoritarian imperial movement known as Meiji Conservatism and was encouraged by Ito and Inoue. Inoue, although more liberal than Ito, was behind the ideals of bunmei kaika – translated as 'civilisation-opening' – which accorded with his call for 'a new, European-style empire on the edges of Asia'.

Perhaps surprisingly for someone not usually seen as partisan, Glover was behind a number of movements to set up Japanese Europhile imperial committees. He supported the establishment of the celebrated Iwakura Mission, an Enlightenment think tank for ryugakusei, soon after Restoration in 1871. This elite group was first proposed by the Dutch missionary Guido Verbeck, and named after and headed by the influential commentator Iwakura Tomomi. Glover's personal friends were amongst its management, and two of its vice-ambassadors were Ito and Kido. Its whole membership was drawn from the old samurai establishment. The Mission had a general staff of 48, and about 60 students, some of whom stayed abroad long term to finish their studies, some of whom returned to found colleges and have various other stellar careers. On 23 December 1871, the Mission left Yokohama to sail to San Francisco – California itself had only been 'opened' in 1848 and federalised in 1850 – then round the US, then to Europe and various parts of Asia on the way home, returning on 13 September 1873. They arrived in London in August 1872 and visited Liverpool, Manchester, Glasgow and Edinburgh, and a connection with the family of Robert Louis Stevenson – and via R.H. Brunton and the Foreign Office, and Glover – appears as the Mission follows Enlightenment back to its source:

Edinburgh provided a chance for sightseeing at the Castle, the Palace of Holyroodhouse and the Museum of Science and Art before continuing the industrial tour . . . [o]n 16 October, as guests of the Commissioners for Northern Lights, they steamed 40 miles on the ship *Pharos* to the Bell Rock Lighthouse designed by the firm of the Stevenson brothers, David and Thomas. For this visit they were accompanied by

R.H. Brunton, the 'Father of the Japan Lights' who had trained at Stevenson's. Brunton had written a letter to *The Times* published on 29 June 1872 in which he had described Japan's lighthouse building programme . . . [t]he next day a coal oil refinery was visited, and the mission divided into three groups. Iwakura and Kume headed for Blair Atholl in the Highlands, Ito went to Glasgow, and Kido stayed in Edinburgh.

As his stance hardened in relation to a lack of recognition in Europe, Ito became more authoritarian and presided over a post-revolutionary Terror of increased surveillance and centralised government, while Inoue spread the new imperial order across Asia. The bad news for Ito was that new rebel samurai soon began agitating against the Meiji government. By the mid 1870s new dots of rebellion were joining up, for example, the Shizoku rebellions and in the Shintoist Shimpuren of Kumamoto – and mid 1870s counter-revolution was, of course, where Glover weapons came in. By now, also following Gloverite–Victorian thinking, domestic wellbeing was index-linked to military reach and national pride. British Consul Harry Parkes put the samurai connection of domestic and imperial ambition with his usual candour, as well as a touch of hypocrisy: '[t]o the *Meiji* mind, international relations in the second half of the nineteenth century were based on a predatory system of might'.

But the Ito government was rattled by the new samurai rebels of the late 1870s, and policing for public meetings was stepped up towards the end of the decade. In 1881 the kenpeitai, military police, were set up, and from then until 1945 they assumed ever more authoritarian and secretive powers. As soon as 1884, 750 political suspects were expelled from the capital. The period saw a rapid expansion of the Imperial Navy, with Glover ships still a central building-block, and the Chinese peninsula of Korea coming into the cross-sights. Comparisons of Japanese development with the development of other capitalist societies – especially Glover's Britain – were popular. The aikokuto – 'patriotic faction' – felt that the domestication of Enlightenment ideas was an incomplete project, and organised talks on European Enlightenment and Utilitarianism. Becoming associated with the term 'Meiji Enlightenment', Fukuzawa Yukichi set out to import European political ideas. He travelled to Britain and returned to set up the newspaper *Jiji Shinpo*, then gathered round him at Keio University an Anglophile group of thinkers. Keio was an elite, and expensive, institution: in samurai thinking as in the

Indian colonial elite, the lower orders needed to be led into a new political dawn. It was this developing class-centred Great Men spirit of samurai with which Glover found common ground. Although he had called for redundancies amongst the miners, he was keen to look after endangered samurai: '[n]ative engineers and mechanics in great numbers would find suitable occupation and good wages. This in itself is very important to Japan at the present moment, and will be so for a long time, until the immense body of idle samurai are employed.'

At least until the 1880s, when Ito drifted towards Prussia, the fact that the model for Japan's new constitutional monarchy was Britain had at least as much to do with Glover's influence as it did with diplomats like Parkes. In the mid 1880s Meiji Conservatism shaded into 'Meiji absolutism', aiming to enforce modernisation and suffocate any pockets of anti-globalising rebellion that still existed. And yet, as with other class societies, there emerged with the new industrialisation a new socialism. Specifically, the Meirokusha think tank was founded in 1873 by Mori Arinori, and in time he was joined in spirit by Fukuzawa, Kato Hiroyuki, President of the University of Tokyo, and Nishi Amane, President of Tokyo Normal College. Initially very small, this group was behind the development of what eventually led in 1932 to the Socialist Mass Party, which tried to talk Japan out of war, with as little success as the German communists. We can imagine how Glover, self-improver and manager during the Takashima labour disputes, would have felt about the growth of socialism from Enlightenment. But then, the extent of Japanese militarisation and free-floating, amoral, unrecognised samurai pride would probably have disturbed him even more.

The movement forward into military and ethnic pride is easy to portray as a native phenomenon – as the natural characteristics of the Japanese – and usually is. But as a tenet of modernisation and as an outlet for empire, samurai uniqueness had been encouraged by the west since the 1860s. After Restoration, modern warfare had arrived, and while the methods of politics were rapidly changed from caste to class, the feudal power elites largely stayed in place to preside over the new order. The process associated with Glover, sometimes drafting him in as an honorary samurai, and usually simply called rebellion, was of the top caste of Japanese society individually adapting to the new military logistics. And not all Scots were uncritical of this process.

ELEVEN

Treasure Islands

S cotland's best known historical adventure novelist, Robert Louis Stevenson, spent some of his youth scheming to visit Japan. When Glover was helping to plot the Meiji Restoration, Stevenson was in his teens. When Glover was struggling to pay off his debts and living in his besso at the mine, Stevenson was studying the still mysterious country. The two figures had almost nothing in common, and yet their stories are closely interlinked.

Stevenson never made it to Japan, because of poor health. He did, however, settle in a more southern area of the Pacific, which he made the setting for some of his most influential work. 'The Ebb-Tide' and 'The Beach at Falesa' describe a mercantile informal empire with a probing irony that would have made Glover uncomfortable. But the northernmost Pacific archipelago, the one he never reached, continued to feed Stevenson's imagination. He was especially fascinated by the generation which had inspired Ito, Inoue and their comrades to form the Restoration government.

By the time of Restoration, Stevenson's family, long established engineers, had become a key supplier of technology to Japan in that most culturally loaded area, lighthouses. As Enlightenment was transmitted from the Scottish context to the Japanese one, light itself became a powerful sign, and the Scottish and Japanese Enlightenments took light and vision to be central to cultural progress. In Scotland, scientific vision underpinned advance. In Japan, bunmei, meaning civilisation, is transliterated 'culture-light'. (And Meiji is transliterated 'light-government'). As suggested previously, with the loss of the way of the sword, vision was used in empire to separate the advanced from the catchers-up. Glover of course was no stranger to the lighthouse business, being the son of a coastguard and having watched the installation of Fraserburgh's Stevenson technology, and both the Stevenson family and the Glover family (as well as the Brunton family) were part of the same enlightening east-coast Scottish maritime engineering network.

Stevenson, sometimes subsumed into a John Buchan-type tradition of boyish adventure, was interested in politics from his youth, and followed Walter Scott's fascination with Scotland's place in Britain. Unlike Glover,

in the joi generation of Yoshida Shoin, he perceived a nationalism comparable
to Jacobite Scotland. The similarities suddenly became concrete in March
1878, when the educationalist Taizo Masaki was in Edinburgh, scouting
for his Europhile institution, Kaisei University. One dinner engagement
during his tour came at the invitation of local academic Fleeming Jenkin,
at Jenkin's house at 3 Great Stuart Street in the New Town – to Meiji eyes,
with its portentous radial avenues, the most Edinburgh-like part of
Edinburgh, and just downhill from Stevenson's home on Heriot Row. The
lecturer position had probably already been sewn up by J. Alfred Ewing,
and Jenkin's dinner party had mainly formal significance. But it gave Taizo
the opportunity to meet a representative group of Edinburgh bourgeoisie –
academics, businessmen and engineers. Amongst them was a 27-year-old
ex-engineering student of Jenkin's, now itinerant travel writer.

As the Restoration had neared, in May 1866, Article 11 of the Custom
Duty Treaty had demanded the standardisation of Japanese lighthouses.
In September of that year Harry Parkes organised for the bakufu to have
new lighthouses constructed, and in November they decided on eight
locations. Japanese lighthouses were thought to be too short, not sturdy
enough, and, significantly, inadequately enlightening. The architect of the
system of lighthouses to foreign specifications, the Japan Lights, was
Glover's acquaintance and fellow engineering speculator, Richard Brunton.
Brunton had trained as a railway engineer before he joined the Stevensons,
now contracted by the Foreign Office to oversee the Japan Lights. Brunton's
employment via the Foreign Office and the Stevensons involved an informal
recommendation from Glover, and there was a degree of quid pro quo:
in his memoirs, Brunton makes a point of advertising the quality of
Takashima coal.
    Brunton arrived in the country in June 1866. Over a period of only six
years, he designed and supervised the building of 26 Japanese lighthouses.
His work in Japan was a direct export of Scottish engineering, specifically
of the Northern Lighthouse Board, largely replicating the design of the Bell
Rock Lighthouse admired by the Iwakura Mission. He stressed its earth-
quake-proofing for the Japanese market – though the replication of design
had more behind it culturally than just safety. Despite setbacks, particularly
the sinking of the *Elleray*, carrying vital equipment, in December 1869, the
lighthouses were finished as soon as 1872. In the remaining time Brunton
turned to the civil engineering of Yokohama – a huge project for which he

is more remembered in Japan than in Scotland – then to education, and finally cartography. After eight years in Japan he returned to the UK in March 1876 to write an account of his trip under the constipated title *Pioneer Engineering in Japan: A Record of Work in helping to Re-lay the Foundations of Japanese Empire (1868–1876)*. When the account was finally published it was through two separate imprints under two titles, corresponding to different parts of the manuscript: *Building Japan 1868–1876* (the one most commonly known) and *Schoolmaster to an Empire: Richard Henry Brunton in Meiji Japan, 1868–1876*.

The year 1872, when Brunton finished the lighthouses and started dabbling in university administration, was a watershed for education in Scotland, as the Education Act was widely perceived as a failure of Scottish universities' attempts to maintain a general, inclusive education system centred on philosophy. In Scotland, traditionally even science had been taught from first principles as philosophy, and Moral Philosophy had been seen as central to Scots' intellectual flexibility. The twist here is that where the practicalism and specialism of Brunton and Glover seem at first to represent Scottish pride in engineering and to be typical of the achievements of the time, the pair both deviated from a Scottish educational tradition which concentrated on more cross-disciplinary and moral questions. Glover's own education had stopped at the Anglophile and practicalist Gym. Had he progressed to Aberdeen University in the pre-1872 years, his thinking might have become more similar to the critical voice of Stevenson. The difference is well demonstrated in a letter dated 25 September 1875 from Henry Dyer of the Imperial College of Engineering, later the University of Tokyo (and afterwards a Glasgow-based organiser of Japanese ex-pats), in response to a complaint Brunton had made about Dyer's courses, in particular relating it to the Stevensons' stance, which Brunton found to be too generalist and not sufficiently practical. Dyer wrote:

. . . the only fault which is found [by Brunton] with the programme of this College [the Imperial College of Education] is, that too much time is taken up with theoretical studies to the neglect of the practical part of the students' education . . .

Is he aware that this Robert Stevenson, when building the Cumbrae Light-house, spent every spare moment he had in going to Glasgow to obtain instruction in mathematics and mechanics at the Andersonian University [Strathclyde]. [sic] Does he know that when engaged on a light-house on the Pentland Skerries in Orkney, he came to Edinburgh University in the winter and studied mathematics, natural and moral philosophy, chemistry, natural history, logic and agriculture? I have no doubt 'R. H. B.' thinks this time was sadly mis-spent, or at least would have been spent to greater advantage in practical work, but Stevenson thought otherwise, and I am very much inclined to agree with him.

Glover and Brunton were great doers, and Glover was a great connector of individuals, but neither ever felt any overarching ethical sense of purpose, and both rejected the theoretical or generalist knowledge which characterised Scottish university education, as seen in Stevenson and Dyer. Intellectually, in many ways Glover diverges from Scottish tradition, which may explain why he missed any connection between the Japanese rebellions of the 1860s and the Jacobite rebellions of the 1740s – a link which occurred to Stevenson straight away. And although Glover had been central to the story Stevenson was to tell of this far-off country, and had smuggled and armed some of the Yoshida-influenced rebels by whom Stevenson was fascinated, the young writer seems not to have heard of him. In his essay on the rebellion, Stevenson doesn't mention the Choshu Five or the Satsuma Nineteen, which would have added to the ronin–Jacobite comparison.

By the time Taizo Masaki reached Great Stuart Street in 1878, and as Glover relaxed into salaried work at Mitsubishi, Stevenson had already become friendly with the technician Fujikura Kinjiro, interpreter to Brunton, appointment of the Stevensons, and another acquaintance of Glover's. Stevenson had enjoyed A.B. Mitford's *Tales of Old Japan* (1871), and Mitford had gathered material for this book touring Japan with Ernest Satow, and for some of the time with Glover himself. The significant literary event comes two years after the dinner party, with the publication of Stevenson's own essay on Yoshida Shoin. This short fictionalised biography has a similar tone of adventure to much of his historical fiction. It is based solely on the story Taizo told him during the evening and caused some unease amongst literary critics.

Stevenson's interest in Japan has been known but little remarked on in Japanese literary circles. There has been no book-length Japanese attempt to show an underlying link between the two figures. Yet Stevenson's show of interest in Yoshida in 1880 is precocious even by Japanese literary standards. It comes well before the Meiji Conservative wave of Yoshida research begun by Noguchi Katsuichi and Tomioka Masanobu in 1891 and followed by Tokutomi Soho two years later. These later Japanese studies established Yoshida as a political figure to revive his fierce sense of national self-definition. Stevenson's account also sees nationalism as a force for resistance, but is silent over the military pride of joi – which Glover, veteran of 1862, couldn't have missed if he tried.

There was only a slight build-up of information on Japan during Stevenson's early life, and in 1878, despite his correspondence and reading, and despite Glover's centrality to government and their families' connections, the writer was still mostly guessing. He claims no specific knowledge of Yoshida and notes that Yoshida was virtually unknown in Britain, as were those comrades of Glover who had been Yoshida's students, even though they had by now become government leaders. He doesn't touch on Ito at all, and doesn't seem to realise the influence Yoshida had on him. Aware of his own lack of expertise in the changing situation Taizo described, at the outset of the paper Stevenson admits, perhaps disingenuously, to imperfect recollection of the story, and even claims at the outset that he is 'not the author' of the work. His account contains a number of factual mistakes, wearily corrected in editorial parenthesis by Jenkin. But the remoteness of the cultural and historical context in 1878, evidenced by Stevenson's wild romanisation of names and pronunciation guide, shows the difficulty for Britons of the time to grasp the scale of Glover's achievements. Unlike Glover, Stevenson's essay continually links Restoration Japan's twin ideals of self-reliance and globalisation on one hand, and the Scottish situation after the Union on the other. Unaware of Ito, Stevenson nevertheless appreciates the influence on Yoshida of Sakuma Shozan, the scholar of Chinese classics known for 'Eastern Ethics – Western Technique', who mentored the young Yoshida from 1850. Stevenson also realises that Yoshida in turn mentored the generation of the Choshu Five – though he doesn't know the fate of the Five themselves. For Stevenson, as for Glover, rebels like Yoshida had kept alive the call for a patriotic stance. But unlike Glover, Stevenson engages with the terms of cultural nationalism in describing his 'enlightened' Yoshida.

By the time of his death at 27, also Stevenson's age when he wrote the essay, Yoshida had achieved widespread political fame amongst the clans of his own country. Unlike the black sheep Robert Louis, Yoshida's fame had arisen in part from the educational methods he inherited from his father – he continued the family business in establishing his matsushitason-juku training school in 1856 and broadly following the curriculum of his father's yamaga-ryu heigaku (military-philosophical training, or logistics). The irony is that the rebels' anger over the Unequal Treaties is directed precisely against the very opportunity which brought the Stevensons to Japan, when the bakufu felt forced to 'import' a new form of light according to European specifications. His family's opportunism incurred mixed feelings in the young Robert Louis, and he shows a deep sympathy with Yoshida's double bind, internationalist and yet anti-globalisation. Yoshida's joi was similar to Scottishness in empire in that it was an aspiration which also meant compromising national traditions. Yoshida's own attempts to attain an international education, from his chasing Russian ships to Nagasaki in 1853 to his attempt to stow away on an American ship at Shimoda in 1859, made him one of the first in a long line who saw advanced education as being abroad, continuing today in those Japanese students who see a foreign degree as being essential to an outstanding CV.

Stevenson extends the Scottish–Pacific connection in 'Records of a Family of Engineers', where he pointedly describes Scottish Highlanders as 'natives', 'barbarian' inhabitants, 'like [those of] Guam or the Bay of Islands'. And in a letter to Fujikura Kinjiro of 1877, he registers his sympathy with Japan's ongoing nationalist revolution: '[i]t is a very fine thing to be born at a moment of your country's history, when there are such great things to be done for her; and above all, to be able to do them'. In Enlightenment-intellectual vein, more sympathetic to France than is Glover, Stevenson's Yoshida the rebel is both an encyclopaedist and a noble savage: although brilliantly self-educated, like Walter Scott's gruff Highlanders he lacks refinement, rarely washes, and is pointedly removed from the gentlemanly image associated with British empire.

In Scotland, the fact that the ban on national dress of 1746 had been lifted by 1782 shows the extent to which a licensed national uniqueness had been assimilated into a wider imperial movement. This is exactly what happened in Japan in the 1860s: as an idea of national uniqueness was frozen into absolute properties and came to be viewed as harmless. Made unique, the nation loses the ability to adapt. A unique national culture is petrified, caught in the headlights of modernity. This duplicity in globalisation is what the young Stevenson relates in his account of Yoshida, projecting his struggle onto the remote territory of Japan, before he turns his gaze back on Scotland later in his career.

That both Stevenson and Yoshida were struggling to maintain a sense of national place despite the demands of the modern is perfectly demonstrated by the fact that Japan's lighthouses were thought to be insufficiently enlightened. Stevenson in effect critiques practical Scots like Glover and Brunton, and, to an extent, his own family: in 'Records of a Family of Engineers', he suggests that the enlightening mission which took the Stevensons to Japan also placed them as archetypal nineteenth-century 'North Britons' of a canny, self-improving nature, industrious and loyalist craftsmen who made good imperial managers, 'decent, reputable folk, following honest trades — millers, maltsters, and doctors, playing the character parts in [Walter Scott's] *Waverley* novels with propriety, if without distinction'.

Stevenson's message was pro-rebel and anti-imperial. Glover's was pro-rebel and pro-imperial. At the time, Stevenson's ideas were dangerously subversive and had to be diluted for publication. Just as Joseph Conrad, deeply influenced by Stevenson, would struggle with a readership that didn't want to hear any criticism of colonialism in *Heart of Darkness* (*Blackwood's Magazine*, 1899), nor was national rebellion popular with the readership of Stevenson's 'Yoshida-Torajiro' (*Cornhill Magazine*, 1880). While the generalist Stevenson struggled with empire, the practicalist Glover had already become a successful self-improver by brokering enlightenment in Japan. It is a perfect envoy to the story of the two families that Glover was the first person in Japan to commission a 'western-style' lighthouse for his own needs, as is noted with admiration by an anonymous letter writer to the *Nagasaki Press* on 10 January 1903.

TWELVE

Cowboy Consultancy

Having weathered the economic storm of Takashima – perhaps better than some of his family – from 1876 Glover settled into a quiet life of consultancy at Mitsubishi and informal diplomacy. He was now free to spend time with his wife, son and newborn daughter Hana. Tsuru's infertility, perhaps largely due to the makeshift conditions in which she had given birth to her first daughter when she was 15, prompted them to seek out Thomas's son, Shinsaburo. The family Glover had wanted as much as his father was now as complete as it would get. But unlike his father, the young Glover had been toughened by foreign trade since the age of 18, and he had fathered at least one other child before Tsuru. Given the chance, Glover would probably have gone the same way as his father and had a half-dozen sons, or legitimate sons, had the birth of Hana not been so difficult. The question now was whether or not he could settle down and look after his new family. And he did look after them financially and, most of the time, attentively.

The year of the birth of Hana and the adoption of Shinsaburo, 1876, also saw Glover beginning to travel between the east and west of Japan for Mitsubishi, as Iwasaki had him working in Tokyo but maintaining Nagasaki links – a tiring journey at the time. The Iwasakis were amongst Glover's very small band of correspondents, and their letters provide hints as to how he felt in later life. His position at the company was already quite senior, and it was felt that he had proven himself both during the days of the revolution and at the mine. As Olive Checkland says:

Glover . . . began a new career as servant and adviser to Mitsubishi. He had known Iwasaki, its founder, from pre-Meiji days. Indeed, they had almost certainly been associates in the heady years around 1868 when Iwasaki in charge of the Nagasaki office 'was buying all the arms he could find for the militant Tosa Han'. At that time Iwasaki and Glover, both buccaneering spirits, had shared in the excitement of the great days of Nagasaki.

Glover's projects of the late 1860s, the three big ships and the Kosuge Slipway, had been central to Mitsubishi's early expansion. Coming so soon after his personal nadir of 1869 to 1874, his will to work and network had won through to bring him a financial security which would never desert him. At Mitsubishi, he was without portfolio: the company created a position specifically for him. And this position became massively remunerative – for at least some of this time he earned more than Iwasaki. When he first moved to Tokyo it was to a well-appointed house in Shibakoen in the centre of the city. Although he was salaried in Tokyo, he kept Ipponmatsu, and Tsuru and the children lived there for some of the time. He would travel back to Nagasaki frequently on business at least until the mid 1890s. It was not until 1895, when he moved to an even more opulent residence in Azabu, that he was established full-time in the new metropolis.

As he had rebuilt his finances after his ordeal at Takashima, Glover had started, a bit vengefully, to pursue small businesses who had owed him money. He had assumed an air of responsibility which verged on the political and at times seemed to have difficulty seeing the distinction himself. As one adjudicator said in 1875, 'It is clear . . . that the municipal council which Mr. Glover claims to represent is not officially recognised by the consular board or by way of the consuls at Nagasaki; save Mr. Flowers, Her Britannic Majesty's consul at that port.' He took to operating on the edges of diplomatic jurisdiction, not always gracefully, being accustomed to the early settler idea that power and wealth belonged together. This assumption had not always endeared him to the Foreign Office, but as far as Mitsubishi were concerned, it was the kind of realpolitik which would make him a valued consultant.

When he moved, times were becoming rough for western Japan: in particular, since the 1860s, the numbers of Nagasaki foreign residents had been diminishing. This was in part because there was less unrest to encourage arms trade, and in part because the native residents were becoming more knowledgeable about international trade. Relieved to have placed one foot in the expanding east of the country and to be surrounded by powerful friends, Glover graduated from hard drinking yujo and the shacks of clubs which functioned as lobby groups and cultural safe havens, and began to move in more refined circles. Organised sports and pastimes came into evidence, as he made a deliberate move towards hobbies appropriate to the family man. The tennis courts near Ipponmatsu had been a social focus for a while. Golf increasingly became a stage for corporate socialising, much as it is today, and a course was developed at Glover's vacation retreat near the temple at Chuzenji in the mountains. There was also a fad for bowling. The sport was disorganised and the venues mostly drinking clubs – the swish lanes to be found in almost every Japanese town today are a post-1945 American import. Glover took part with good spirit and no great aptitude, though one report of 1880 has him winning 'very decisively' over an unnamed opponent. Songs were composed in praise of bowling, and the newspapers carried match reports. When the Glover Garden still had a Scotch kitsch giftshop and tartan skirts were part of the uniform, a young assistant explained to me how Glover's participation proved that bowling had been invented in Scotland.

It was at Mitsubishi that Glover began to take on the studied appearance of a VIP. But his move to the company also coincided with a number of disasters. In 1876 the last of the three great Glover ships, the *Wen Yu Maru*, sank – the only one to perish within its working lifetime. In April 1877 his eldest brother and long-term business partner Charles died of cancer. The young Thomas had always looked up to Charles, and, normally tight-lipped, he wrote that his passing came as 'a terrible blow'. When Charles died, he had been owed $125,430, and it may be that, like Alex, he suffered from the financial stress that Takashima had brought on the family. William died the following year, and, most traumatically, his father died on 11 March 1878. The two elder brothers, respectable clerks while Thomas had been growing up, and the coastguard head of the Glover clan, all died within the space of two years, and Glover posted long absences throughout 1877 and 1878. During these two years his business dealings are quite anonymous within the company. He was relieved to have a new family but struggled with the disappearance of the old one. Living far from home and losing relatives, he was also losing any sense of home itself.

Although Thomas didn't write home often, he conveyed messages through other family members – the siblings kept in touch through their business contacts – and there was always a sense of closeness with the family. The consecutive deaths had an emotional impact, but he didn't go home to join his family during the period. As far as we know, he didn't return to Scotland at all after 1868. Still, the distance between him and his childhood began to play on his mind, as his family shifted from one generation to the next. He knew that the country he still called home was disappearing from him – though he would always describe himself as primarily British. (And he maintained the pragmatism of this 'national' identity: 'Britain has no friends and no enemies, only opportunities.') Another critical moment in his relationship to his dwindling family came when Alex's ship *Star Queen* was wrecked in January 1879. Although Alex was not on board, by the end of the 1870s both he and Thomas were possessed of a spirit of carpe diem, and were hatching plans to travel to the US, where they would once again take on the role of prospectors. Meanwhile the growing Shinsaburo, whose lukewarm ambition in later years became something of a trial, was inspiring nothing but pride, and Alan Spence is right in portraying Glover as someone desperate to pass on his own experience to a son.

What Iwasaki was looking for in Glover was expertise on an international scale in arms, ships and trade relations. Glover's role in Harry Parkes's coming to Satsuma territory a decade before had not been forgotten by the rebel clans. From 1876, he advised on the management of Mitsubishi's fleet of steamers, his own slipway, increasingly used for naval production, the shipyards, privatised by the government and now hugely profitable for Mitsubishi, the new currency, and, as ever, coal production. He had kept an eye on Takashima throughout the 1870s, cringing at the management of Goto Shinpei, and Mitsubishi came to see him as a troubleshooter in the coal market.

Goto had struggled with the 1878 riots, which had partly arisen through underpayment of wages that made Glover look philanthropic. When Mitsubishi bought the mine outright in 1881, Iwasaki began sending Glover back to Takashima on regular and increasingly lengthy trips. But the mine's labour disputes were far from over: from 1885 to 1886 the journalist Matsuoka Koichi anticipated the investigative mine journalism of George Orwell by working at Takashima, living with the miners, and writing a withering exposé of conditions. Matsuoka's book described overcrowding, underpayment and exploitation. To Glover's and Iwasaki's dismay, the account didn't disappear quietly but was taken up by a number of prominent journalists, including Inukai Tsuyoshi, who would later become Prime Minister.

During one of Glover's trips to Takashima, on 9 May 1878, a phone cable was laid from the mine to the Nagasaki mainland to the island with the help of a Norwegian engineer who had been a collaborator with Alexander Graham Bell, and the Glover brothers used this cable to make experimental calls. The experiment can legitimately be described as the first telephone call in Japan, and the *Nagasaki Express* described it as being of great importance. However, the reporter did admit that there was so much background noise that the phone was practically useless. Glover himself confessed that the sound quality was never better than 'exceedingly poor', and the brothers abandoned its use soon after. The phone line is nevertheless a good example of a fascination with communications technology from steam rail to television which preoccupied Scots in the context of British union and empire.

Although comfortably in upper management, Glover hadn't given up on innovation and his interests spread in two new directions. From as early as February 1881 he was experimenting with dynamite, a significant development in military logistics, and a demonstration was reported in the *Nagasaki Express* of 9 February:

> A good number of the foreign residents, including ladies, and a large concourse of native officials, and others interested in mining and engineering, were present . . . [the dynamite's] destructive properties were well illustrated by the entire demolition of a solid block of granite, and the breaking of a massive casting, weighing half a ton, into a thousand pieces . . . [i]ts harmlessness was equally as satisfactorily convincing, as a charge was burnt in an ordinary charcoal fire without the slightest sign of an explosion, and a box containing 10 lbs. was afterwards blown into the air by a ten pound charge of gunpowder, completely destroying the box without in any way affecting the dynamite. Various other minor examples were also given, and at 4 o' clock the proceedings adjourned to the bay, where experiments in the water were made. To illustrate torpedo warfare, a small native boat was destroyed by a charge of dynamite connected by insulated wires with a dynamo electric battery, contained in a boat at a safe distance away, and when the current was connected the doomed craft was blown to atoms and a column of water thrown high into the air. Several other torpedoes were also cast into the water and exploded by the same means. Those afloat in the vicinity had a rather unexpected windfall in the shape of fish killed by the explosions, of which great quantities were picked up.

The 'windfall' of fish represents a precedent in fishing with explosives, for which poorer countries are now often criticised, but the dynamite experiments were mainly carried out with an eye to use in mining and weaponry. Both Glover and his young son were thrilled by the results. It had been only 15 years since dynamite had been developed by Alfred Nobel, and so far the technology had not been used in Japan at all. So unknown was the technology that a representative of the Nobel Explosives Company had to be present to supervise the experiments.

Later that year, Glover got some of the diplomatic recognition he had craved, in election to public office as Portuguese Deputy Consul in Nagasaki. As with Mackenzie's French appointment, there were no particular qualifications required for diplomatic status, beyond being locally well-connected. By this time, though, with an established foreign population, the Portuguese appointment was a significant one. In the couple of years before, still recovering from the deaths in his family, Glover had staged semi-diplomatic parties at Ipponmatsu, intending to establish his reputation as a non-partisan play-maker and host. On 26 July 1881, Foreign Minister Inoue Kaoru received a letter from Joakin Jose de Graza, Minister Plenipotentiary (Acting Consul) of Portugal in Macao, offering Glover the position as Deputy Consul in Nagasaki.

Glover would be Portuguese Deputy Consul from 1881 until 1887. He was the fourth Portuguese Consul in Japan after E.H. Evans, the first boss of the prominent company Dent & Co., Jose Loureiro and Willie P. Magnum. The duties were largely honorary, but Glover was becoming increasingly interested in diplomatic affairs and made sure he was in a position to influence leading politicians. The position was not a token one: the Portuguese had been, along with the Dutch, the only Europeans to have lived in Japan through sakoku. However, Portugal represented a technical exception in that diplomats on-site in Japan didn't have the authority to deal with juridical matters in the kyoryuchi – they were instead passed to the Consul in Macao. This meant that Glover's position involved few formal duties and a lot of informal ones, perfect for a noted networker with no formal diplomatic skills. His greatest asset remained his ability to connect disparate groups of people. Perhaps because he still lacked confidence about his standing in the foreign community after Takashima, he took a couple of weeks before accepting the offer on 20 August. But as soon as he was appointed, he threw his weight behind the job, celebrating the 42nd birthday of Don Luis I at Ipponmatsu as early as 31 October 1881. Fortunately, no one spoke to him in Portuguese, or asked about the health of Don Luis.

In an echo of his father's move to Bridge of Don, he also accepted the Portuguese position in part for the sake of Shinsaburo, using it to claim that a consul's son needed a fitting education. The appointment also revived the spirits of Alex, who, changed by his near-death experience, left Shanghai for Nagasaki the day after Thomas was offered the post, giving up his job there with Jardine Matheson. But Alex was as restless in business and love as was Thomas, and despite Thomas's responsibilities, soon persuaded him into rediscovering their adventuring past by leaving the country for another new territory, the still unfederalised American West.

By the end of 1881 Glover was glad of the chance to get away. Despite his Mitsubishi position, his Portuguese honour, and the opportunity to spend time with his family, the political landscape had been shifting against him since 1878, as Meiji bureaucracy started to give him more than he had bargained for. The day before the letter of Glover's appointment arrived from Macao, the government had begun dividing up Hokkaido land under the Satsuma samurai Kuroda Kiyotaka, involving a displacement of the northern Ainu people which has become notorious, and inviting accusations of the old clans using their power undemocratically. On 25 August 1881, Europhile liberals protested that this advancement of Satsuma suggested continuing nepotism between Satsuma samurai and a government which was supposed to be post-clan, transparent and meritocratic in the European tradition. The same year also saw the establishment of the kenpeitai. The liberals pushed against Satsuma prominent in government for a British monarch-in-parliament model of government, which was delivered only after a struggle in the form of the 1889 Constitution by Ito, who had belonged to Choshu, the clan which had, significantly, been at war with Satsuma until 1865. But Ito's Choshu were equally invested in the European-style Executive, and a rift appeared between Glover and Ito in 1881, as Ito drifted away from the British model to a more absolutist idea of government which he would retain for most of the decade. On 11 October 1881 Ito, Iwakura and many of the apparently liberal service intelligentsia, stunned Glover by virtually abandoning the British idea of monarch-in-parliament in favour of a version of the old joi idea of supra-parliamentary allegiance to a divine emperor. Ito's persuasion away from the position of monarch-in-parliament, by now a cornerstone of Glover's conception of a civilised mercantile society, towards one which stressed the supremacy of the monarch, looked as if it would be sealed by Ito's fact-finding trip from Yokohama to Prussia, scheduled for 14 March 1882.

On 29 January 1881 these tensions had also led to the creation of Japan's first political party, the anti-absolutist Jiyuto, usually translated as Liberal Party. The party was seen as such a threat to the government that its leader, Itagaki Taisuke, would be assassinated on 6 April 1882, in an old-school joi attack by loyalists. Naito Hatsuho has speculated that Iwasaki and Glover, along with luminaries of the Meiji Enlightenment such as Fukuzawa Yukichi, were involved with this anti-absolutist fight in 1880–1 – though Glover was never, in the sense in which we now understand it, a liberal. And in the 1860s Fukuzawa, father of the Japanese Enlightenment, hadn't been a rebel but an active member of the bakufu. Mitsubishi's Iwasaki, increasingly accused of funding the pro-liberal faction, also became distanced from the Ito government. There ensued something of a smear campaign against Mitsubishi, and on 18 August 1881 Iwasaki felt compelled to give a speech to his employees defending accusations made against Mitsubishi and adding, with some bitterness, that his employees should 'steer clear of politics'.

For Glover, Ito's Prussian trip was a reminder of his friend's thrilled journey to England in 1863. For Ito, leaving his regime to the temptations of liberals was a gamble: only two days after his departure, the reformer Okuma Shinenobu duly took advantage of his absence to set up the Rikken Kaishin party (Constitutional Progressive Party), to advocate the British system over Prussian absolutism. Government was becoming increasingly factional, as was usual for European-style governments, but in a situation where samurai tensions were still high and absolutist joi was still present. Extraordinarily, Mitsubishi, given its corporate reputation today, remained under suspicion as a hotbed of liberals.

During this period, Glover's interpersonal skills were tested as much as they had been in the mid 1860s. Two of his closest and most important friends, Ito and Iwasaki, were now involved in a serious ideological dispute, and he was a lifelong supporter of the former and an elite employee of the latter. Glover remained unloved for his efforts at mediation: around New Year 1882 he struggled, over the course of several carefully worded letters, to arrange an invitation to Ito to visit Mitsubishi's Takashima mine. Ito refused, resulting in an indirect loss of face for Iwasaki because of an invitation he would never have made himself. This feud may account for the fact that Glover didn't receive his famous national decoration before 1908, even though he had been central to the formation of Restoration Japan. The political disenfranchisement became a reason to take a break from the country with Alex.

Glover stayed loyal to Ito in that he wisely never became involved in opposition parties, for his own safety. In general Glover was never interested in party politics. He was, however, worried about how the foreign commercial community would react to Ito's trip to Prussia, and the spectre of recidivist joi fundamentalism. Again he began to complain of pains in his back, probably exacerbated by the political stress, and now certainly linked to the kidney complaint which would remain with him for the rest of his life. Even in Ito's absence, on 3 June 1882, loyalist samurai authorities clamped down further by passing a kind of Criminal Justice Act which limited the extent of political assembly. If Glover had had high ideals for the Saccho rebels in the mid-1860s, or, more likely, if his free trading principles had seen an outlet in a British-style empire recreated in the east, he was now becoming disaffected. The government he had backed was drifting towards repeating the totalitarianism of the old bakufu, and his employer, despite its economic standing, lacked the political power to do anything about it. He was increasingly estranged from one of his oldest Japanese friends, his most important political ally, and the most important statesman of the age. And Ito was a formidable opponent, intelligent, pragmatic and as quick with a political excommunication as he was with a sword. Their emerging differences were a personal sadness for Glover, and a sign to take care in public life. His activities in the years to 1882 remained muted and were largely limited to apolitical forays like the telephone and dynamite experiments, in-house reports for Mitsubishi, and carefully pitched Portuguese functions. He would lie low from July 1882 for almost a year by quitting Japan entirely.

Leaving on 28 July, Thomas and Alex surprised their employers and loved ones by embarking on an open-ended journey to look for opportunities in Oregon and Washington. The next day the Gloverite *Nagasaki Express* lamented his leaving:

> Mr. T.B. Glover, accompanied by his brother, Mr. A.J. Glover, left by the *Nagoya Maru* last night *en route* for Oregon. We understand he will return to Nagasaki in about six months' time, the trip being partly for relaxation from business, and partly with a desire to investigate on the spot the resources of the Far West. Mr. Glover's name has so long been associated with Nagasaki, and he himself the centre and active agent of every movement for the social welfare of residents and visitors, as well as in other ways having done so much for the improvement of the port, that he will be widely missed.

In 1882 the American Pacific coast was still frontier territory, and during their time in this new Anglophone wild west, Thomas and Alex speculated in land, much as Thomas had in 1860s Nagasaki. Despite Thomas's responsibilities in Japan, both brothers considered staying long-term. Few records remain of this time, but it is tempting to imagine something like a rerun of the adventures of 1860, this time enacted in a common language.

The American descendants of Alex Glover are these days rediscovering their roots. Recently, Alex Glover's great-grandson Tom Glover has shed new light on the brothers' American adventure, based on information gathered at Spokane County Library, Washington. He has, for example, noticed designs in the brothers' houses in Washington which are unusual compared with those of their American neighbours. Aware of the possible cultural significance, he is now attempting to have the houses placed on the state historic register. His research also illuminates the brothers' western American road trip, and the way in which they revived their pioneering spirits in this new frontier land. Alex has been the lead into this part of the Thomas Glover story: after Thomas returned, not having turned much of a profit, and not leaving any record of his activities, Alex stayed and made a life in the west of America. The 21st-century Tom Glover's account is worth quoting at length here, since, although unrehearsed, it captures the scene vividly:

Alex homesteaded there [Spokane, Washington] about 1885 or thereabouts, I guess just after having arrived from Japan. [If it was 1885, this would be after a gap of three years]. He purchased 160 acres, and built the house and barn that are there now. I noticed a few new planks in the barn walls, and the owner said he was trying to restore it.

The story that my dad's [Alex's grandson's] cousin told was that Alex and Thomas went to America, to what is now the State of Washington, which was still a territory at that time . . . I don't know why the brothers chose Spokane, which seems like a very out of the way place for people used to living in more settled areas. Spokane is about 300 miles from Seattle or Portland, so getting there would have been no easy task back in the 1800s [i.e. nineteenth century]. Probably they arrived from Portland by train. Still, to have known about it from Japan seems a stretch.

Spokane was founded by [a] James Glover, but James was born in Missouri, so I doubt he is a relative. Spokane was a wild west town at the time, and remote, so maybe they were looking for land in America, but without too many eyes watching them? . . . I'm certain that with their accents and style they must have drawn a lot of attention to themselves without meaning to.

. . . we know that Thomas returned to Japan so if he had purchased land he must not have held on to it for very long. Alex's original 160 acres has since been subdivided, but the original homestead is intact.

. . . My dad told me that his grandmother [Alex's wife] told him, that when she first moved into the house (she may have been the housekeeper at first) that the Indians were still living in the area, and would pick berries on the property.

It would be interesting to know what Tsuru made of her husband's new adventure, full of speculation, disgruntled natives, footloose young house-keepers, and uncertain futures. It would certainly bring us close to *Madam Butterfly*-type abandonment if Thomas was seen as feeling out possibilities for a long-term move, but Tsuru's feelings on this as on everything else remain a mystery.

In any case, the early 1880s American west coast was as ripe for speculation as had been the early 1860s Japanese west coast: there was cheap land available and, like newly opened Nagasaki, it was seen as a lawless, hard-drinking, young man's playground. The brothers were reliving their adventures of the wild west of Japan, under similar circumstances of oppor-tunism, speculation and native joi-type danger ('Indians'). As Ito was rethink-ing his political views in Prussia, Glover was revisiting his own youth in Washington. Thomas Glover did eventually leave his second speculative adventure behind – though not within the six-month limit the *Nagasaki Express* had promised – and recognised the idea of abandoning his Japanese career and family as a form of midlife crisis. Still, many Japanese residents saw frontier America as a natural home for Glover, and his friend W.B. Mason later expressed surprise at his coming back to Japan:

[Glover] went to Spokane, in the State of Washington, where he invested in land, and, for a brief period, enjoyed the novelty of a farmer's life, a life for which one would have thought he was peculiarly fitted . . .

Had the American option proved more attractive to Glover, it would have changed the whole story of his life. His search for permanent opportunities, at least in the beginning, throws into question the common story that he committed himself in his twenties to stay in Japan and stuck to his decision. On Alex's part, the resolve to start a new American life represented a final emotional acceptance of the failure of his first marriage: as soon as it was legally possible, he divorced Ann, with a bitter account of their marriage, in the 'District Court of Washington Territory for the Fourth Judicial District . . . at Spokane Falls'. For no reason we know of – other than the speculated affair between Ann and Ryle Holme – Alex's lawyers seem desperately keen to demonstrate that Ann abandoned him, and to stress that Alex had, through his own effort, earned all of his own property in America:

> . . . in the year 1886 [t]he said defendant [Ann] disregarding her marriage vow willfully deserted and abandoned plaintiff [Alex] and still continues to desert and abandon said plaintiff and lives separated and apart from him without any sufficient cause or reason, moving from plaintiff's resident [sic] and being cause of the following circumstances.
>
> For three years after the said marriage of plaintiff and defendant they lived together as husband and wife at their home in Japan where plaintiff had business. Thereupon, they went on a visit to their old home in England [that is, Aberdeen] for six months and when plaintiff was ready and desirous of returning to his business and home in Japan, defendant refused to accompany him and gave as a reason therefore that she would not again leave the old country [in fact the split was almost definitely decided before they arrived in 'the old country']: then plaintiff went back to his business and home in Japan without the defendant. Two years thereafter plaintiff returned to England to induce defendant to return with him to their home in Japan but defendant still refused to do so. Plaintiff then returned to Japan and there remained several years and then came to this Territory where he has since resided. That after plaintiff's second visit to England he frequently at different times wrote to defendant telling her that he had a home for her and requesting her to join him at such home [Glover descendants have uncovered no such letters]. Defendant once wrote him that she would not do so. Would not leave England and that she did not desire to correspond with him. Thereafter, plaintiff wrote to her at different times but defendant returned to him his letters unopened. Plaintiff always provided properly for defendant when she lived with him and has always since had a good home and been ready and willing to share it with her and properly provide for her . . .

... since his residence in said Spokane County, plaintiff has acquired by his own exertion the following real property ... [list of real estate and effects follows] Therefore plaintiff prays the bonds of matrimony between himself and defendant be dissolved, that the above property be awarded to him as his separate property ...

As well as his desire for financial security, Alex took with him his restless libido, which may indeed have been the final motivation for the formal divorce. He married Julie Belle Davis on 9 July 1889, and although he died only six years later, in that time they had three children, Victoria, Thomas and Julia Belle – the middle child named after his uncle. When Alex remarried, he was 49 and his new wife 19. Along with Charles's and Thomas's descendants, these are the only surviving kin of the original Glover siblings we know of. Thomas matched Alex's American enthusiasm, much as he had Mackenzie's at the turn of the 1860s, but never matched his financial or romantic ambitions. Ultimately he accepted that his home was in the Far East.

When he returned to Japan in March 1883, he found that the political situation had worsened. The Jiyuto, which, in the beginning, had been trying to bring to bear the same pressures on the government as had Mitsubishi, were now targeting the company for its wet stance, feeling that the zaibatsu had caved in too easily to Itoist absolutism. Mitsubishi boss Iwasaki Yataro's health was beginning to fail him. On 6 February 1885 he died of cancer and was replaced in corporate-feudal tradition by a brother 17 years his junior, the New York-educated Iwasaki Yanosuke, who would later represent the whole Japanese business community in the Imperial Assembly. The years between 1883 and 1885 had been the cruellest possible time for Yataro to watch the Jiyuto stage demonstrations in which model Mitsubishi ships were burned. This was also a personal heartache for Glover, who had been responsible in large part for the early development of the fleet.

Worse, Ito had returned on 3 August 1882 a confirmed Prussian convert, and from late 1882 had set about countering the liberals and advancing his country towards a form of absolutism. This was difficult for Britons abroad to take, whose imperial rivalry with Germany was becoming increasingly clear, as the power blocs of World War One were already beginning to form. Tensions within East Asia itself had also deteriorated since the military coup in Korea of 23 July 1881, when a government broadly disposed towards Japanese imperial protection had been deposed by Korean nationalists, a prelude to Ito's later fate. Back with his legitimate family in 1883, Glover wondered if he had been right to return from America after all.

But his corporate and diplomatic positions remained beneficial for his family, despite his American sabbatical. Shinsaburo was massaged into the high-profile school Gakushuin, which would eventually prove beyond him, academically and socially, in part, apparently, because his ethnicity played on his mind and affected his relationships with his classmates. By 1883, the Glovers' domestic life was relatively peaceful. Privately, Thomas Glover had put the family deaths of the late 1870s behind him – partly thanks to his midlife road trip – and publicly he was ready to settle into a quiet and low-profile phase of Mitsubishi consultancy. Financially, he was doing better than he had ever imagined he would, even during the Mackenzie days. Yet, the political and ethical standoff with Ito, and the spectre of an absolutist, surveillant and possibly xenophobic government, was making it stressful to cope day to day in the nation he had helped to create. He needed a drink.

THIRTEEN

Beer and Honour

The legend is true: the whiskers on the fabulous giraffe–lion on the labels of Kirin beer are based on Glover's own moustache. Returning from beer-rich America, it dawned on Glover that while imported beer was too expensive in Japan, the foreign community was dissatisfied with the domestic product. But he was now a regular salaried worker with no investment capital of his own. If he tried to borrow enough to set up an enterprise as speculative as a brewery, there was every chance that he would over-reach, as he had with the mine. And by this time and age he was more eager to remain solvent than he was to resume the life of a speculator. As a compromise, he decided on a shareholder system.

Kirin's website associates the company's beginnings with William Copeland's Spring Berry Brewery, which started production in 1869 on the site later chosen by Glover for his project (although the brewery celebrated 2007 as its official centenary). This claim is surprising, since Spring Berry folded long before Glover's Japan Brewery Company was set up, and although Kirin inherited the location, it has no connection to Copeland's ill-fated brewery. If anything, Glover's fame in Japan seems to make Kirin's connection with Copeland's obscure product disingenuous – unless, that is, Kirin are equating age with trustworthiness: walking around Tokyo today, it's not unusual to see corporate logos which read 'Since 2002'. But Copeland was not the first foreigner to attempt brewing in Japan: Henrik Doeff, also the compiler of the first Dutch–Japanese dictionary, brewed beer in Dejima in the early nineteenth century. We know little about Doeff's product, which catered to only a few pre-Ansei Dutch settlers. We do know that Copeland's Spring Berry Beer couldn't find the market to keep going, and the company went bankrupt in 1885. At this point Glover moved to fill the niche. Not everyone agreed that it was possible to produce domestic beer to the standards of foreign beer without incurring impossible costs, and the project was far from risk-free.

Glover bought the site of Copeland's brewery not long after it went bust, in partnership with a M. Kirkwood, who was then working for the Ministry of Justice. Together they formed the Japan Brewery Company, and, so as not to over-borrow, set out to raise the capital via 500 shares of only $100 each. This method of investment was new to Japanese business: stung by his experience at Takashima, and more considerate of the financial wellbeing and education of his family, Glover tried to protect himself by involving as much of others' capital as possible. Although he was first to recognise the potential for the project, he also felt that his own time at the cutting edge of entrepreneurism was over, deciding to 'defer judgement [of Brewery policy] to the members'. He was also, unknown to these members, in increasing pain from his kidney complaint, which, would have been less serious if he had stuck to beer instead of moving to sake with Ito in 1863. But the ninth section of the minutes of the company meeting from 25 March 1887 shows that the other interested parties were determined to keep him on the board, suggesting that the name and reputation of Glover, Mitsubishi consultant and retiring Portuguese diplomat, may have meant the difference between success and failure:

> Mr. Talbot [a director of the Japan Brewery Company] gave notice that he would, at the next meeting of shareholders, second Mr. Kirkwood's proposition that Mr. Thomas Blake Glover should be elected a director of the company. As by article No. 77 the number of directors is limited to five, it was resolved that an extraordinary general meeting, to be held on the same day but subsequently, to the next annual general meeting, should be called for the purpose of passing a special resolution empowering the directors to substitute the number of seven for five as the highest number of directors, the secretary to give the necessary notices. This resolution was deemed necessary in order to retain the services of the present directors in addition to those of Mr. Glover, whose accession to the board is considered to be most advantageous & desirable.

In the flotation of the brewery, Glover's loyalty to Mitsubishi and other samurai worthies paid off, as he had calculated it would: Iwasaki Yanosuke bought shares, as did a number of senior politicians, and these names were enough to open the floodgates and sell all 500 shares quickly. The seven-director Japan Brewery Company finalised its negotiations with the licensing authority on 5 July 1887, its signatories being Glover and the local entrepreneurs James Boddo, Edgar Abbott and W.H. Talbot. To qualify for its licence, the company agreed to recognise any rules 'the said governor may deem proper', and on 23 July 1887, declared that they were 'registered as a limited liability Company in Hong Kong'.

Significantly, amidst the rising popularity of Meiji Conservative nationalism, Glover was now also beginning to show support for the renegotiation of the Ansei Treaties: although the brewery business was inside the foreign concessions, it was to observe Japanese law, and 'the undertaking becomes, in many respects, a Japanese industry'. During the company's foundation it was suggested that they should pay taxes, and Glover declared himself to be in favour. This meant that he joined his estranged comrade Ito as a critic of extraterritoriality, recognising the responsibility of foreigners to the emerging empire, and hoping to heal some of the wounds caused by Japan's movement towards Prussian authoritarianism.

Glover had other, more personal reasons for being a critic of extraterritoriality. After almost two decades of marriage, he was still living with the fact that he wasn't free to travel throughout his wife's land, and that she had no rights as a Japanese citizen in the kyoryuchi. She moved little, while her husband dotted around the Pacific and the Sea of Japan. While Glover had now lived in Japan for twice as long as the country he still called home, he had no rights under Japanese law. For Ansei reformers, without taxation there could be no access to Japanese law, and no moral ground from which to argue for the right of free passage through the country. This long-term resident now saw himself as pioneering the voluntary payment of tax, as a statement against extraterritoriality. As a lonely, frantically ambitious youth in 1859, he had been one of the traders in Shanghai pushing for a strengthening of the Unequal Treaties which opened up Japan's markets hugely in favour of the west. Three decades later, the Japan Brewery Company was the only foreign-run company paying Japanese national tax to show solidarity.

The Company planned to begin brewing in October 1888, but as it turned out its first yield was available by May of that year. The product was immediately popular, being cheap domestic beer of an unusually high quality, and the company soon returned profits. Since the board had suspicions about how successfully neutral third parties might market the product against domestic beers, they set up a specialised shop in Kanagawa, tellingly called Meijiya (Meiji-shop), in partnership with returning ryugakusei Isono Hikaru who had spent six years in Britain. Again Glover's habit of checking on all points in the production process proved to be key. With beer as with

coal, he was as concerned with quality as with yield, knowing that this
would give the company an edge against products already on the market.

It was during Glover's involvement with the set-up of the brewery that
his mother died, on 21 August 1887. She was buried in St Peter's Cemetery
in King Street, Aberdeen, near her husband and son James Lindley. Both
parents were now gone, and a heaviness set in. Sister Martha had been the
main carer of her mother at Braehead, dutifully resisting the temptation to
go to Nagasaki. But in 1889, with no domestic commitments left, she
decided to make the voyage. Glover didn't go back to Braehead after the
death of either of his parents (there was of course no way to make it in
time for the funerals, or even the immediate emotional fall-out, and practical
arrangements were better handled by those already there), but with his
mother's passing and then Martha's move to Japan, his last major link to
the country of his birth disappeared. If he was now at the peak of his success,
he was also adrift from his country of birth.

Despite his initial reticence, Glover eventually became outright head of
the Japan Brewery Company in 1894. By this time JBC beer was widely
regarded as the single quality domestic product, and was significantly cheaper
than imported varieties. He had found the higher quality/lower price balance
that had never quite come off at Takashima. Today, Kirin is still the default
beer in many restaurants and bars. The product is now backed up by a
massive advertising budget, but originally it had nothing but local newspaper
advertising and the logo of a giraffe–lion designed by daughter Hana, who
adapted a figure from Chinese legend. Hana had noticed that beer bottle
labels almost always used animals, and abandoned her own first idea of a
dog for something more original. 'Kirin' means giraffe, and the name on
the labels is in archaic kanji, implying Chineseness, or, more nebulously,
tradition. Hana, perhaps more than Tomisaburo, loved the reflected glory
of her father's achievements and added that the first yield of beer was 'a
time for [Glover] to feel proud'. Beer certainly had a central place in the
life of the kyoryuchi, for better and worse.

Despite the passing of his parents and most of his siblings, in his plans
for the brewery Glover continued to maintain the local connections of his
dimly remembered youth: William Watt, a Fraserburgh man and veteran
of the Battle of Kagoshima, was appointed as general manager of the brewery,
where he would work for eleven of the company's formative years. Watt's
obituary in the *Fraserburgh Herald and Northern Counties Advertiser* of 7
March 1916 tells of his death in a far-off country, now, mid World War

One, described as 'our staunch Ally':

The deceased was born at Fraserburgh, Scotland, on May 15th, 1847, and was thus in his sixty-ninth years [sic]. As a young man he left Scotland in the year 1868 in the barque 'Ellen Black' [the ship which took the Kosuge Slipway to Nagasaki], which made the trip to Japan by way of the Cape, arriving at Nagasaki in June of the same year. An engineer by profession, he joined the Tosa Company, later merged in the Mitsu Bishi and then in the Nippon Yusen Kaisha [the company into which Mitsubishi morphed briefly in 1885]. He was on board the 'Shinagawa maru' at the time of the Kagoshima rebellion, and had some very interesting experiences in the civil strife of those early days. At a later period he was for some time connected with the Imperial Government Railways during the construction of the Kanzaki bridge, between Osaka and Kobe. He then joined the Mitsu Bishi Steamship Company which was later absorbed by the Nippon Yusen Kaisha.

   On retiring from the sea, Mr. Watt joined the Kirin Brewery Company [the Japan Brewery Company] at the time of its formation, erecting the plant and running it for over eleven years. He was later employed by the Yokohama Engine and Iron Works, where he remained for over fourteen years, and then with the Zemma Works, retiring from active life in the early part of last year.

The Japan Brewery Company was bought outright by Mitsubishi in 1907. It was at this point that the moustache was added to the giraffe–lion design in honour of Glover's foundation of the company. An advertisement in the *Rising Sun and Nagasaki Express* of 25 March 1896 of that year says:

KIRIN BEER

CHIEF BREWER   H. Heckert
ASSISTANT BREWER   R. von Mann

THE PUREST BREWED OR SOLD IN JAPAN
WON THE HIGHEST AWARD FOR BEER AT THE NATIONAL
EXHIBITION

Tokyo   1890
Kyoto   1895

AND ALSO THE 'JIJI SHINPO' GOLD MEDAL

There may be a hint of insider dealing in this last claim – *Jiji Shinpo* was the project of Fukuzawa Yukichi, Anglophile, reformer, father of the Japanese Enlightenment, and friend of Glover. The quality of the beer, though, was undoubted.

Under Mitsubishi, Kirin would diversify to produce soft drinks as well as coffee and tea – Glover's first speculation in Japan, and later a booming and notoriously tough market. Its share of the domestic beer market is now around 50 per cent. Despite the heritage, what we know about the early days of the company is limited by the fact that some of the original company documents were lost in the Kanto earthquake of 1923.

In the mid 1880s Glover was also, gingerly, continuing to spread his diplomatic and semi-diplomatic network beyond his role of Portuguese Consul. He became involved with, and in 1887 became honorary secretary of, a celebrated institution aimed at well-to-do foreigners called Rokumeikan – transliterated as 'deer-cry-pavilion', the title of a book by Pat Barr on the subject. Rokumeikan was one of a number of business clubs set up quickly during the Enlightenment of the 1870s to 1890s to encourage the westernisation of the country and to bring together business leaders and local bureaucracy and gentry. Rokumeikan's idea of a party caused some conflict in Meiji Conservative circles towards the end of the 1880s, at a time when Japanese imperial pride was seen as being ignored by the heroic empires of the west. When politicians wore European fancy dress to balls, quite seriously intending to show themselves as cultural equals, those samurai who had retained the joi but not the internationalism of the Meiji isshin (reforms) sensed a betrayal. Glover remained tight-lipped about the silly fancy dress, but recognised that a serious cultural dislocation was taking place.

In 1886–7 the political situation had again heated up, as Ito's push for the renegotiation of the Ansei Treaties had become increasingly irresistible to liberals in the west. Japan was still an oddity, but it had too much potential to be ignored entirely as a modern force – as hard as the British Foreign Office tried. Within Japanese elites, the debate rolled on over whether it was better for empire to copy European fashions or strike out in a new form of quasi-unique ethnic pride, and the cultural battle became mixed up with the question of trading rights. The government fancy-dress balls were supposed to show the country's status as European-modern with a uniquely non-European twist, but this didn't always satisfy the Conservatives, who wanted a return to traditional dress and protocol, and a purely functional use of western logistics. Foreign Minister Inoue was left with the impossible job of commissioning diplomatic functions to please everyone, trying to cement Japan's membership of the club of great empires without appearing weak to the Conservatives. The roles of the clubs Glover frequented were less party-political and more ground-level than those of the politicians, who moved in rarefied and strategic circles.

Rokumeikan's activities sometimes verged on the peculiar: in an odd anticipation of the Nazi Joy Division, they encouraged intermarriage to produce 'mixed-blood' children between natives and settlers. They also set out to replace Japanese script with romanised script, which anticipated today's tendency to write out public signs alphabetically. By now the imperial family had also turned Euro-modern: at New Year 1887, the empress turned up to a ball wearing a hugely expensive German dress, which delighted Europhiles as much as it upset Eurosceptics. (And the trend continues: today's Princess Masako had a diplomatic career in the Japanese Ministry of Foreign Affairs before she married, under pressure to produce an heir.) Ito and Inoue held their own fancy-dress masques on 14 and 15 January 1888 – Inoue even had his event MC'd in English. Glover was on the guest lists of both balls, and rehearsed the gentlemanly habit he had cultivated of going round the tables greeting each party, personably, if stiffly.

In the minds of Japanese politicians, the entirely serious point to the costume play was a demonstration of support for the end of extraterritoriality, and the key cultural target was usually Britain. Britain was still not paying Japan enough attention – placing the long-term key trader Glover in a lonely intermediary position. Another party held by Ito on 20 April had an explicitly British theme, with guests dressed as Victorian gentry. Ito was careful to state that he intended the theme of this ball to show his support for the opposition to the Treaties. In what can be related to a Scottish Enlightenment form of thinking, perhaps communicated in drunken conversations by Glover, Inoue was attempting to convey the ideal that the Japanese empire was equal in its common goal of civility, quickly learned from traders and diplomats. As ever, Glover went along with the Victorian gentry theme enthusiastically, albeit with an awareness of how outsiders would probably view it as odd. But the samurai were entirely serious in their opposition to the Unequal Treaties: in the latter half of the 1880s, anti-Treaty, mostly Conservative, hawkish factions within the government were becoming increasingly vocal. Glover showed support for European-style imperialism not only by attending the government masques, but also by helping to organise the more proactive activities of Rokumeikan. He even listed the institution as his home address at one point in 1887. It was a touchy time, and in an increasingly conservative atmosphere, Inoue was perceived as being too compromising in his Europhilia, in particular by merely asking that more foreigners should be employed in Japan when he should have been demanding a renegotiation of the Treaties. Conservative patriotic opinion went against him, and he resigned on 17 September 1887.

Despite his Prussian overtures, Ito established a cabinet and civil service in 1885, and then a privy council in 1888, showing himself to Glover after all to be reforming in an acceptably British sense, after his struggle to remain loyal during the culture wars of the mid decade. Compromising his absolutism of seven years before, Ito saw through the high point of liberalism of the age, the Meiji Constitution of 1889. This was the first time that Japan had attempted in a European sense to write down the responsibilities and rights of a citizenry. The 1889 Constitution represented a relief for Glover, who had feared a tightening of absolutism, as well as an unexpectedly positive cultural outcome to the zany culture of masques. The drafting of the Constitution took six years, and Ito now aimed at a British-style tricameral government – there were two debating chambers and the emperor again had a proper say in policy, via his genro, or senior advisers. Ironically, Britain has since moved down the opposite route, avoiding the writing of a constitution, turning the head of state into a token presence, and encouraging the appointment of peers, pointing towards a unicameral government and the possibility of absolutism by stealth.

Having missed the passing of his two older brothers and both parents during this decade, Glover was greatly relieved to see Martha in 1889. After acclimatisation – her brothers had been much younger when they made the same trip – Martha set out to help with raising Hana, giving the girl a female European role model. Before the arrival of the nuclear family proper, the movement of children around households in extended families was common, as in the adoption of Shinsaburo. As well as becoming a second mother to Hana, Martha became active in the church, as would, to a lesser extent, the ageing Thomas. Martha had at some point converted to Catholicism, and she became involved with the upkeep of Oura Cathedral, an imposing European-style dome near Ipponmatsu, and now a tourist attraction.

After the Portuguese job, his rise through Mitsubishi, and the recovery of his friendship with Ito, Glover was back in an exalted social position by 1889. At work, the situation was more mixed. The coal market, always close to his heart, was showing signs of falling apart, and he was one of the first to foresee the fall. Of the few letters which remain from Glover's consultancy period, almost all are to Iwasaki, and almost all talk about coal prices. Mitsubishi's aggressive policy was to squeeze out smaller coal producers when they became unable to cope with dips in the Hong Kong market. This strategy had been successful throughout most of the 1880s, with Glover shuttling back and forth between Tokyo and Nagasaki, but he now produced a number of worrying reports for Iwasaki and Holme Ringer on the potential for a downturn in coal prices. His instincts proved right later in 1892 when there were serious fluctuations, and the Hong Kong market, in which until then Takashima had been supreme, virtually collapsed. Although Mitsubishi had already diversified and the collapse didn't threaten either company or government, Glover still felt responsible, describing the crash as 'a disaster'.

Meanwhile, his working hours became more Japanese than British. While younger brother Alfred was complaining about having to work for Mitsubishi on Sundays in a letter of 5 January 1892 – 'it really is too much' – Thomas is not on record as ever criticising the Iwasakis for overwork, despite indications that while on-site during 1889–92 he occasionally felt the danger of becoming mired again. During this period, he had little to say that wasn't linked to the expansion of Mitsubishi or a carefully pitched gesture of solidarity with Japanese imperial expansion. His frequent missions back to Takashima, where he had spent some of his worst times, were perhaps beyond the call of duty, though he went with a sense of melancholy rather than anger or panic. 'I am very lonely here,' he wrote in 1892, in a dim echo of the frantic times of 1870.

He watched as his government-favoured Mitsubishi progressed through a period of rapid expansion. Shipping and coal remained Glover's main fields during the early 1890s, and, now recognised in diplomatic circles, he increasingly was in demand at society functions. In 1896 he would dip a toe back into independent ship brokering, acting as agent for Yarrow & Co. in the construction of torpedo destroyers, which would be decisive in the Russian war. The fleet of torpedo destroyers included the *Viper* – 'the fastest vessel in the world' at 32 knots. As with the Kosuge Slipway, he obtained and sold designs for similar vessels to be built in Japan itself, and suggested China as a potential market. The Nagasaki Dock & Engine Works was the first recipient of his offer of one detailed technical drawing for £6,000 or two for £10,000.

In general, from the turn of the 1890s Glover no longer viewed himself as a venture capitalist or exhausted himself trying to think up money-making schemes. His job at Mitsubishi gave him more money than he could ever use, and his diplomatic appointment had provided him with the status he had craved. Now, as befitted a long-term resident with an outside perspective, his concerns became more strategic. As the prospect of an Asian war as an outlet for imperialism became more realistic, he became preoccupied that his vision of a modern Japan, now a constitutional, militarily strong empire, was not being accorded the importance it warranted by the British Foreign Office. The exception amongst the British diplomats was again Satow, now a long-term acquaintance of Glover's and Envoy Extraordinary and Minister Plenipotenitary in Tokyo from 1895 to 1900.

When the domestic political victory of the seikanto — the Korea hawks — took concrete colonial form in the Sino-Japanese war in 1894, Glover supported it vigorously, and participated in it to the best of his abilities. However, by the mid 1890s it had become clear even to an arms dealer that militarism was over-dominating Japanese national policy, despite the Europhile masques and the Constitution. Both Glover and Satow realised the seriousness of the lack of recognition of the Japanese empire as a viable modern force by the west. In the heads of Japanese statesmen, policy was merely carrying out what it had been shown to be necessary in becoming modern. The seikanto in fact closely resembled earlier nineteenth-century British imperial policy in their aim of opening the Korean peninsula both economically – as a market and source of natural resources – and emotionally, for a sense of national pride.

Glover declared himself entirely behind a strike on Korea, but when it came he would struggle with Japanese aggression. Writing of the war for the diplomatic reader he seemed to be trying to convince himself: 'I cannot believe . . . that this [colonial massacre] is true.' The killings at Port Arthur, puzzling to Glover because they were apparently beyond any economic rationale, caused his mood to shift from careful support of Japanese empire to a confused combination of public solidarity and private denial. His psychological state was not helped by his kidney problem, for which he rejected all treatment, and which was not yet properly diagnosed. Tomisaburo was less ambivalent about expansion than his father, returning from college in the States with great patriotic enthusiasm. (And it is worth noting that American McKinleyism was even more expansionist than most European policy at the end of the century.) Even daughter Hana, artist of the giraffe–lion spinning around the vision of millions of beer drinkers today, would move to the newly opened Japanese territory of Korea straight after marriage. She remained there until her death in 1938, which was perhaps wise, since, although she was still on Japanese territory at a time when it was uncomfortable for those of 'mixed blood', she missed the horrific fate that awaited Tomisaburo.

FOURTEEN

At the Edge of Empire II: Japan

The shareholders of the Japan Brewery Company accepted Glover's resignation in 1894. When the business was sold to Mitsubishi, Glover was presented with the sum of 3,000 en, enough to last through several retirements. The old clans' problem was no longer money or power, but the fact that while they were transforming into a modern empire, they were still being treated as a part of Europe's own informal empire. Their imperial competence would be proven only by a war. Again, Glover recognised his centrality to the international situation.

In the year Glover gave up brewing, Japan made its first major imperial move to annex Korea, a conflict which had been long pressed for by Meiji Conservatives, specifically the seikanto faction. The samurai executive knew that in weaponry Japan hugely outranked China, the 'sick man of Asia', and felt that empire demanded an outlet and an international demonstration. They understood that Glover, arms dealer and hero of the 1860s, would be a useful spokesman for the war. But this was not as easy a job for Glover as it sounded, and involved serious self-deception. The scoop of the Port Arthur massacre, which Glover worked so hard to convince the public he didn't believe, came in the American newspaper *The World* on 12 December 1894:

> Yokohama, Japan, Dec. 11 – The Japanese troops entered Port Arthur on Nov. 21 and massacred practically the entire population in cold blood. The defenceless and unarmed inhabitants were butchered in their houses and their bodies were unspeakably mutilated. There was an unrestrained reign of murder which continued for three days. The whole town was plundered with appalling atrocities.

This was a shock in terms of what Glover thought he had achieved for the country. The end-career stage remains a plateau of existential difficulty for all businesspeople in Japan: when the economic imperative is removed, and if there is no lasting legacy to be worked on, their lives can seem to be suddenly emptied out. Glover reached this stage around 1892–93. But the government, gearing up for the Korean attack, had already decided that his next major project should be a public show of sympathy with empire, with the aim of giving the country a position recognised by Europe in the twentieth century. When the news of unexpected aggression came in, his role was to assure the settlers and the Japanese nobility new to imperialism that the massacres were simply 'part of the business of killing' entailed by war. Coming from a westerner who had brought a new logistics to the country and who had risen up through Mitsubishi, this was liable to be widely trusted, and he played it well. Privately, though, he was less sure that civility entailed carnage.

In 1893, Mitsubishi reorganised as a limited company, and management was taken over by Iwasaki Yanosuke's nephew Hisaya – though Yanosuke would keep hold of the reins. By 1890, the company had made one of its most iconic investments, in real estate in Marunouchi, central Tokyo, which would become known as Japan's first modern business district, and house Glover's office. During the war, the company based Glover in Tokyo, but from 1894 to 1896 he was also officially a resident of Nagasaki. He was encouraged to participate in the set-up of the new Nagasaki Club, in which Tomisaburo was becoming active. Tomisaburo had already been consulted on the design of the building, for which he appropriately advised a 'neocolonial' style. The club was, like Rokumeikan, a semi-diplomatic gathering point with a more genteel atmosphere than Glover's earlier clubs, and was also intended as an international meeting place for local business leaders. It was situated in Dejima, in the foreign concessions, the barbed irony being that in 1894, the whole ground of Japanese–foreign relations had shifted, as anti-extraterritorial policy was finally passed which would turn the kyoryuchi into normal Japanese territory by 1899. When the club was being built, extraterritorial Dejima was already becoming an anachronism.

Early in 1895 Mitsubishi put Glover into semi-retirement and rehoused him in Azabu, central Tokyo, where he was pensioned in great opulence. His support of Korean expansion meant that he was more favoured than ever by the government. The Azabu house was more pointedly western than Ipponmatsu. A villa with a large garden, it was furnished partly by Mitsubishi and partly by Ito, suggesting a reconciliation after the 1880s rivalry. Azabu is in the centre of Tokyo, and is a district strongly associated with foreigners. Here Glover's house was of a size that no one, rock stars, CEOs or aristocracy, could live in these days. The land of the house now comprises a number of office and apartment blocks. Anyone looking at Glover in Azabu from 1895, in a metropolitan mansion which spilled onto conservatories and patios, would have had to assume that his entire career had been successful.

As extraterritoriality had been legislated in 1894 but not yet enacted, Glover had to register his residence in Azabu in Tomisaburo's name. Tsuru and Hana stayed in Nagasaki, but moved from Ipponmatsu to Minami Yamate lot 1, where they would stay until they joined him in eight months. Martha's whereabouts during this period are uncertain: still in a state of grief but close to Hana, she was undergoing a religious rebirth. She had converted to Catholicism, but when this occurred, and how Thomas felt about it, we don't know. The youngest Glover brother, Alfred, was now looking after Ipponmatsu and flourishing in the house in a regrowing city which he enjoyed much as Thomas had in his youth.

But Meiji Conservatives, creating their empire in a vacuum of non-recognition, were worried that the strength of their combination of ethnic pride and expansionism was creating 'new rebels' amongst the foreigners, and Glover came under suspicion as one of the highest-profile foreigners in the country. The increasingly powerful police watched him, despite the fact that in the mid 1890s he had almost definitely been enlisted to conduct covert operations above and beyond his known propaganda, about which the details have, of course, never been made public. It may be that he was put in place in the west of the country to infiltrate anti-war elements gathering in the Nagasaki clubs, since his later recommendation for decoration hints at a mediating role during the Sino-Japanese war between the pro-war faction and foreigners on the ground in Japan.

The war had provided exactly the expression of national pride the growing military had been looking for – not only the expansionist Conservatives but also Ito, who had retained some of the Prussian ideals of a 'greater nation'. But the reports of military excess worried foreign residents, who were a more mellow group than the buccaneers of the 1860s. Glover's comment that the atrocities were all in the 'business of killing' may have done little to reassure them, though it was by now becoming dangerous to speak out, even in the company of Glover himself. Aside from being an object of surveillance, the problem he had with the war was, as with the samurai elite, his growing perception of other imperial powers' failure to acknowledge the extent of Japan's desire to be seen as equal. For Conservatives, this made all Europeans potential rivals: some voices within the government expressed concern that, as one historian has it, 'the foreigners who had been promoted into positions of influence in Japan could themselves turn against the country, as Japan's empire threatened to rival those of European countries'.

If Glover had been younger, or more idealistic, or if he had developed a pacifist streak, perhaps he would have turned rebel again. He had started to become uncomfortable with the suspicions which had grown up around him despite his pro-clan history. He organised celebrations for Japanese victories, but, as a wealthy adviser to a large company, he was no longer economically dependent on arms, and some of the younger settlers were unimpressed by his 'business of killing' comments. Increasingly uncomfortable as a propagandist, he retreated as much as possible from his former military role. As a memoir of a rising Satsuma bureaucrat later wrote, 'It was in Meiji 28 [1895] that [Glover] drew back from active public life, and his support came under question by a few.'

Glover certainly never became anti-Japanese. Rather, in the 1890s he looked for ways to distance himself from the old joi thinking of the Conservative faction while negotiating on behalf of Japan's imperial standing. The source of the Conservatives' paranoia was not a lack of strength or ambition, but a lack of European acceptance of Japanese empire, as they ploughed through Korea. Assured in his own insight into Japan's double-bind, Glover hardened his defensive stance towards both the academic pundits of the day – who were increasingly appearing in the mid 1890s to comment on the Asian situation, but who seemed not to understand old samurai ambitions – and the *Lonely Planet* writers of their day, who had happened on a relatively unknown land and were keen to explain it. Both types he dismissed out of hand. W.B. Mason recalls:

> Latterly, he liked to pose as an authority on Japanese politics, as one who had access to the workings of the Japanese mind in its international relations; and he did not spare condemnation of the globe-trotter or visitor who ventured to air views on the subject after a two or three weeks' sojourn in the city.

Of the *Daily Telegraph* journalist Sir Edwin Arnold, Glover wrote, 'He may gush about geisha as much as he pleases, but when he writes such rot as he did the other day on Japanese politics, it is another matter.' These invectives were frequent, but were not simply a matter of ill temper, or even of influencing Conservatives within the country, who were by now swept up by their own ambitions. Rather, Glover could see factions developing within London politics according to whether MPs and peers were pro- or anti-Japan – meaning, willing or not to accept the empire on equal terms and form some kind of pan-imperial bond. He watched the movement of these factions carefully from the time of the Sino-Japanese war, and began to align with the pro- faction, using semi-formal institutions such as the Nagasaki Club to influence diplomats and businesspeople – as well as, possibly, to keep an eye on pockets of resistance to the war.

By the time the Korean killing had calmed, both Glover and Ernest Satow were pressing the case for a deeper understanding between the British and Japanese empires. As Satow had feared, when he accompanied Prime Minister Ito to England to celebrate Queen Victoria's diamond jubilee in 1897, the Japanese party found that their respect for the head of state was not reciprocated. The scale of the snub, though, shocked the already touchy Ito, when Foreign Minister Lord Salisbury, whose overseas knowledge was known to be flaky, gave the most important Japanese statesman of his age an audience of five minutes. Salisbury, during his four spells as Foreign Minister in Glover's time (1878–80, 1885–6, 1887–91 and 1895–1900) was, if anything, of the anti- faction, and showed a marked lack of interest in Japan at the very time that Japan was keenest for promotion into the first division of imperial powers. Under Salisbury, policy remained resolutely European, and he disdained advisers who tried to draw him beyond the continent.

Satow's struggle for recognition for Japan was therefore an uphill one. His authority should now have been irrefutable, his career had been long and distinguished, if not straightforward. After graduating from University College London just before the Choshu Five arrived, he had become a dedicated linguist from his teenage years, was very rapidly promoted within the Foreign Office, and as early as the 1870s was suggesting equal alliance with Japan as the only way forward – 'They are the only Asiatic people who could adopt our civilisation *in toto*.' But within the mid Victorian Foreign Office, being brainy just got Satow sidelined: at a time when the English public school system was being reformed to stress fair play and gentlemanliness, the critical voice was rarely prized. Both more outspoken and more junior than Parkes, he was exiled to Bangkok in 1883 and then Uruguay in 1889. (This was intended as a serious disgrace: Salisbury was said to be uncertain about where Uruguay was.) Morocco in 1893 represented something of a revival, and returning to Tokyo in May 1895 as Consul a vindication. From 1895 to 1904 in Tokyo Satow built up a wide network of literati, politicos

and merchants who shared his views, and when he pressed the case that
Japan was a necessary ally in Asia, one of his long-term models for British–
Japanese exchange was the relationship between Glover and the Europhile
samurai. As soon as he returned to Tokyo Satow had reconnected with
Glover, and many of the rest of his network were mutual acquaintances.

After the treatment of Ito in London in 1897, Satow was warning that
since Russia was threatening to hold sway in the East Asian sphere, the
Japanese government, on the back of its Chinese victory, was developing
ambitions to make a decisive stand against European empires. If Japan challenged Russia, it would be reaching right into Europe – and for Satow and
Glover, Britain had to be made to understand the seriousness of this possibility
before it happened. Japanese ambitions in Russia seemed a timebomb ticking
too far away for the British Foreign Office to hear. Satow reckoned that
Britain had until a couple of years into the new century to recognise Japanese
ambitions. The only course open was an agreement between Britain and
Japan before Japan moved on Russia with unpredictable and possibly
disastrous consequences.

By the turn of the century, Glover was coming to the office most mornings
in his French deluxe car – one of the first in Japan – to a read of newspapers
which reminded him of how the Japanese Imperial Navy had grown to the
stage of threatening the world's largest land mass. It's hard to believe that,
despite his pride in his own achievements, there wasn't some regret at the
killing that had already taken place and a hope that it could at least be
slowed before an advance on Russia. Spending time with Satow from the
end of the nineteenth century, Glover's position gradually shifted from one
of simply ignoring amateur Japanologists to being more strategically pro-
in relation to British politicians, whose ignorance of Japan he found to be
'simply beyond belief'. He began to meet more regularly with others related
to the pro- faction in the exclusive leather-lined clubs which bulged out
into the narrow streets of Tokyo. The aim of the on-site pro-s was not to
stop Japan expanding – they were not anti-imperialists – but to stop it
expanding in an ideological vacuum, by having its empire recognised on
European terms – they were counter-imperialists.

Glover's support for Japanese expansion, especially after his covert ops of
1894–5, completes three phases of imperialism in his life. His early years had
propelled him into the Victorian arena of global adventure. In his youth he
helped the clans rally round emperors Komei and Meiji while pursuing British
free trade, and finally he became a spokesman for his adopted country's right

to global spoils. Even though he continued to proclaim himself as British first and always, his imperialism-gone-native was now quite different from that of the Foreign Office, who maintained a policy of using Japan instrumentally to maintain their interests in the Far East, while holding on to strategic points like Shanghai. Glover was increasingly worried by the latent attitude that Japan could still be brushed aside, as it had been in 1863–4. He took note when Lord Spencer, of the Lady Diana line, and a soft-pro- politician who would soon become pivotal in Glover's and Satow's plans, wrote: 'Even with the Japanese in a state of exaltation after their victories [the Sino-Japanese war], they would not be mad enough to resist us for they would know that they would not succeed, even though their ships might in the first instance of their lighter draught elude your [the Royal Navy's] heavier vessels.' Japan may still have been no match for the British Navy, but it might soon become a powerbroker in the Eurasian sphere and potentially even form an alliance against Britain. It had been, after all, little more than a decade since Ito's Prussian conversion, and the conditions for the World War One were becoming increasingly clear. Glover was exasperated that peers like Spencer, for all their pro- sympathies, seemed not to realise this.

Glover was nevertheless less subtle than Satow in his diplomatic under-standing that 1890s militarism had been a symptom of the unevenness of the modern development of the country, for which Glover's own rapid rear-mament of Japan after the Ansei openings had been partly responsible. The country had the military hardware, but culturally it had been denied the long period of national self-creation allowed to Germany, France and Britain, and had to pick up what it could about what empires were supposed to do. The Glover of the years after the Sino-Japanese war at times showed a similar degree of confusion about Japan's future role, and he never quite recovered from the massacres in Korea.

However, Glover and Satow soon saw a significant opportunity to inter-vene in the British perception of Japanese ambition. Satow planned to have Lord Spencer take a guided visit to Nagasaki as part of a general Far Eastern inspection and asked Glover, in a letter dated 23 February 1896, to look after this lukewarm but important peer:

My Dear Glover,
    Herewith a card of introduction to Lord Spencer to whom I have written to Hongkong about you. He said he should travel by the C.P.R. Steamer reaching Nagasaki March 22. I shall be very glad if

you can do anything to help them. I have spoken about Lord Spencer
to Ito, who said they would gladly show him everything, including
Sasebo and Kure. Very likely I shall hear by telegram from Hongkong
what his wishes are with regard to those two places, and if in time
will endeavour to let you know.

Satow's eventual aim here was to have local pro- Japanese issues raised via
the House of Lords before the hawks in the Japanese government got out
of hand. He knew that Glover had been an informal go-between for the
clans and Harry Parkes during the Saccho alliance of 1866, when Parkes
had visited Satsuma territory, and the trip had influenced his ideas about
the direction of Japanese politics. Immediately after returning to Tokyo in
1895, Satow had announced his desire to swing more peers towards active
lobbying in the pro- camp in British government. In the next year he set
out to convince Glover that some amateur pundits were worth engaging,
and on this occasion he persisted with his faith in Glover as Nagasaki envoy
to Spencer. On 12 March 1896 he wrote:

> My Dear Glover,
>   yours of the 9th has just reached me. Very many thanks for all
> your kind intentions with regard to Lord Spencer. A telegram came
> from him yesterday in which he speaks of visiting Kure in the 'Edgar'
> and of reaching Kobe about the 25th. So I infer from this that he
> does not think of going to Sasebo, and that his stay at Nagasaki will
> be short. Nevertheless I hope you will see him and Lady Spencer,
> for I am sure they will be pleased to make your acquaintance.
>   Yours very truly
>   Ernest Satow

The next month a letter came from Spencer himself, showing that although
his visit to Nagasaki had been 'short', he had been impressed by the speed
of Japan's modernity on recognisably European terms, both military and
cultural. Assuming that Glover still had the kind of persuasive powers he
had shown over Parkes three decades before, Spencer's conversion to a
recognition of the power and ambition of Japan would seem quite genuine.
(A product of the Victorian public school system, Spencer had difficulty
distinguishing between the sentence and the paragraph):

Miyanoshita
8th April 1896

Dear Mr. Glover,

A pouring day enables me to take up my pen for letter writing and my first must be to thank you for your note of 30th March.

. . .

We are delighted with Japan, our visit to Kioto was most enjoyable and I went then to Kure and Itsukushima in H.M.S. Edgar. It was most interesting to see the energetic and intelligent development of the Japanese D. Yards.

Very wonderful that all the complicated and costly machinery enough to equip an arsenal and Ship-building Yard should be set up and put together without a single European.

We go to Nikko to-morrow and stay for a week, then to Tokyo where we are to have much entertainment.

I am greatly flattered by the attentions and civility of the Japanese government.

I saw for a few minutes Sir E. Satow on Sunday. He kindly ran down to see me.

Thanking you and your daughter for all your attention to Lady Spencer and myself,

Believe me, Truly yours,

Spencer

The significance of this exchange lies not in the elevated level of Glover's hobnobbing, but in the part Glover and Satow hoped Spencer would play in pressing for an Anglo-Japanese alliance before a Russian disaster took place. Spencer duly became a noted supporter of Anglo-Japanese relations and one of the few peers to understand that an attack on Russia without British approval could create a dangerous west–east axis. Parliamentary records show that Glover's persuasiveness strengthened Spencer's will to speak up in the Lords. For the next half-decade Spencer would be amongst a growing group of peers proposing a movement to ally with Japan. As Ian Nish puts it:

. . . many were rather attracted by the idea of a treaty with Japan . . . in the Lords, Lord Spencer and Lord Rosebery, who had been associated

with the Liberal ministry which had first called Japan into the comity
of nations by the treaty of 1894, were inclined to support the new
measure [negotiations towards an alliance around 1900].

Glover's part in the Spencer episode went largely unsung at the time. Diplomatic praise of merchants in print was still bad form, and Glover had
developed a taciturn attitude towards public affairs and didn't invite praise.
Still, towards the end of his life, his influence in the field was thought of
as comparable to that of the diplomats. In 1918 W.B. Mason noted that:

Lord Redesdale, in his 'Memories', published in 1915, speaking of the
services of Mr. Satow (now Sir Ernest) in the early days through his
tact and knowledge of the language, towards establishing friendly relations
with the leading men of the country, adds: 'There was another man,
Mr. Thomas Glover, a merchant in Nagasaki, who also rendered good,
though hitherto unacknowledged, service, in the same sense'. Lord
Redesdale was mistaken, as I have shown, in believing there had been
no recognition. Glover was one of the few men who found admission
to the inner shrine of Japanese life in days when the stranger from
abroad rarely penetrated further than the *genkwa* [presumably genkan,
entrance].

Perhaps the most important aspect of Glover's service between 1895 and
1900 was simply being in the right place with a sympathetic, if sometimes
slightly coerced, ear for Japanese ambitions. Although he was often graceless
in his dismissal of politicians and diplomats, his attitude was much more
nuanced than the usual one between settlers and natives: despite the fact
that much of the fleet of the Japanese Imperial Navy was British (in 1900
combined British and British Indian imports made up 37 per cent of Japan's
total), as a Russian war loomed there was still great Japanese suspicion of
the British chicanery that had seen the Ansei Treaties prolonged until 1899.
It looked quite possible that Japan might make its next imperial move with
its suspicions of Britain intact. Ito himself had been hypothesising during
the Sino-Japanese war that 'England is rousing the foreign powers against
Japan'. Pro- London journalists such as the Printing House Square Group
were important in the late 1890s in maintaining the idea of a friendly
British–Japanese environment, but so also were veteran concession-dwellers
such as Glover, living day to day in an environment of extraterritoriality

and increasing tension. In one way they were even more important than London journalists and diplomats: they cut out the still lengthy time it took for communications to pass from London to Tokyo. At ground level, Glover maintained amicable relationships with power-brokers in the gentlemen's clubs, not saying much but making his sympathies known. This was a simple role, and wasn't always performed with great finesse, but it helped to temper the righteous anger that was propelling Japan towards Russia.

This puts into perspective the oak-panelled, crystal-decantered opulence of the Nagasaki Club, the Naigai Club, Rokumeikan and the many other clubs springing up in Tokyo. These clubs may have had an odd atmosphere and fairytale modus operandi, but they did house important shows of mutual trust, and Glover was often central to their functions. They might have been merely frivolous had other, less experienced concession-dwellers' opinions not been so vocal — and hostile:

> . . . the British merchants in the Japanese treaty ports . . . were skeptical of the [Japan's] modernization because they detected behind it so many remnants of the old Japan; they were aware of the anti-foreign feeling in Japan and expected at any moment a recurrence of the violence of pre-Restoration days which would be directed against themselves.

Glover was aware that he represented an exception and felt this to be his primary responsibility as his Mitsubishi work slowed in 1897, partly for family and partly for health reasons. His role in the company was turning into a largely honorary one of sitting behind a huge desk drinking tea and dictating memos. But he was increasingly persuaded by those around him of his importance in connecting pro-Japanese British officials and local immigrants. Along with Satow, he had found another kindred spirit.

Joseph Henry Longford worked for the (British) Japan Consular Service from 24 February 1869 to 15 August 1902. When he retired he became Professor of Japanese at King's College London, and during both his diplomatic and academic careers, produced a number of influential textbooks on Japan. A regular guest at Glover's Tokyo house, he joined Glover and Satow in pressing the Foreign Office for an Anglo-Japanese alliance before a Russian attack, particularly appealing to its sense of pragmatism by stressing that Singapore and Hong Kong could only remain British with the cooperation of Japan. The three had become the major Anglo-Japanese cultural brokers of their time — so much so that their formal titles seemed to matter little amongst themselves. In his diary on 13 February 1897 Satow dryly recalled how the trio were casual about the rules of diplomacy in a region so geographically and intellectually remote from the Foreign Office:

> [Glover] also said Longford had asked him whether the work of the Consulate required an assistant. He inquired whom I was going to send down. Tho' this was rather indiscreet on his part, I replied that I had no one to send and had given a promise to sanction the employment of a clerk. Glover talked also about the 'dignity' of a consul, so I told him I thought it unnecessary to have an assistant simply that a consul might sit in a back room and do nothing.

In 1899 the atmosphere of Anglo-Japanese mistrust calmed slightly with the dissolution of the laws of extraterritoriality. Foreign nationals were now free to travel beyond the old concession areas, but they would no longer have diplomatic immunity while within them. It took some residents longer than others to get used to the idea that they could now be arrested by Japanese police. According to Nagasaki lore, the old concessions continued to attract foreign residents into the 1900s, making the city look more like overseas than like Japan (begging the question of what Japan itself is supposed to look like). Not surprisingly, many parts of the country make the same claim, in particular Glover's old real estate jewel of Hyogo/Kobe. If Nagasaki did have a special claim to cosmopolitan status during this period, it was as a result of Japan's first big imperial war: after taking Korea, Nagasaki's proximity to China made it a major centre of commerce again. Brian Burke-Gaffney notes that in 1899 there were 2,000 foreigners living in the city.

The following two years saw something of a vindication of the pleas of Glover, Satow and Longford, especially Longford's appeal to British pragmatism. Despite Salisbury, British politicians had realised that Russia was pushing Japan south towards the Philippines, and in part through the efforts of the pro- party, there was a delayed acknowledgement of the expansion of Japanese power in the shipyards. An Anglo-Japanese alliance was, to the relief of all three, signed on 30 January 1902 after much procrastination. This was only a first volley in a series of agreements and was renegotiated in 1905, 1911, 1920 and briefly in 1923. The 1902 alliance said little but it did help to defuse the Russian doomsday scenario, in which a post-Restoration Japan would rival European empires still bearing a grudge. Having forced Europe's hand, some Japanese politicians felt that the country had made it as an imperial power in 1902. For Aoki Shuzo, Vice Foreign Minister under Ito: 'We may congratulate ourselves on having . . . with one stride entered into the "Fellowship of Nations".'

The alliance was a relief to Glover personally, in that he had given Japan the weapons and the rationale to take on Russia without British recognition. After the free-for-all of his twenties, and the dubious propagandism of his fifties, he was now able to look back on a career which had at least encouraged the empire's sympathy towards British forms of government. As Ian Nish says:

> It was the main aim of the new Japanese government to modernise the country; and naturally it could not ignore Britain as the most economically developed country in the world. Japan's industrial missions, which went overseas, naturally sought advice in Britain, where the Industrial Revolution had first taken home in Europe.

Many British politicians nevertheless viewed this 1902 alliance in functional terms, that is, to subdue Russia, rather than as an acceptance of any shared civility, which Glover and Satow realised Enlightenment Japan wanted. Nevertheless, it worked in the short term, and Glover became recognised by many as a bridging figure. One reason Brian Burke-Gaffney makes so much of the Spencer visit in his account is that Satow doesn't accord Glover's persuasive powers their full importance in his own official memoirs, despite what he says in his diary: even for the otherwise generous Satow, traders still didn't belong in diplomatic histories. There were doubtless dozens of other smaller intrigues and omissions which have gone unrecorded. When the official dithering in London about the 1902 alliance is considered, local traders and professionals look quite important. In the hands of the diplomats, alliance negotiations had been slow and clumsy, to the disdain of Glover, who wrote to Iwasaki of the trials of 'damned politickers'. His own place had become more crucial by 1902 even as it had become less official.

Despite the 1902 alliance, Satow and Glover still had concerns about the lack of recognition for Japan by Britain. After the uncomfortable Ito visit, Satow had written to Salisbury: 'I am convinced that the Japanese are ambitious of being a great naval and military power and they are confidently persuaded that they possess the necessary gifts.' If he didn't already know it, the imminent Russian war led Satow to confirm that the country's ambitions were global: 'I give the world ten years' peace in this part of the world. During that time Japan will be able to recoup her losses and be ready to begin again.' In 1903, with the alliance in the bag, Satow actually began to press for an attack on Russia, largely to keep the war as minor and Anglo-friendly as possible while showing Britain the capabilities of the Japanese Imperial Navy. With the elderly Glover publicly in support, Japanese expansionism continued to prevail. In June 1903 Glover had a series of private meetings with Ito, in which he reiterated his imperialist and expansionist credentials but implored Ito to use his influence not to force a war of a scale which could seriously provoke Europe. Ito was so enamoured of the gains in Korea – to his eventual cost – that he listened to his old friend politely, but without taking much notice.

It was during the typhoon season of 1905 that the pine tree around which Mackenzie had had Ipponmatsu built was blown down (the name Ipponmatsu transliterates as 'one pine tree'). The house which had acted as a base for the struggles of 1863, as a diplomatic hub through the 1880s and 1890s, and as a home for Glover and Tsuru, now looked strangely bare. There was something terribly lonely, and ominous, about the new Ipponmatsu without its pine. It was as if some seismic shift had taken place. The garden had to be extensively rebuilt. It lost its shape and, to an extent, its character, as the leafy central plot gave way to open space. With the fall of the tree, Glover's outlook also darkened. The Japanese Imperial Navy had by now overrun Russia, the domestic situation had become so authoritarian that it would have been dangerous to criticise any aspect of policy, and the Japanese objective seemed to be veering towards a show of strength rather than a civilising mission.

Appropriately, the opening volleys of the Russo-Japanese war had been fired on 10 February 1904 by a veteran of the Battle of Kagoshima and personal friend of Glover's, Togo Heihachiro. Both the *Ho Sho Maru* and the *Jho Sho Maru*, though now ageing, saw active service in the war. The Glover brothers remained immersed in the loyalism of the Imperial Navy, while Glover senior privately dreaded the possible implications of the victory. His support for this war, as for the Sino-Japanese war, is mentioned in the citation of achievements which accompanied his decoration by the country. This time, though, it was Tomisaburo who led the celebrations at the victory party at Ipponmatsu, minus its iconic pine. Glover did his usual rounds of the tables, looking distracted in photographs, now often in pain, greeting and congratulating the assorted dignitaries. Tomisaburo feted the outcome in the casual manner of one who expects great things of his country: '[t]omorrow, if the weather is good, we plan to celebrate Japan's war victory.' Glover senior's celebrations were less exuberant. In the past half-decade, there had arisen more personal reasons for him to become muted.

FIFTEEN

The Butterfly Effect

W hen a butterfly flaps its wings in Nagasaki, lifts in tower blocks break down in Coatbridge, and there are storms of frogs in Saltcoats. When a local dignitary makes a comment to the press in Aberdeen, the birth rate in Gifu increases, and tourists in Nagasaki 'flock' to local spectacles. The lives of Great Scots are retold via a kind of chaos theory, where small events have unfathomable faraway circumstances. It has usually been thought to be vital to the corporate Glover haiku, itself thought to be key to international goodwill, that there was a concrete connection between the Glover family and the opera *Madam Butterfly*.

In the Ansei ports, marriages of convenience had the same economic logic as the Treaties themselves. The temporary wives were usually all but destitute, and the uneven-development economics of free trade made it natural that they stayed that way. Marriages were usually worked out through a professional intermediary. Until recently, when the ideal of romantic liaison has been raised above it practical possibilities, and second-hand feminism has persuaded some middle-class women that marriage means admitting career defeat, the arranged marriage has remained a common pattern. The romance-marriage pattern is so recent that there is a separate term for it (ren'ai kekkon). But the Ansei Treaties brought a new starkness to marriage economics, since a group with over-inflated buying potential, the Euro-American settlers, were able to choose partners at will. This economic differential is reflected in the story of *Madam Butterfly* and made tragic: Puccini understood the situation and created the opera with an ear open to the sexual exploitation that was taking place, albeit a nostalgic one. Yet something as stark as the international division of labour has led to ideas of Asian women which are still common today, when we still often look at structural economic differences as if they were differences of ethnic thinking. The original opera was not so naive. Only when Japan had been fully subsumed into a tradition of orientalism, did the story take on the mantle of European tragedy. In 1968, Pat Barr wrote:

In spite of its sentimentality and its distance from the rather sordid truth, the story of Madame Butterfly made its point: it was not the light-living, amiable, frivolous, simple Japanese women, but the ruthless, sophisticated, selfish western men who committed the worst moral sin; the Japanese were not pretty playthings to be petted, admired, laughed at and left at will, like dolls, dragonflies, or elves – they were people who got hurt, made jokes, felt love. Perhaps the worst fault of the Japanese was that some of them have always helped to sustain the westerners' illusions. Some forty years after the Madame Butterfly syndrome had reached its climax [that is, 1957], the Japanese opened the Nagasaki residence of a former prosperous English merchant, Mr T B Glover, as a museum; to draw the crowds, they called it 'Madame Butterfly's House'. It would have amused Madame Butterfly, had she ever existed; it might even have amused Mr. Glover – a hospitable and courtly gentleman, apparently, who lived in the country for nearly fifty years and had great sympathy with and understanding of Japan, at both its best and worst.

Barr's pithy comments seem to leave little room for a concrete connection. But if Barr wrote this with such conviction in 1968, why has there been so much argument over the nature of the Butterfly–Glover links since? There were two parallel phases which pinned Butterfly onto the Glovers between the 1960s and the 1990s.

Firstly, after World War Two an association between the Glover Garden and the opera arose because the Garden was atmospheric, western-looking, bore a resemblance, perhaps coincidental, to one source of the story, and seemed to encapsulate a formative period in Japan's history – in Barr's words, it was used 'to draw the crowds'. During this phase, Tsuru was enlisted as Butterfly, even though her first husband, Murayama Kunitaro of Oka han, had never left her – she left him of her own will, and he made no fuss about their baby, Sen, who remained amicably attached to Tsuru and came to stay at Ipponmatsu in 1880–1. One iconic connection with Tsuru was a butterfly-like, actually more moth-like, design on her kimono, a family crest. But despite this embroidered crop circle, the idea of Tsuru as 'the real' Butterfly was discounted long ago because of evidence of family registers that show she was not the natural mother of the abandoned son supposed to be a model for the snatched child, Shinsaburo. Besides this, her tough childhood and her inability to conceive after Hana notwithstanding, there wasn't that much tragedy in Tsuru's life, compared with other yujo. Her life wasn't long, but most of it turned out to be comfortable. The only serious exception to the rejection of Tsuru-as-Butterfly now is represented by Noda Shizuko, a descendent of Tsuru, who has gone to great lengths to interpret family registers to try to keep the story alive. Noda's interpretations are worth reading, and we await more research which claims to corroborate a link to Ipponmatsu after Glover's death, but with Tsuru there is simply no scene of abandonment to lead to Puccini's 'tragedy'.

It is worth remembering parenthetically here that although the marriage of convenience was a common pattern, not all of the early settlers in Japan practised a smash-and-grab sexual policy. Glover was a long way from being faithful and disappeared for as much as eight months at a time, but he did look after Tsuru and provide for her until she died, and described her in public as 'my wife'. A distinguished precedent for a European who went native in romance was the Dutch doctor and scholar, Philip Franz von Siebold, who arrived in Dejima in 1823, a figure who is commemorated in Nagasaki as fondly as Glover, and whose son became adviser to Foreign Minister Inoue Kaoru. Siebold built up an enormous amount of knowledge on Japanese nature and customs, and Commodore Perry used his book as reference in preparation for his move on the country. There was certainly a degree of exploitation in the marriage of convenience, but scenes of abandonment were not universal.

When it was found out that the biological mother of Tomisaburo was the yujo Kaga Maki, who was left, or not, by the 'fair-haired devil' (balding merchant) who returned later with his new wife to take the son they had had together, Maki became the second possible abandonee. One immediate problem is that Maki, a low-ranking sex worker, would never have expected Glover to stay with her. For local prostitutes, unplanned pregnancies were a professional hazard. Another problem is that Glover, unlike Pinkerton in Puccini's opera, never left the town to spark the tragedy of separation. In fact when Shinsaburo was born, he was posting a strong intention to stay and clear his mining debts. And Nagasaki being a small and gossipy town, he and Maki were probably always vaguely aware of one another's whereabouts.

By the late 1980s, Alex McKay was bringing to Scottish attention the fact that Nagasaki-shi was advertising a Glover–Butterfly connection, and that the only plausible source remained Maki. McKay suggested persuasively that the Nagasaki-connected writer C.S. Long may have seen Tomisaburo as the child in the story, and that Maki may have become distraught after having her son taken by the infertile Glovers. This argument bolstered the second phase of speculation which saw Maki as Butterfly. Some corroborated this by pointing out that Tomisaburo was in Philadelphia in 1889–91 at the same time as Long, and others by suggesting that Long later mentioned Tomisaburo by name. As McKay asks:

> Long elaborated on his earlier admissions by telling her [Miura Tamaki, famous for playing Butterfly in the opera in Japan] that the real name of the boy in the story . . . was Tom Glover and that this boy was known to his sister . . . [d]id Thomas, or perhaps Tsuru . . . unfeelingly offer to take the child from Maki? Did Thomas completely reject her?

If this was the source, there would still have to have been major changes made to Long's story before it reached Puccini: Glover would have been sent to sea, Tsuru would have been made an American, and Maki would have been hidden from the incomer over whose loss she was weeping. But Maki never considered herself to be married to Glover as we understand it. She was intrigued by him, but didn't know him enough to love him. She was professionally disconnected. Yujo were, as Pat Barr points out, only ever that naive in male western fantasy. Maki was certainly unsettled by the sudden loss of Shinsaburo, especially because she had never expected Glover to come back – which he only did because of the discovery of Tsuru's infertility – but it was also common for babies to be re-adopted by wealthier or more conveniently-placed families. Glover himself did the same with Nakano Waka, who later became his daughter-in-law, with no hint of the tragic. Nor did Maki commit suicide as did the opera's tragic heroine, in fact she lived until 1905, longer than Tsuru.

Perhaps most importantly, Kaga Maki couldn't have lived in Minami Yamate as a wife-of-convenience, since this was within the foreign concessions. There were two classes of yujo, and normal 'interference' between a western man and a Japanese woman was technically forbidden except for the upper level of yujo who paid registration fees. Unlike Tsuru, Maki didn't have the licence which allowed her to live in the concessions. She was of the common unlicensed strain, stuck on the outside, while Tsuru was of the licensed, prestigious strain, able to enter the concessions and become Glover's recognised wife.

Absorption of Maki and the Glovers into the Butterfly story misses our willingness to retain an orientalist twist in order to celebrate Glover. The story is expensive in terms of gender and ethnic stereotyping: white men are explorers with a tendency to be taken off by the affairs of the world, native women ('girls') sit at home pining. Men move, women stay still. Men go outwards, women retreat inwards. But unlike Pinkerton, and apart from his brief midlife crisis ranching in Washington with Alex, Glover had made it clear from the mid 1870s that he was staying – in conditions which don't trigger images of exploration, but rather embracing corporate management. While Butterfly's Pinkerton recovers from going native to leave Butterfly for an American wife, Glover stays initially somewhere near Maki, to consolidate his relationship with another yujo, Tsuru. If Maki is Butterfly, this show of permanence comes six years before the traumatic scene of Shinsaburo's adoption. And it was in the year of his son's adoption that Glover got his peach job, with an offer that not even a fair-haired merchant could refuse. Moreover, although Glover dedicated himself to Tsuru in a closed-doors but formally arranged ceremony in 1870, the partnership still lacked the quasi-Catholic, Italian-American sense of unbreakable permanence with which Kate became Pinkerton's wife in the opera. Glover and Tsuru stayed together for almost 30 years and felt a deep bond, but merely extended a temporary arrangement typical of the time. How did the Butterfly story come about?

The story evolved into Puccini's opera via a couple of routes. Firstly, through Nagasaki kyoryuchi gossip overheard by Sarah Jane (Jennie) Correll, wife of Irvin Correll of the American Methodist Mission and briefly headmaster of Chinzei Gakuen school, Shinsaburo's alma mater. During the Corrells' five-year stay in Higashi Yamate lot six, at a loose end, Jennie turned overheard scraps about a 'tea-house girl' – perhaps entirely made up by foreigners – into a story to tell her brother, would-be author C.S. Long, whom she visited in Philadelphia in 1897. Long's story survived almost intact in the libretto of *Madam Butterfly*, though it was joined there by elements from a similar, earlier story by Pierre Loti (real name Julien Marie Viaud), who had come to Nagasaki in 1885, when his ship arrived there for repairs.

In Loti's story, *Madame Chrysanthemème*, an American sails into port and arranges via a broker a marriage which the bride takes seriously, but which the American sailors laugh off. When he leaves, she has his child and refuses all other offers of marriage to await his return. When he does return it is with a blonde woman. His wife-of-convenience, realising that he had never taken the marriage seriously, tries to commit suicide. Loti's story parallels and prefigures *Madam Butterfly*, and Jennie Correll may have known the story already when the 'tea-house girl' gossip was arranging itself in her head. She may or may not have had Ipponmatsu, one of Nagasaki's best-known foreign houses, in mind. As Jan Van Rij points out, Long uses a great deal of Loti's detail but also exaggerates the itinerant sailor into the crass caricature that would become Puccini's Pinkerton. Van Rij also notes that Loti's immediate inspiration was probably a French vessel anchored in Mitsubishi docks in 1887 – though Loti doesn't mention Glover's tenure as Mitsubishi's most important foreign employee.

Loti's book was turned into a mini-opera by André Messager, and when Messager composed the music in 1892 in Italy, he was a guest of Giuli Ricordi – along with Giacomo Puccini. Puccini had become interested in an idyllic Japan as early as 1872, when portrayed by Camille Saint-Saens in *La Princesse Jaune*. Saint-Saens was the first composer to popularise the pentatonic scale in western music, a scale based on five notes and intended to sound 'oriental'. Saint-Saens's pentatonic scale was immediately post-Restoration, but also well before the peak of Japonisme in the arts. *La Princesse Jaune* describes an unlikely match between a Japanese woman and a Dutch doctor, who bears a resemblance to Siebold, and who acts with an integrity incompatible with Pinkerton. Saint-Saens's non-tragic version of *Butterfly* is now often overlooked, even though he can be identified with some of the musical and cultural themes of Japonisme.

Crucially, Van Rij notes that Long, author of the later version, was motivated not just by literary ambitions, he also aimed to raise awareness of the Japanese campaign to abolish the Ansei Treaties. In this, he certainly did recognise that the situation was an economic one, rather than merely one of loose and easy eastern ways. In the context of a society in which the Unequal Treaties had become a national crisis, Long's Butterfly begins to look quite political when set next to that of Loti: marriages of convenience were revealed as a domestic form of Unequal Treaty. Long's story was immensely popular on its publication in 1898 – a year before the enactment of the repeal of the Treaties – and was taken up by the playwright David Belasco. In 1900, a production of Belasco's play, based on Long's story, was seen by Puccini, who had now experienced both dramatic threads – those of Long and Loti.

Puccini was now ready to act. He had since become aware of a number of 'oriental' musical experiments which had followed in the wake of Saint-Saens, for example those of Claude Débussy, from whom Puccini may have taken the use of the pentatonic scale. Pietro Mascagni's *Iris* (1898) added to the momentum, its libretto written by Luiga Illica, who was also the librettist for *Madam Butterfly*. Illica also took ill-advised clues from the Japanophile Judith Gautier, whose view of Japanese women was slightly batty – the women in her account are in the business of 'selling smiles'. In *Iris* there are clear hints of Puccini's drama to come, including the extended tragic scenes when Butterfly is waiting for Pinkerton and of her ritual suicide. Less influential but also worth mentioning is Gilbert and Sullivan's *The Mikado* (1885), which, though it looks Monty Python-like today, seriously adopted Saint-Saens's pentatonic scale.

Not all Japonisme, meanwhile, was so nostalgic: at exactly the same time as Puccini was adapting the stories of Loti, Long, Belasco and Illica, Japonisme was having a serious influence on Scottish artists including Patrick Geddes, Phoebe Traquair and Charles Rennie Mackintosh. These Celtic Revivalists used the bold, clean lines of Japanese art and fed it into a movement which would become known as the Glasgow Style. It would have made for an interesting cultural legacy if Glover had known of the early trips to Japan of the Scottish artists Edward Arthur Hornel and George Henry in 1893, especially if he had supported them as he had supported students making the trip in the opposite direction. Perhaps more important than the question of whether Glover knew of the opera, is whether he knew of the effect Japanese art was having on his fellow Scots – the answer almost certainly being no.

Japonisme as a whole helped Meiji Conservatives to sell the country as culturally and ethnically unique, which they did with some pragmatism, reckoning this to be a prerequisite for imperial pride. A state company was set up as early as 1874 to regulate the cultural export of things marketable as typically Japanese. In Europe, Japonisme became whatever Meiji Conservatives said it was, and all but the most critical of western artists and critics failed to keep an eye on the economics, going along with the exported images. For example, for Ernest Fenollosa, the celebrated American scholar of Japanese aesthetics and an influence on the poet Ezra Pound, who in turn influenced the Scottish poet Hugh MacDiarmid, kanji – Japanese characters – were imagined to carry an essence of the object they described. Kanji were pictures. This implies that Japanese language is simply experience itself, an idea so nostalgic it makes Gilbert and Sullivan look gritty, and that the Japanese language has no ability to refer to things or feelings outside of whatever is present and visible. The abstract remains impossible to the Japanese mind:

like Butterfly, the Japanese can only talk about things which are in front of their eyes, having no past and no future. Thus, Butterfly waits every day as if it were the first day, and the tragedy is her inability to grasp the passing of time. Japonisme lifts her clean out of the flow of history. Dating from half a century later, some of the most striking exhibits at Japan's first atomic bomb museums are the clocks which melted and stopped telling the time simultaneously.

Puccini worked on *Madam Butterfly* between 1901 and 1904, a writing period that spanned a car crash, a divorce and an excruciating wait for a libretto from Illica. Illica's story in the end was a mixture of Long and Belasco, with the editorial aid of native informants, particularly Oyama Hisayo, wife of the Japanese minister in Rome, who helped repair the Americanisms. The restraints put on Illica's story by the libretto format, particularly in having to collaborate with the notoriously difficult Puccini, meant, ironically, that the story was brought closer to the Glovers' than its original version. For example, in the original stories, Butterfly's child is left with the mother, but at the end of the opera Pinkerton's wife wants to adopt him, as did Tsuru with Shinsaburo. This certainly shows a similarity to the Glover–Maki story, but at two removes, and via the chance conjunction of two interpretations.

Unsurprisingly, much of Illica's early draft was scrapped. Puccini then stunned his friends in November 1902 by telescoping acts two and three into one long act, a decision against which all tried to persuade him, but of which he was only cured after the opera's disastrous opening in Milan in February 1904. Further changes were made for the opera's US tour in 1907, which predictably portrayed the Americans in a much more sympathetic light. In this version, the haughty American wife Kate, responsible for stealing away Pinkerton – our would-be Glover – almost disappears, and we return to a tragedy brought about by simplistic native thinking.

Although the increasing popularity of the opera coincided with Glover's last years, in which he allowed himself more time to pursue hobbies, there is no indication that he knew about the phenomenon. (Alan Spence's background music to Glover's famous last interview in *The Pure Land* involves a handy piece of poetic licence.) Even if Glover had known about the opera, it is unlikely that he would have seen any resemblance with his own life story – as Spence carefully shows. More likely he would have described the opera in bah-humbug tones as an example of sub-standard Japanology.

Long's version achieved prominence in Japan, since he told his story directly to Miura Tamaki, who is still known throughout the country as a veteran of the role of Butterfly and who brought the opera back to the country. Miura's name is almost inseparable from the role. Her statue is to be found front-and-centre in the Glover Garden in Nagasaki. The Japanese adapted the story in their own way: Kawakami Sadayakko performed a version of Belasco's play in Osaka in 1916, then in Tokyo in 1917, and both versions boldly stressed the irresponsibility of abandonment, rather than tragedy. Miura Tamaki finally premiered the opera in Tokyo in 1936, as it turned out with the worst possible timing, when the country had little time for western sailor-rogues. Even post-war, the opera never gained a great deal of popularity in Japan, despite the efforts of Miura, the speculative linking of the story to a real place in Nagasaki, or, since 1967, the 'Worldwide *Madama Butterfly* Competition', the finals of which, significantly, take place in the Glover Garden.

For her part, Jennie Correll gave an interview in March 1931 in which she claimed to be the only person who knew the real Butterfly story. But her dim recollection, her taste for sensation, and her lack of detail, only served to throw her account into more doubt. This left the door open to Nagasaki city to make an explicit Glover connection after the war, which it duly promoted when the Garden was set up as a tourist attraction in 1957. In the interview Correll states mistakenly that Tomisaburo was the natural child of Butterfly and 'an English merchant'. This line was taken up by Noda Heinosuke, father of Noda Shizuko and a source of the first round of Glover–Butterfly links which had Tsuru as Butterfly. For Correll, Tsuru-as-Butterfly was corroborated by a bemused nod by Tom in answer to a question about whether his parents could have been connected to the story. Who knows what Tom was thinking? He may have been bored by being interviewed about his father again. He was also scrupulously diplomatic. And probably nervous: various unpleasant experiences at school had turned him from an anxious boy into an anxious adult.

We might think that Nagasaki city authorities would want to hush up the possibility of a connection between their genteel city, the Glover family, prostitution, child-snatching and the manipulation of official family registers. But even sceptics connected to Nagasaki have pushed the Glover connection. Van Rij, for example, described on his book jacket as an 'opera buff' (making us wonder how many ex-diplomats are jazz-fusion buffs or hip hop buffs) follows the movement of the two other Glover brothers, Alex and the young Alfred, and suggests that either one of them could have been the father as they passed through Nagasaki, while Thomas was moving between Shanghai and Hyogo. For Van Rij, the brothers' absence from the young Shinsaburo represents a possible scene of abandonment; this is a well-argued and plausible idea, though it remains hypothetical in terms of journey times, paints a slightly sordid picture, and still assumes from the outset that Ipponmatsu was the site of the original story, when our evidence that this house was the scene is so far after the fact.

The placing of Butterfly in Nagasaki is itself debatable. After keeping the possibility of a connection between the Glovers and Puccini's opera uncertain from 1957 till the 1990s, the Glover Garden in Nagasaki itself now claims no definite influence – at least in their English brochure. The Japanese brochure is pointedly equivocal, framed in a 'what if' voice. Looking back with the English leaflet in hand, it is hard to deny that the search for the 'real' Butterfly is an anachronistic approach. Few studies have been written on who was the real Jane Eyre. Or the real Luke Skywalker. Or the real Fred Flintstone. The answer to the question of who was the real Butterfly is that there was no real Butterfly: Butterfly was made up.

But it's telling that the connection is still emphasised in the Japanese version of the Garden brochure, while it has been abandoned in the English version. The Japanese version maintains the original Noda hypothesis as one of a number of possibilities, and at the time of writing, a Japanese-language video in the garden still strongly suggests that Butterfly related to the Glovers' story (moderu datta desho ka). Tsuru's butterfly–moth is pointed out, as is the statue of Miura Tamaki. It is almost as if the Japanese authorities themselves want to be seen as fulfilling the Butterfly role whereby the natives are obligingly simplistic. In English, mention of the opera is worded as a careful denial: '[a]lthough there is no direct connection, the Glover House has been referred to as the "Madame Butterfly House" because it is reminiscent of the hillside setting in Puccini's famous opera'.

'Reminiscent' is a key word: although Long's story is based on his sister's jumbled fantasies, and Loti's experiences were in Nagasaki, Nagasaki is not the only possible stage for the drama. The first traumatic sight of Perry's American ships was at Shimoda in central Honshu, far fom Nagasaki's western peninsula in Kyushu. The 'white ship' to which Illica's libretto refers may also be an oblique reference to Perry's black ship. Even if the scene was set in Nagasaki, why was a Glover link emphasised later? When interest in the opera was at its peak in Japan there was little interest in Glover himself.

The critical ground shifted when it was suggested that the connection of Ipponmatsu and butterfly motifs came about only post-World War Two, and from an American source. In 1997 Brian Burke-Gaffney demonstrated in correspondence with those involved that the description of Glover's house as 'the butterfly house' derived from the time when Ipponmatsu was occupied by an American family during General Headquarters (GHQ) occupation after World War Two. GHQ serviceman Victor Delnore attributed the butterfly house comment, which had no particular historical referent, to a Joe Goldsby, another GHQ serviceman then living in Ipponmatsu, and in turn embellished by Goldsby's wife Barbara. The naming of the butterfly house would come only a decade before the thematic connection with Puccini's opera was seized on by Nagasaki-shi.

The Glover–Butterfly connection then found its destination in tourism, an industry necessary in 1957 to a city still recovering from the war. The story probably did arise from this same city, probably did involve mutual acquaintances, and Tsuru's family did have a butterfly–moth emblem. But everything from then on is embellishment, specifically for economic reasons – which reminds us of the uneven development described by the story itself. The Butterfly tale may be an appealing one, but, as it has come to be portrayed as more nostalgic and less economic, it also demands a degree of cultural aggression. It overlays tragedy on a society where Aristotelean tragedy doesn't belong. Butterfly becomes an easy victim, then as today sacrificed to globalisation. The 'syndrome' of the pining native girl fits two ongoing marketing niches: tragedy and sexual surveillance. It's not surprising that the story hasn't been beloved of the Japanese any more than other lascivious tales of the orient which are still popular in the English-speaking world.

The GHQ connection even suggests that the Butterfly story's relation to the Glover house is entirely bracketed by American interventions. In 1853 at Shimoda, Perry practised a form of gunboat diplomacy beyond even the British Navy's tradition of maritime threat. The story subsequently arose from the gossip of an American visitor to Japan, was taken up by her American brother, turned into an opera whose prize market was the US, and was then linked to Glover during the post-war American occupation of Nagasaki. Japan becomes a miraculating ground onto which American ideas can be projected and played out, since the country itself seems so culturally distant, strange and blank – as in, for example, Sofia Coppola's film *Lost in Translation*.

It turns out then that the concrete connection I was looking for is a mirage. In a sense this had been obvious from the start. Sexual conduct in this grimly economic context is difficult to look at without some kind of lyrical sweetener. The Butterfly story shows early traders' conduct pared down to its bones, and it is a story which is far from picturesque. In later life, Glover showed signs of trying to distance himself from the institution-alised system of yujo for foreigners. But under the strict rules of free trade the system made perfect sense. It was all too rational and in need of romance. And only through many retellings of the story by foreign agents could it become tragic.

SIXTEEN

Cultivation

When Tsuru became sick in 1897, Ito gifted the Glovers a 'Japanese-style' (wafu) house extension, thinking she would feel more at home there. Such was Tsuru's life: even at home she was under orders to feel at home. A traditional Japanese wife to a foreigner with a taste for samurai style, she was now to recuperate in a Japanese-style extension to an imitation western Japanese house, gifted by a Europhile Prime Minister. Tsuru's existence was layered with pallid authenticities. They are inevitable when national identities are exaggerated and separated out to show them come together again – which is why celebrations of 'our traditional culture' are counterproductive. 'Traditional' tends to mean 'old', and the search for a pure Japanese cultural form only provokes bemusement now in Tokyo, where culture is quickly hybridised. The Glovers had enough problems living with the hangover of 'race' which separated them in public vision. Tsuru's sickness was one reason Glover's Mitsubishi work slowed at the end of the 1890s.

Glover wasn't even close to being monogamous with Tsuru, but from the time of the adoption of Shinsaburo, their relationship was quite similar to the ideal of European romantic love. He was distraught beyond the normal bounds of the marriage of convenience when she died on 23 February 1899, and expressed it in a well-known note to friends about 'my poor wife'. As a hard-drinking workaholic brought up on a Scottish diet, he couldn't have expected to outlive a Japanese 17-year-old.

Ironically, Tsuru died in the year in which the extraterritorial laws ended, when she and her husband would have had the freedom to travel throughout their country, rather than continue to be abroad at home. She had remained loyal and left him to his own affairs – business, diplomatic and romantic. Financially she had been very comfortable – though her first joining him when his debt was deepening in 1869–70 showed a leap of faith perhaps only possible in a teenager with nothing to lose. But from her early childbearing to her period of destitution to the trials of bringing up children who 'looked foreign', Tsuru had had a tiring life. By her forties, photographs show her looking worn. When it came, her death was fairly sudden: although she had had stomach cancer for two years, it had been left untreated by western medicine. She accepted her passing when it came, with perhaps more of a bushido attitude towards death than many of Glover's samurai heroes of the 1860s. Newly widowed, he took a while to get back to work, and quasi-diplomatic social gatherings were his only serious activities of 1899 and 1900. Despite his high social standing, he never remarried. By the 1900s, he had few loved ones left in Tokyo and relied for company on the gentlemen's clubs and visitors to Azabu.

Tsuru was cremated and her remains moved to Taiheiji to be left until Glover himself died, when her ashes were exhumed and taken to Sakamoto International Cemetery. Tomisaburo's decision to go ahead in the year of his mother's death with his marriage to Nakano Waka, his pretty and mannerly sister by adoption, was a careful one: traditionally, celebratory events are put off for a year after a death in the family. The wedding was low-key and caused no changes in the structure of the household, since Waka was already a part of the family. The two would never have any children – probably not by design, since, according to letters of the 1910s, they discussed adopting a child in the way that Waka herself had been adopted. Waka, though more Europeanised and a regular presence at many of her husband's social gatherings, remained on the fringes of public life and in many ways remains as mysterious a figure as her adoptive mother.

After his wife's death and his son's marriage, Glover lived alone in central Tokyo with at least two helpers, including, giving in to old habit, one young woman. Nominally he continued to work for Mitsubishi in Marunouchi, then becoming a fashionable shopping and business district, though his visits to the office became less frequent from 1899 and less so again after two bad turns of health in 1905 and 1908. He still spent holidays at Chuzenji, the family retreat in the mountains, sometimes with Tomisaburo and Waka, and here he took to fishing, as he had in the River Don. A *Japan Weekly Chronicle* report of 21 December 1911 recounts a yarn of his having been recommended to visit Australia to fish, only to find out that all the rivers were dried up. (There are no known records of an Australian trip, though he was advised by his doctor to escape the Japanese winter by going there in 1907.) Throughout the 1900s he still offered the company a lot in terms of reflected status. After his help with government propaganda in the 1890s, his financial position was absolutely assured, but he continued to work sporadically when able, until he became infirm towards the end of the decade. He never retired, because he never had an official position from which to retire.

Meanwhile, his generation of the family began to disappear. Martha died on 20 March 1903, Alfred on 18 May 1904. Martha had become close to Thomas during his later years, making up for the fact that he hadn't known her during her prime. Her funeral was held in Oura Catholic Church, to which she had dedicated so much energy in her last years. She was greatly missed by Hana, with whom she had spent a great deal of time. Alfred fell ill suddenly near Hong Kong on the way back to Scotland and passed away on the ship. His body was brought back for a service in Nagasaki's Episcopal Church to which Thomas may have given some financial aid later in life. Alfred had been an organiser of pseudo-Scottish events in Nagasaki and was loved as the baby of the clan, yet he too died while Thomas was still relatively well, and for the last seven years of his life Thomas was the sole survivor of the seven siblings. We don't know if he was aware of Alex's death in the US, as no letters remain, but unless they had had a major falling out, it seems likely. Despite his risk-loving, unhealthy, stressful lifestyle, Thomas had proved to be a survivor. Since Hana, always a loyal supporter when she was in Japan, had gone to Korea, he was now isolated except for his son in Kyushu.

In 1903, perhaps as a reaction to his father's dwindling family, Tomisaburo made an effort to get to know what was left of this side by journeying to Aberdeen. This was probably the only time he visited the country. Little information remains of the trip, but photographs show him looking chilly and slightly ill at ease in Fochabers. He was glad to get home to Japan, a fact that makes it especially ironic that he would be viewed as a foreign threat there during World War Two. He returned as the Russian war loomed, which he enjoyed a lot more than his father. In 1905, his natural mother, Kaga Maki, also died, but neither he nor his father is known to have paid her passing much attention.

Later, Glover was often confined to his house and garden with his back pain. In the middle of the decade what was now clearly a kidney complaint became so serious that he was bedridden for periods. Never much of a correspondent, in more reflective mode he began to write the occasional non-business letter to Tomisaburo or Iwasaki during the last three years of his life. Had his 1908 decoration by the nation come two years later, he would have been unable to attend without a struggle, and Ito was probably aware of this when he chose the timing of the award. After 1905 Glover was a quiet figure, sometimes taking the sun, sometimes doodling on a piece of woodwork, and he is best understood through his last famous interview and his attempts to consolidate his family. With Tsuru dead, Hana in Korea, his siblings all gone, and his work for periods stopped due to constant discomfort, he increasingly turned to his son.

Tomisaburo was a thin and fragile-looking boy. During his American college years he grew a wispy moustache, parted his hair in the centre, and wore small round glasses, giving him the polite society look of a character from a Henry James novel. His first education was in Chinzei Gakuen, run by the Methodist preacher C.S. Long – one weak link to the Butterfly story. He entered Gakushuin, now Gakushuin University, in 1884, boarding with Iwasaki Yanosuke in Tokyo. Gakushuin is not a conservatory catering to the intellectually gifted, it's a middling-prestigious private university known for its openness to the Japanese gentry. In Tom's case, all went well academically until December 1887 when his grades plummeted. He dropped out of Gakushuin in March 1888. His father's explanation was that the naturally bright Tom was bullied because of his appearance, and his sensitivity worsened the situation until he became unable to concentrate on his studies. Here, we get a picture of a father trying to smooth an academic path for a son whose strengths were not really academic. This became especially apparent when, despite Tom's patchy results at Gakushuin, his father arranged via the US ambassador for him to pursue further study at Wesleyan University from 1888, and at Ohio State from 1891. But in the American college atmosphere Tom was equally at sea. The same ethnic sensitivities may have been at work, since he was again described as the only foreigner in his class at Ohio State, and, although a native English speaker, he was regarded as Asian, while almost all of his classmates were second-, third- or fourth-generation European. He left the college in 1892 and is described with leaden diplomacy in the Japanese records as having been an excellent (yushu) student, although he never took a degree.

He was strongly patriotic and never showed any great interest in his Britishness, despite his gentlemanly appearance. He was comfortable with Japan's militarist-nationalist atmosphere and threw himself into support for the country's imperial wars. His return from college had immediately preceded the second growth period for Nagasaki, boosted by its proximity to Japanese Korea, and he became a representative for Holme Ringer in 1895. After settling comfortably at Ipponmatsu, on 12 June 1899 he married Waka, daughter of James Walter, a locally celebrated, Liverpool-born silk merchant with an affable nature and a flamboyant handlebar moustache, and became fixed into Nagasaki social life, where he would remain contentedly.

Despite a chequered educational past, Tom would never have any financial or social difficulties in a city in which his father had climbed to such a position of authority. The legacy was double-edged: Tom admitted to feeling that his 'father has the presence of a mountain in this country' (in Japanese animism, mountains have quasi-religious connotations), and as a salaried worker from his youth he felt overawed by his father's record of entrepreneurism. Nevertheless at Holme Ringer his social circle increased, as is evidenced by the way the locals consulted him over the set-up of the Nagasaki Club. The club first met on 8 January 1899, inviting, with a hint of sangfroid, the Japanese to socialise within the obsolete borders of the concessions, and ironically, given his discomfort away from Japan, Tomisaburo's English-gentleman look became a feature of the gatherings. His look anticipated the well-to-do Europhile Taisho fashions of the 1910s.

One of Glover senior's main pleasures in his widower years, having established his son's position, was watching his progress through these social and diplomatic circles. Most of his few later letters are to Tomisaburo, but he doesn't betray much emotion, commenting on coal prices, fishing, shipping and the upkeep of Ipponmatsu. Tom's letters describe entertaining, family and vacations at Chuzenji, now a leafy retreat in the mountains where he and Waka often joined their father during the crazy summer heat. Although apparently secure, he often ends letters with a worry about his own lack of funds: 'I am awfully hard up and I do not know what I have to do unless I receive some money from you.' Even though Thomas senior was clearing the way for his son's career and allowing him to use Ipponmatsu – Tom had moved there in September 1903 at a token rent – the income required for the house's upkeep remained a source of worry to the younger Glover: '[I require more funds] as well as sending me a remittance which you have [sic] promised that you would at the end of last year. You know what I get from the firm is not enough to pay my own expenses and upkeeping [sic] Ipponmatsu property. Please give your kind assistance as soon as possible.' Glover remained patient with his son's dependency, though it was in stark contrast to the dynamism of his own youth.

Glover senior's own greatest honour came in 1908, when he was famously the first foreign national to be decorated by the Japanese government to the level of second-class Order of the Rising Sun (kyokujitsusho), sometimes cited as the second most prestigious national award after the Order of the Chrysanthemum. It is an extraordinary award, was a long time coming, and was probably delayed by Mitsubishi-Ito politics, and only granted as his health

seemed in danger. The recommendation to Emperor Meiji came jointly
from Ito and Inoue in the same year, but Ito had been sitting on it for
some time. On 21 July 1896 in a letter to Ito, Iwasaki Yanosuke, still acting
cautiously because of his company's reputation as dangerously liberal,
described Glover's work at Mitsubishi and suggested his nomination, dramat-
ically offering to 'give away all my own property' to assure Glover's award.
Ito needed no description of Glover's actions, having fallen under his political
spell in 1863, battled the British Navy with his new weapons in 1864, and
sparred with him ever since. Even though he wrote the initial letter of recommendation, Iwasaki was probably surprised at the level of honour eventually
awarded. The official recommendation to the Emperor cites Glover's various
innovations and diplomatic work, and also hints at espionage, recommending
him on the basis of his negotiation 'between Japanese and foreigners' during
the Sino-Japanese war, as well as for unspecified help with foreign navies
and press. The medal reflects his place in Japan's young parliamentary governments, and it is remarkable that a lucky trader was the first foreigner to
receive the award, rather than a scholar-diplomat like Satow, Parkes or
Siebold. Such was the prestige of the award that 20 pages of achievements
were listed as evidence. Photographs of Glover receiving his medal show
him stiff and well-groomed, though showing signs of strain.

One of the most painful deaths for Glover at the end of a decade that had
seen the last of his siblings disappear was that of Ito himself. Having lived in
Japan since the age of 21 with only short breaks, he had come to know Japan's
first prime minister better than some of his own brothers. On 26 October
1909, while working as governor of the colony of Korea, Ito was shot by a
nationalist, An Jung-Guen, in a train station in Harbin. The reaction of the
authoritarian Japanese government was to strengthen further its control over
the territory. Glover had dark feelings about this decision: although the younger
Ito would have accepted his own death fighting for what he felt was a noble
cause, by the end of the 1900s both harboured unease about the old joi
sentiments collapsing into globally militarist ambitions. By the time of Ito's
death, Japan had consolidated Formosa, Korea, parts of mainland Russia, and
the 'Northern Territories', disputed even today, and had sent settlers as far
as the diasporic independent region of Hawai'i (which is why Japan's attack
on Pearl Harbor, after its annexation by McKinley through the Newlands
Resolution of 7 July 1898, was not as unpredictable as is sometimes imagined).
Around the turn of the century, the American government was taking note.
Just before Ito's death, Theodore Roosevelt wrote:

Japan . . . is a most formidable military power. Her people have peculiar fighting capacity. They are very proud, very warlike, very sensitive, and are influenced by two contradictory feelings; namely, a great self-confidence, both ferocious and conceited, due to their victory over the mighty empire of Russia; and a great touchiness because they would like to be considered as on a full equality with, as one of the brotherhood of, Occidental nations, and have been bitterly humiliated to find that even their allies, the English, and their friends, the Americans, won't admit them to association and citizenship, as they admit the least advanced or most decadent European peoples.

This, of course, was the message Satow, Glover and Langford had been trying to get through to the west since the mid 1890s. Frustrated at its lack of imperial recognition, Japan had tightened domestic policy, and the late 1900s were in a new way as restrictive as the early 1860s, leaving the dying Glover with the realisation that his legacy had partly rebounded on itself. A parallel native account of Japan's expansion at the end of the 1900s comes from Okuma Shinenobu, who was aware of the stand-off between foreign views of the country and samurai policy, but since he had also been encouraged by Glover to think that Japan's imperial growth was natural, bursts with Europhile pride:

By comparing the Japan of fifty years ago with the Japan of today, it will be seen that she has gained considerably in the extent of her territory, as well as in her population, which now numbers nearly fifty million. Her government has become constitutional not only in name, but in fact, and her national education has attained to a high degree of excellence. In commerce and industry, the emblems of peace, she has also made rapid strides, until her import and export trades together amounted in 1907 to the enormous sum of 926,000,000 yen. Her general progress, during the short space of half a century [almost exactly the time of Glover's residence], has been so sudden and swift that it presents a rare spectacle in the history of the world. This leap forward is the result of the stimulus which the country received on coming into contact with the civilization of Europe and America, and may well, in its broad sense, be regarded as a boon conferred by foreign intercourse.

After his honour of 1908 and now seriously unwell, Glover listened to this kind of statement of pride with some scepticism. As Japan joined the European empires in jostling for position in the run-up to World War One, his last two years were spent in his rooms and conservatory staying out of trouble. The furniture which had been provided for Tsuru was kept in place: he had resigned himself to his final romance. He spent his time with various untaxing hobbies, including his woodwork, hunting when possible, and, perhaps surprisingly for an ex-arms dealer, gardening. As an acquaintance recalled:

> His favourite recreation at home was in a workshop where he would spend hours together with a lathe, in the use of which he had acquired considerable skill. His greenhouses with their wealth of flowers in all seasons – conspicuous in his Tokyo home as in Nagasaki – showed another pleasing side of his character; and friends were always being reminded of his sporting and gardening achievements both by presents of game and flowers.

He had another health scare in December 1909 which confined him to bed over the New Year. Aware that he didn't have long left, he gave his famous interview to Nakahara Kunihei, which remains a major source of information about his life, though the reader has to dig through some bravado (and inexplicably obscure Japanese). By 1911 he was virtually housebound, and by the later months of the year in almost constant pain. On 13 December, the doctor was called, administered treatment, and the danger seemed to pass. He sat up in bed and his spirits seemed to recover. But three days later, after managing to eat some soup and fish at lunchtime, as the next course was being brought to him, he fell over and died quite suddenly. The cause was given as kidney failure – what is known today as Bright's disease (chronic nephritis).

His funeral was held in Tokyo at 2 p.m. on 21 December 1911. Hana returned from Korea, joining Tom and Waka and distinguished foreign diplomats and senior government officials. Glover split his estate, including Ipponmatsu – Tom's final home – between the two children and showed a magnanimity towards his helpers less common in his youth: 'I also beg you give my servants Kiyo and Kitaro 1,000 yen each.' The city of Nagasaki observed a day's mourning, and British flags were flown at half mast. An envoy from Emperor Meiji was dispatched to lay his medal on top of his coffin, although this medal, it seems, was later reclaimed. According to members of the family descended through Hana, it was probably sold along with the belongings of Herbert, her son, and may remain with her husband's family, the Bennetts.

It was not a decision taken lightly by Glover to choose to die and be interred in a foreign country – against all odds, and contrary to his lifelong assertion that he was first and always British, he had come to see as his resting place a country which would not allow him free movement until the last decade of his life, and where he would always be an outsider. This determination to be at home away from home was duly recognised by his contemporaries, and his willingness to engage with Japanese gentry was admired by those who knew him more than his ability to make money. After his death one newspaper obituary read: 'No foreigner was so greatly trusted by the Japanese, or understood them so well . . . [and his confidants included] the late Prince Ito, Count Okuma, Marquis Inoyue [Inoue], and others.'

Still trying to live up to his father's reputation, Tomisaburo increasingly felt ill-equipped as entrepreneur and innovator. Nevertheless, he had his own achievements, and his life work can be split into two parts. Firstly, he was general editor of a manuscript entitled *Fishes of Southern and Western Japan*. The 700-page illustrated volume, having taken 21 years to produce, is now kept in Nagasaki University. He employed at least two illustrators, and few of the highly detailed illustrations are his own work. His university career had not equipped him as an anatomist, marine biologist or daughtsman. Nor are we sure if scientists ever did use the book for reference, as is sometimes claimed.

Secondly, he helped to introduce trawl fishing to Japan, one of a number of fishing experiments in the later years of Glover senior, along with dynamite and commercial whaling (the irony of which need not be laboured). Japanese fishermen recognised at the time that trawling was liable to deplete fish stocks, and initially they opposed it when Tom pushed for a licence in 1908. The annual meeting of the Fisheries Association in February of that year passed a resolution to prohibit steam trawling in Japanese waters, to which Tom replied by questioning the extent of Japanese waters. He arranged a meeting with the director of the Ministry of Agriculture the following year and started trawling on 1 June 1909. The Ministry, perhaps because this initiative was seen as another in a line of Glover-backed technological advances, even allowed some subsidies to be given to trawl fishers. In 1910 Japanese-built trawlers received 8,000 en each, and the first speculators, in classic Meiji style, sent students to Europe and the US to study and produce reports. Captain Frost was brought in around the turn of 1911 to supervise the building of the trawler *Tsurue Maru* – named after Tom's dead mother. Tom continued to manoeuvre around the question of territorial rights: a seven-and-a-half mile limit had been agreed for Japanese vessels, but within this limit there were few places suitable for trawling. Following in his father's pragmatic footsteps, he sailed under the British flag, allowing him to dodge Japanese laws and taxes. The results of the trawling boom were depleted stocks and cheap fish. Fish became a diet staple throughout the whole country, leading to the mountain-and-sea Japanese cuisine which we now call traditional.

Despite his breaks in trawling, by the end of the 1900s Tomisaburo seems to have developed a grudge towards the Meiji administration. Apparently frustrated by the restrictions on trawling caused by ongoing territoriality disputes, he wrote to his father: 'It is very strange that they subsidise on one hand and prohibit on the other. It is like many other things we have been misled [sic] by our government.' The 'other things' are unsubstantiated, but there may be a veiled reference to Glover senior's latent sense of ambivalence towards Ito.

It is a cruel twist that both father and son were persecuted as spies, Thomas by the shogun's secret services in the 1860s and then by the paranoid militarists of the early 1900s, and Tomisaburo by the now ferocious kenpeitai of the 1930s. Waka, Tomisaburo's wife, passed away in 1943 when rations were low and stress was high. The kenpeitai who hounded Tomisaburo were still nominally working on behalf of the state authorities his father had helped to set in place. There is no denying that the two Glovers were indeed both spies, of a kind: of necessity, they both had information about the other side that was withheld or used according to their business purposes. For Tom, having knowledge of the other side was a result of his heritage as the son of a British father and a Japanese mother: living in Japan and benefiting from British trade contacts, a double knowledge was his lot. He had thrown himself into Japanese imperial celebration, organised street parties for the 1905 war victory, and was more gung-ho than diplomats like Satow – or even the older liberal samurai of the Meiji Enlightenment. Yet during his mature years, leading up to and during World War Two, there was a hint of the totalitarian purge as the kenpeitai

rooted out counter-revolutionary forces on behalf of a government as blink-
ered as the one his father had helped to depose, and Tom felt betrayed
and abandoned as he was increasingly subjected to kenpeitai surveillance.

Hana was born on 8 August 1876. She inherited her mother's soft features
and mild temperament, supported her husband in his business dealings and
built up mannerly achievements in a Jane Austen-type manner. Glover senior
was proud to introduce her at functions of the 1890s and 1900s, and in
part due to her own adoration of her father, she was from an early age
interested in things cosmopolitan and European. As soon as she reached
school age she left western Japan for Tokyo and developed the genteel
Europhile manner later fashionable for ladies of the Taisho era. On 26
January 1897 she married Walter George Bennett, an Englishman who
worked for Holme Ringer in Nagasaki. In 1898 Bennett was posted to a
branch in the new territory of Korea, near Soeul (by the current location
of Incheon airport). In 1904 he set up his own company there and later
acted as Consul. After having four children with Walter, Hana died in 1938,
after which he returned to his family's homeland near London, where
Bennetts of his line remain today.

Hana's son Thomas moved to the US in 1912, at the age of 15, and a
new line of Bennetts settled there. Thomas entered Dayton State University,
studying in the same state as his uncle Tomisaburo. He trained as a fighter
pilot during World War One and later worked for General Motors, leading
the family towards a typical American life. The dangers of being Japanese
in the US from the 1920s to the 1940s meant that the generation beneath
Thomas (Hana's son) had their ancestry hidden from them, and only found
out about it much later. After the war Thomas told his own son Ronald
about his Japanese ancestry, but Ronald only realised its significance going
through his father's family heirlooms.

Charles, the oldest of the six sons of the coastguard, had married Margaret
Isabella Mitchell on 21 May 1868, and named their third son after his
father. This Thomas Berry Glover, although based in Calcutta, was in Yokohama when he died on 17 March 1906, and in contact with his uncle
Thomas Blake. It is the second Thomas Berry Glover who led to the only
known British-based descendents of the seven – other than, possibly, Edith
Bennett, who followed her father to England – through Gertude, later Lady
Gertrude, Carmichael, who returned to India after her father's death, and
later settled in Gloucestershire. Gertrude Carmichael reached maturity just
in time to become a rare correspondent of both Tomisaburo and his father.

In a letter of 28 August 1906 she describes preparing to go to Charles's adopted home: from the untropical climes of Fochabers, she is looking forward to 'get[ting] ready to start again in India'. Her son, another Charles, followed Thomas Blake's 'improving' education, beginning in Edinburgh around the same time: 'The Carmichaels arrived in Bombay about 10 days ago and are now stationed at Poona. Little Charlie has gone to School near Edinburgh where he seems very happy.' She thanks the increasingly frail Glover senior for seeds in another letter of late 1908 – suggesting that, as in W.B. Mason's recollection, much of the time of Glover's last few years were spent in his garden.

By the time he died, Thomas Blake Glover had known four of his grandchildren. Tsuru died just before she was able to meet any of them. All four of Hana's children were born in Korea – Thomas in 1897, Herbert in 1899, Edith in 1901, and Mabel in 1903. Mabel would become the keenest correspondent of the four, and much of the information that remains from the generation of Glover's grandchildren in the 1920s and 1930s comes from her. Like Thomas, Hana's son, Herbert also moved to the US, as did Mabel, following her great-uncle Alex, to the west coast – Stanford, then Palo Alto, where she passed away as recently as 2001. Since Alfred died on his way home, as far as we know, none of the childbearing Glovers ended up in Scotland during their last years, helping to explain why the Glover story remained a mystery in Scotland for so long. Tomisaburo died childless and of Hana's US-bound children, those who are known to have had children themselves were forced to conceal their backgrounds, only later reassociating with the family name.

The legacy is bittersweet: Glover opened up bakufu Japan and helped a number of elite samurai to global educational and diplomatic opportunities they would never otherwise have had. On the other hand, his arming and priming of the Japanese imperial forces and encouragement of expansion helped lead to war between Japan and the country which almost all his descendants now call home. These descendants understand that Glover's rise to fame as an arms dealer was typical of Scots' mercantile desires in empire, leading both to an adventurous history and a heavy sense of responsibility.

And I was back where I had started, with a jumble of conflict and friendship, war and peace. It was hard to imagine, for example, that a figure who had helped the arming of World War Two Germany would be used as a basis for international exchange. Glover is a double figure, pragmatic, amoral and often apparently devoid of emotion, yet generous and admired by a wide range of friends. From these origins have grown attempts to spark international friendship. It was a sensitive paradox. I decided to consult a more engaged party, a direct benefactor of the Glover legacy.

SEVENTEEN

Dejima

One good example of Japanese culture is Starbucks. The logos and products in the Dejima Starbucks are the same as those in the branch in Aberdeen, but there are other fragments of local difference. The Dejima branch is filled with ronin cramming for university entry tests, dozing executives, and unmarried office women escaping office gossip. The Aberdeen branch is louder and messier, and closes at seven, emptying customers out for a compulsory evening of drinking. This only left me an hour to use their wifi spot to write to a new friend in Nagasaki, under the same logos. Glover would have appreciated the efficiency of this new zaibatsu and worked with its inequalities rather than fought them.

I was missing Nagasaki's typical September weather and its semaphoring waiters. But I was also aware of having failed to account for how simply digging up historical connections between two countries promotes friendship and goodwill, whatever the nature of those connections. I knew that, if the book were to be published, some of the tax money raised would go towards restoring the UK's Trident programme, in case the state needed to melt another Asian city to preserve trade advantages. And yet I was going ahead with it, rather than risking breaking the law by refusing to pay taxes. It was a terrible hypocrisy. I had begun to feel an empathy with the predicament of the younger Thomas Glover.

I had found someone who had had first-hand experience of travel under the Glover banner, a recipient of the Brig o' Balgownie Rotary fellowship which organises exchanges of students between Aberdeen and Nagasaki, using Glover as a spectral intermediary. The next morning before work, in a mid-priced suit and a compulsory necktie that had the air conditioner boosting global warming, my correspondent came to the Dejima Starbucks for its wifi spot (for this was back in the mid 2000s, before everywhere in urban Japan was wifi). He was salaried in a successful company and he was busy, but he'd agreed to reply to these uninvited emails from someone in Aberdeen, where he'd spent an enjoyable trip five years ago, and for which he thought he'd paid his dues. He took the seat nearest the air conditioner, 146 years to the day after Glover had arrived in fog behind him, and tried to work out what I wanted.

I had suggested five questions about his trip to Aberdeen. One: do you think your stay in Scotland brought the two countries closer? Two: what's your impression of Glover as a person? Three: in what ways do you think Glover was a founder of modern Japan? Four: does it bother you that Glover sold arms to both sides during the 1860s and encouraged the colonisation of Asia? Five: would you have accepted a fellowship to visit Scotland under the name of any historical figure? I asked him to be as honest as possible, but was ready to compensate for the fact that he would probably veer towards answers he thought I wanted.

One of the first things he told me was that the Scottish tradition of adventuring made Scots' part in the opening of Japan unsurprising. (And unlike many young Europhile Japanese, he noted the Chinese envoys who had continued to act as foreign diplomats during the period of sakoku.) Glover transmitted the spirit of international speculation to the natives – though my correspondent believed like most that Glover had been responsible for the smuggling of Ito and Inoue. Arms dealing, he said, may not have been the ideal occupation, but Glover played the hand he was dealt, and 'personally, he deserves respect as an extraordinary adventurer. After being born in Aberdeen, eager for success, he was prepared to travel to Hong Kong and Japan. We should learn from his spirit of challenge.' [my translation] This wasn't reverence, but an admiration for Glover's energetic pragmatism. The young people selected for fellowships are not under the misapprehension that all of Glover's business dealings had wholesome results, and sitting in Aberdeen Starbucks helping to build Trident I was in no position to comment.

The answer to question three cited both rearmament and helping to overthrow the bakufu as typically modern activities. I remembered that my correspondent was an ambitious young executive when he went on to explain how important it was that Glover had 'supported modern Japanese economics' and 'helped Japan understand the rules of international business'. Despire Glover's personal financial problems, he saw his greatest success as being in Takashima, since he had imported an industrial revolutionary idea of production (keiei). The question of arming both sides brought the frank answer that in the context of the times this was not troubling (anmari ki ni shite imasen). The speed change in logistics was seen as being one of the pains of modernisation. My correspondent realised that Glover had been a cornerstone of the Imperial Navy – and to anyone brought up under clause nine of the Constitution, the military always flags up an ethical problem. But he also noted that if the Japanese government hadn't bought arms from Glover, it would have bought them from another foreign trader – borne out in Godai Tomoatsu's demands after Kagoshima, and daintily negotiated in Alan Spence's novel, when Glover has to be persuaded that arms are the emerging market whether he likes it or not. The question of Japanese imperialism, though, was approached by suggesting that Japan was under threat from other Asian countries. This was the most unexpected answer because, unless we count Russia as part of Asia, Japan was far ahead of the rest of Asia in military terms soon after 1868. Rather, largely because of Glover's influence, Japan came to see its Europhile mission as one of empire-building. The ethical bases of globalisation were now too readily accepted to be a meaningful source of debate for an ambitious young executive.

My last question was in a sense the key one, the one which would help me to see how friendships might arise from Glover's mixed legacy. Were Glover's personal qualities in the fellows' minds as they went abroad, or would they have accepted a place under any figurehead? My correspondent's answer was an unqualified yes to the latter. He was shrewd enough to realise that it was only through the Glover name that he had been able to go abroad and make the ground-level connections he had made, and that this pragmatism echoed Glover's own relationship with Jardine Matheson. We agreed in our respective Starbucks that Glover would be viewed for the fore- seeable future as an icon first and a person second. He was both a pioneer and a speculator in fear of anonymity in his ambitious family. He was a keen amateur diplomat and an imperialist relying on inequality and expansion. He was an important go-between full of personal sympathy and someone who never developed any real ethical beliefs. His innovations were crucial to the emerging governments of the time and led to some terrible long-term damage. He was a charismatic humanist, capable of connecting the most diverse groups of people, and an intransigent reactionary. He is known in Japan for reasons which mainly have little to do with his life. All of this, my correspondent understood. He loosened his tie, and the ozone layer snatched a breath. He would have to remember to do it up again before he reached his office, which demanded impeccable western business protocol.

My new friend was the fourth Japanese recipient of a Rotary scholarship.

Given his realistic answers, a spokesman for the scholarships commenting on the second Japanese recipient in the *Aberdeen and District Independent* on 14 August 1997 might have been closer to the mark than he imagined when he commented: 'We are delighted to give [Kondo] Erika the chance to see Scotland . . . One of Thomas Blake Glover's first visitors subsequently became Prime Minister of Japan [the Choshu Five myth], so we have great hopes for Erika.' But what if Erika, like Ito, was trying to overthrow her own government? What if, like Ito, she revealed a history of arson against foreign diplomats? What if she resented her fellow travellers because they refused to respect her status? If she really had used Ito-like protocol, she would have become famous well beyond the Aberdeenshire press. A large publisher would have taken her memoirs, and thousands of disaffected young people would have started talking about her in Starbucks across Japan. She could have stood for parliament under Japan's more democratic system, which uses a degree of proportional representation. Similarly, much of Glover's success came from avoiding a diplomatic status quo which he felt was missing the point. A benign Glover also fails to fire the imaginations of young exchange students, who could easily feel like pawns in a rehearsed performance of traditional culture.

Like my correspondent, the best answer I could find to the question of Glover's diplomatic power today was in looking critically at the legacy, learning from both the creativity and the damage. Another image which gets in the way is that of Japanese tourists as a high-spending and malleable resource. This is misleading for various reasons. The rate of tourist spending gets mixed up with the absolute amount: since there are fewer holidays in the normal Japanese working year, the same amount of money is spent over a shorter period, making tourists seem richer than they are. In fact, to Japanese people life in the UK is frighteningly expensive. Housing in the least salubrious suburb of Aberdeen costs more than housing in a fashionable area of central Tokyo. In Japan, most people eat out a number of times every week. Service and quality are high, and in no Japanese restaurant will the request for water be answered with the question 'Tapwater?' Nor is it easy these days to sell people their own history as bequeathed by the west – as is seen in the sceptical reaction in Japan to *Memoirs of a Geisha* and *Pearl Harbor*. People are more enquiring than they were during the post-war censorship before the opening of the garden, as is evidenced by its economic problems.

Two reasons are usually given for the garden's decline in popularity: the availability of overseas travel, and the fact that people want more historical context. Although almost every deadline-pressured Scottish newpaper report of the last twenty years has cited the annual number of visitors as two million, it has fallen from a figure above this to one well below it. From a peak in 1988 of almost three million, it has gone down by about 8 per cent a year, to an official figure of 801,506 in 2005. Korea sends the biggest share of visitors – ironically, since Glover supported the seikanto movement to colonise the peninsula. The total working budget of the garden in 2005 was 364,673,000 yen (then about £1.8 million), and almost all of this, as laid out in Nagasaki-shi plans, went to the upkeep of the grounds and meeting 'tourist needs'. The city acknowledges that the main attractions of the garden are its scenery and its atmosphere.

As the young scholars realise, Glover's willingness to do things his own way allows the story to be told differently. A tentative move away from a Scottish hero approach in part reflects how much things have changed in the UK itself. When Alex McKay was finishing his pioneering book, Margaret Thatcher had just handed over to the most Anglocentric prime minister in living memory (warm beer, ball on willow), and it was essential to demonstrate Scottish achievements. Today, a more confident Scotland can stand up to its own history. Nor is Japan too sensitive to look squarely at its own history. To date, it has seemed almost taboo to link Glover's legacy to World War Two. But the Basil Fawlty school of diplomacy, unlike Japan's own atomic bomb museums, goes against Glover's own internationalist legacy by preventing us from learning about the real and raw differences he faced, his improvised reactions to globalisation. As many younger Japanese people now realise, since 1945 their country has been denied access to its own history to a dangerous degree, leaving little space for a proactive national culture, and risking passivity as Asian values are relegated to static past-ness by the west.

With these caveats, research of Glover's world offers great opportunities for semi-formal links. The Aberdeen Glover House, after various funding troubles, is open for visitors and is thinking ahead. Over the last couple of years, numerous exhibitions and celebrations with Glover-related themes have taken place in Aberdeen, Fraserburgh – the unsung home of Glover research – and Edinburgh. A memorial garden has been set up in Fraserburgh, and photographic exhibitions have taken place in all three towns. On the anniversary of Glover's birth in 2006 the first of what was hoped to be an annual event commemorating his life took place in the Scottish Parliament. The Thomas Glover Foundation in Fraserburgh ceded its student exchange remit to the Brig o' Balgownie Rotary a few years ago, but has gone on to support other cultural activities. The Foundation was set up on 3 September 1996 to, amongst other things:

> provide funds and make or assist in making arrangements for initiating or sponsoring projects or research or study relating to the Foundation and for publishing the useful results of research including educational and cultural exchanges between Japan and Scotland.

All of these events and more are to be welcomed, and are valuable if they are undertaken while looking straight at the contexts of Glover's life. If we repeat that he was Scottish and modern and therefore great, then revert to displays of piping and origami, we condemn ourselves to repeated failures to generate friendships, to losing younger people's interest and to forgetting what was pioneering about him. By looking at both his vision and its cultural fall-out, we can hope for a new understanding. This is probably what the old man, looking back on his life in his conservatory in Azabu in 1911, would have wanted.

Works Consulted

Alcock, Rutherford, *The Capital of the Tycoon: A Narrative of Three Years' Residence in Japan* (London, Longman, Green, Longman, Roberts & Green, 1863)
Memoirs of the first British Consul to Japan: revealing about the impressions of the early western visitors and Britain's strategic aims, and used here to show the impressions of the first diplomats.

Allan, John Buckley, *The Gym* (Aberdeen, Taylor & Henden, 1885)
One of the few memoirs left of Glover's old school. Short and very nostalgic, but gives a useful impression of the institution at the time.

Barr, Pat, *The Deer Cry Pavilion* (London, Macmillan, 1969)
A general account of turn-of-the-century entertainments in Tokyo as patronised by Glover, not just the institution of Rokumeikan itself. Contains almost nothing about Glover, surprisingly given the level of his involvement.

Bathurst, Bella, *The Lighthouse Stevensons* (London, Harper Collins, 1999)
The story of the engineering work of the family of Robert Louis Stevenson. The first time, apart from Stevenson's own autobiographical account, that the information has been gathered together in book form. Used here, along with sources from the time, to connect the Stevensons, the Bruntons and the Glovers.

Berryman, John, 'Britain and the Sino–Japanese War: The Maritime Dimension', *in* Keith Neilson, John Berryman, Ian Nish, *The Sino–Japanese War of 1894–5 in its International Dimension* (London, Suntory-Toyota International Centre for Economics and Related Disciplines, 1994)
Academic study of Britain's place in the Sino–Japanese war, used to give context to Japan's growing imperial confidence at the turn of the twentieth century.

Black, John Reddie, *Young Japan. Yokohama and Yedo. A Narrative of the Settlement of the City, from 1858 to 1879* (London, Trübner & Co., 1880–81), two vols
Contemporary account of the opening of the eastern cities at the time of Glover's

first years in Japan, and a rare introduction of the country for an 1880s English-language audience.

Brailey, Nigel, 'Sir Ernest Satow, Japan and Asia: The Trials of a Diplomat in the Age of High Imperialism', *The Historical Journal* 55–1 (1992), 115–50
Tucked away in an academic journal, this is an important and detailed description of how the British government ignored the scale of Japanese imperial ambitions during the latter part of Glover's career.

Brunton, Richard Henry, *Building Japan 1868–1876* (Folkestone, Japan Library, 1991)
Important account of engineering changes made to the country in the post-Restoration period, by the Scottish engineer to the Stevenson family, who was put in situ partly by Glover. Brunton's work can be split into four: the lighthouses, the planning of the city of Yokohama, education and cartography.

Burke-Gaffney, Brian, trans. Sachiyuki, Taira, *Hana to Shimo: Gurabakei no Hitobito* (Nagasaki, Nagasaki Bunkensha, 1989)
Probably the first proper account written in English of the Glover family, by a long-term resident of Nagasaki (himself decorated by the city). Burke-Gaffney also treats the Glover children with great diplomacy, dedicating a chapter to Tomisaburo.

Burke-Gaffney, Brian, *Chocho Fujin o Sagashite* (Kyoto, Kurieietsu Kamogawa, 2000)
A summary of knowledge on the Butterfly story and its sketchy relations to Nagasaki, using local records and contextualising the mass of other stories already accumulated.

Checkland, Olive, *Britain's Encounter with Meiji Japan, 1868–1912* (London, Macmillan, 1989)
Famous account of the time, forthright about the role of traders, used here for secondary corroboration. Checkland, critical of traders like Glover, is also highly respected as an historian of Scotland.

Checkland, Olive, and Checkland, Sydney 'British and Japanese Interaction under the Early Meiji: The Takashima Coal Mine, 1868–1888', *Business History Review* 37 (1963), 139–55
Very early and well-informed account of Takashima, and the three-way power struggle between Glover, the clans, and the Dutch.

Cobbing, Andrew, *The Japanese Discovery of Victorian Britain: Early Travel Encounters in the Far West* (Richmond, Curzon, 1998)
Brilliantly researched and readable account of the first Japanese students to come to Britain, pre- and post-Restoration, those smuggled by Glover and others. Used here, extensively, to understand Glover's role in student defections.

Cortazzi, Hugh, *Victorians in Japan in and around the Treaty Ports* (London, Athlone, 1987)
Famous and authoritative account of various western figures around the time of the Restoration and after. Used as an account of the encounters of the period. Satow is one of the figures discussed at length, but Glover doesn't appear at all.

Dale, James, *The Myth of Japanese Uniqueness* (London, Croom Helm, 1986)
Slightly more polemical version of the argument of Yoshino Kosaku below. A reminder that the idea of a changeless distinct Japanese race can itself be placed in a historical period. Here I suggest that Glover and other traders encouraged a form of uniqueness in the 1860s, keeping the ground of the multicultural and the modern for themselves, a similar process to that of the late 1940s.

Daniels, Gordon, *Sir Harry Parkes – British Representative in Japan 1865–83* (London, Curzon, 1996)
Academic account of the career of Parkes as British consul during and after the Restoration period. Parkes was the figure that Glover claimed to have converted to the rebel cause with crucial results, and he did become an important early spokesman for the Restoration cause.

Davie, George Elder, *The Democratic Intellect: Scotland and her Universities in the Nineteenth Century* (Edinburgh, EUP, 1961)
Highly influential account of how Scottish education struggled to maintain its difference from British norms in the nineteenth century, seeing itself as more generalist, philosophical and inclusive. Helps underline that Glover's education was, on the contrary, relatively specific, practical and Anglo-British.

De Bary, William Theodore, Gluck, Carol & Tiedemann, Arthur E., (eds), *Sources of Japanese Tradition, Vol. 2*, second edition (New York, Columbia University Press, 2003 (1964))
Huge collection of historical documents important to the development of modern Japan. Used here as a sourcebook for contemporary writings.

Dilke, Charles Wentworth, *Greater Britain: A Record of Travel in English-speaking Countries*, first and second editions (London, Macmillan, 1868, 1894)
Account of a shift from the ideal of formal empire centred on occupation to informal empire and culture. After the 1860s, regions touched by empire, especially Anglophone ones, were expected to identify themselves as British. The second edition was extended to cover Japan.

Dumoulin, Heinrich, *Yoshida Shoin: Meiji Isshin no seishinteki kigen* (Tokyo, Nansosha, 1988)
Dumoulin is a noted scholar of Yoshida even amongst native Japanese academics. Here he talks of the mentality of Meiji leaders influenced by Yoshida's joi.

Forrest, Vivienne, 'Thomas Blake Glover: The Scottish Samurai', *The Highlander*, June 1992
Enthusiastic but slightly confused account of McKay's research in an American Scottish-interest magazine. It wasn't then known that Glover's descendants were American.

Foucault, Michel, trans. Hurley, Robert, *The History of Sexuality*, three vols (London, Penguin, 1990 (1976–86))
Helps us to think about how, in modern times, ideas of childhood have been region-specific, and why Asian women are still often called girls. Highly applicable to the *Butterfly* story.

Fox, Grace, *Britain and Japan 1858–1883* (Oxford, Clarendon, 1969)
Now a standard resource for this period. Its area of interest is slightly skewed towards the opening and reforms, and it is used here as one of the authoritative histories.

Fraser, Hamish W., and Lee, Clive H. (eds), *Aberdeen 1800–2000: A New History* (East Linton, Tuckwell, 2000)
Scholarly political and social history by 18 contributors. Illuminating on Aberdeen, but no mention of Glover.

Fry, Michael, *The Scottish Empire* (Edinburgh, Birlinn, 2001)
Account of some of the mercantile successes of individual families during the British empire. It recounts stories of some families related to Scotland, and leaves open the complex question of how Scotland as a nation behaved during empire.

Glover, Thomas, 'Cho-satsu-ei no kankei', *Bocho Shidankai Zasshi*, 27 (1912), 49–73
In this famous interview Glover reminisces about some of the key points of his life, exaggerating many of them but illuminating more. Alan Spence's *The Pure Land* ends with an account of this interview. Some quotations are in my translation, some have been left in the translation of Alex McKay, to whom I am indebted for a copy of the interview.

Glover, Thomas, Uncollected Letters, 1858–1910
Mostly available as copies in Nagasaki Prefectural Library, brought together in part because of the research of Naito Hatsuho. Almost all the letters until the 1900s are business-related, though clues can be had as to Glover's mood from his professional dealings with, for example, the various branches of Jardine Matheson.

Glover, Thomas, Records of Takashima Colliery, 1869–70
Collected in Nagasaki Prefectural Library.

Harvie, Christopher, *Scotland and Nationalism: Scottish Society and Politics, 1707 to the Present* (London, Routledge, 2004 (1977))
Incisive cultural–political history of Scotland, accounting for Scotland's thinking during various domestic and foreign happenings since the Union. Used here to fill in some of the cultural–political contexts for Glover's life.

Hawks, Francis L., *Narrative of the Expedition of an American Squadron to the China Seas and Japan, performed in the years 1852, 1853, and 1854, under the Command of Commodore M.C. Perry* (report presented to US government) (Washington DC, AOP Nicholson, 1856)
One of the best preserved propagandist accounts of the benefits to Japan of the American ships' opening the country. This was published just before the Ansei Treaties, and though Glover is very unlikely to have read it, it is typical of contemporary western attitudes towards the opening.

Henley, W.E., review of Stevenson's *Familiar Studies of Men and Books in Academy*, April 1882, reprinted *in* Paul Maixner (ed.) *Robert Louis Stevenson: The Critical Heritage* (London, Routledge and Kegan Paul, 1971), 98
One influential example of how Robert Louis Stevenson's account of Yoshida Shoin was greeted with suspicion.

Hook, Glenn D., Dobson, Hugo, Hughes, Christopher W., and Gilson, Julie (eds),
Japan's International Relations (London, Routledge, 2005)
Extensive account of Japan's recent relations with the rest of the world. Used here
as a reference for Japan's formal relations up to the 2000s.

Jansen, Marius, *Sakamoto Ryoma and the Meiji Restoration* (Princeton, NJ, Princeton
University Press, 1964)
Useful account of the Restoration in general, not only Sakamoto's part in it. Explains
Glover's place as an arms dealer to the rebels, and vividly recreates the atmosphere
of 1860s Kyushu.

Jansen, Marius (ed.), *The Cambridge History of Japan Vol. 5: The Nineteenth Century*
(Cambridge, Cambridge University Press, 1989)
One volume of Cambridge's massive history of the country. Extremely thorough
and authoritative on the politics of the period, but doesn't refer to Glover. It was
this kind of gap that demanded a rethink of Glover as provided by Alex McKay.

Kamura, Kunio, *Guraba-tei Monogatari* (Nagasaki, Nagasaki City, 1969)
*Gentle summary of Glover's life for a general audience, using the scanty information
then available.*

Takayoshi, Kido, Devere Brown, Sidney and Akiko, Hirota (eds), *The Diary of
Kido Takayoshi* (Tokyo, University of Tokyo Press, 1983–6 (1868–71))
One of the main primary sources of information about the early Meiji period,
written by a Choshu diarist, activist and statesman of the time, well-known to
Glover. Noted as a reference for all scholars of the period.

Lang, Andrew, review of 'Familiar Studies of Men and Books' *in Saturday Review*,
January 1886, *in* Maixner, Paul (ed.) *Robert Louis Stevenson: The Critical Heritage*,
(London, Routledge and Kegan Paul, 1971) 199–202
Another contemporary review discussing Stevenson's 'Yoshida-Torajiro', again in
unflattering terms.

Lighthouse Examination Committee Lighthouse Facility Preservation Facility,
Preservation of Meiji Period Lighthouses (Yokohama, Japan Aids to Navigation
Association, 1991)
Beautifully illustrated guide to the lighthouses built by Glover's acquaintance
Brunton and others, as well as of Brunton's plans for the city of Yokohama.

Long, Juhn Luther, *Madame Butterfly* (New York, Century, 1898)
Long's story, one of two main sources for Puccini's *Madama Butterfly*, cobbled
together from Nagasaki gossip passed on by his sister. Originally serialised in *Century
Illustrated Magazine* in 1897–8.

Loti, Pierre, trans. Esnor, Laura, *Madame Chrysanthemème* (London, KPI, 1985 (1888))
Loti's story of Butterfly, the other of Illica and Puccini's main two sources for the
opera.

Kirin Corporate Reports: www.kirinholdings.co.jp/irinfo/settlement/annual/pdf/
ar2006.pdf
Breakdown of the company finances related to each business sector.

Kusudo, Yoshiaki, *Mo Hitori no Cho Cho Fujin* (Tokyo, Mainichi Shinbunsha, 1997)
An account of the secret life of Tsuru, again speculating on a possible connection
between Tsuru and the *Butterfly* story.

McKay, Alexander, 'Thomas Glover: Aberdeen's Samurai', *Aberdeen Leopard*,
July/August 1988, 31–3
An early account which would feed into McKay's 1993 book. This may be the
earliest use of the 'samurai' tag for Glover.

McKay, Alexander, 'Madame Butterfly's Scottish Samurai', *The Scotsman* weekend
section, 30 December 1989, 2–3
This contains some of McKay's 1993 book's arguments, summarised for general
interest in a national newspaper feature.

McKay, Alexander, *Scottish Samurai: Thomas Blake Glover 1838–1911* (Edinburgh,
Canongate, 1997 (1993))
The book which opened up the Glover field in Scotland. It has also been influential
in Japan in translation. Painstakingly researched over many years, and arrestingly
told. My account is highly indebted to McKay's research.

McKay, Alexander, 'Dr. Jekyll and Mr. Hyde . . . and Yoshida Shoin', *Proceedings
of The Japan Society London*, 124 (Autumn 1994), 76–9
An extension of the Stevenson chapter in *Scottish Samurai*. McKay's pointing up
the importance of the literary connection with Stevenson in Glover's otherwise
unliterary life is very useful.

McKay, Alexander, 'From Aberdeen to Nagasaki: Thomas Blake Glover in Japan', *in* Fladmark, J. M. (ed) *In Search of Heritage: As Pilgrim or Tourist* (Shaftesbury, Donhead, 1998), 153–62
A short but updated account of Glover research, first presented as a conference paper.

McKillop, Malcolm L., *The Glover Trail in north-east Scotland* (Fraserburgh, privately printed, 1994)
Short guide to local landmarks' significance in terms of the earliest part of the Glover story, arranged by place.

Macmurray, John, *The Self As Agent* and *Persons in Relation* (London, Faber, 1969 (1957)
Seminal lectures by a Scottish philosopher used here to distinguish between shared experience based on touch (as in swordfights) and time-differentiated experience based on vision (as in gunfights).

Mason, W. B., 'The Foreign Colony in the Early Meiji Days: II – Thomas B. Glover, A Pioneer of Anglo-Japanese Commerce', *New East*, February 1918, 155–7
An important anecdotal link made by a Nagasaki resident who remembers Glover and illustrates some of the contexts and stories not provided by Glover himself.

Mishima, Yasuo, *Mitsubishi Zaibatsushi* (Tokyo, Kyoikusha, 1979)
Company history of Mitsubishi, not easily found in the UK. A zaibatsu is a company supported semi-formally by the government, creating a virtual monopoly.

Mishima, Yukio, speech before ritual suicide: www.vill.yamanakako.yamanashi.jp/bungaku/mishima/nenpu/his65_70.html (and many other accounts)
Mishima, and particularly his nationalist ritual suicide speech, is important here because the novelist saw how Restoration Japan's rejected attempts to imitate Europe led to the annexation of Japanese culture by the US after 1945, and how the late 1940s turned Japan into what we now know as a client state, transmitting globalised economics to its own people and the rest of Asia.

Mitford, A.B., *Tales of Old Japan* (London, Macmillan, 1871), two vols
An account with contributions from Glover, and perhaps co-research. Popular in Britain at the time, it was read by Robert Louis Stevenson, and was the first introduction to Japan for many English and Scottish literati.

Morris-Suzuki, Tessa, *The Technological Transformation of Japan* (Cambridge, Cambridge University Press, 1994)
Tessa Morris-Suzuki is one of a very few scholars to have applied Cultural Studies models to Japan (see also work by Yoshimi Shunya). Some of the ideas in this book are used here to contextualise modernisation since the Meiji Restoration.

Morton, Graeme, *Unionist Nationalism: Governing Urban Scotland, 1830–1860* (East Linton, Tuckwell, 1999)
A convincing and influential model for the simultaneous working of Scottish and British objectives during the most unionist period of the mid-nineteenth century, helping us think about how Glover could be strongly Scottish, yet also strongly British.

Nagasaki City Council, Glover Garden guide
Glover Garden materials in Japanese and English. If possible these are worth reading in both languages, since, as with much tourist and public information, the English version is not so much a translation as a rebranding for a foreign market. The English-language brochure is beautifully produced and accurate. This is not the small leaflet given out at the entrance to the garden.

Nagasaki City Council, *Heisei 17 Nagasaki-shi no Kanko* (Tourism financial plans, 2006)
Financial account of the running of Nagasaki's tourist attractions. Breaks down the visitors to Glover Garden according to age, place of origin, length of stay, and other factors.

Nagasaki Institute of Applied Science, various articles on university website: www.nias.ac.jp
Short guides to Glover written by Brian Burke-Gaffney, an academic at the institution.

Naito, Hatsuho, *Meiji Kenkoku no Yosho: To-masu B. Guraba- no Shimatsu* (Tokyo, Atene Shobo, 2001)
Vast and exhaustive list of Glover-related events, comprising research from an extremely wide range of sources. The most factually complete account of Glover's life in any language. Used here for corroboration of various events.

Nish, Ian, (ed.), *The Iwakura Mission to America and Europe: A New Assessment,* (London, Routledge/ Curzon 1998)
Thorough account of the journey of the mission, area by area. The Iwakura mission,

which travelled to Europe and America, was a classic expression of the success of westernisation by diplomats and traders, and was supported by Glover.

Nish, Ian, *The Anglo-Japanese Alliance: The Diplomacy of Two Island Empires, 1894–1907* (Westport, CT, Greenwood, 1976 (1966))
Thoroughly researched and chronological account of the background to, and negotiation of, the 1902 alliance.

Noda, Hiranosuke, *Guraba- Fujin: Rekishi no Hida ni Hikaru Shinjitsu* (Tokyo, Shinnami Shobo, 1991)
One of Noda's key Butterfly-mythologising accounts of Glover. There are others, but much of Noda's work now attracts scepticism because of new information concerning Tsuru.

Noda, Shizuko, (ed.), *Guraba-Fujin: Rekishi no Hida ni Hikaru Shinjitsu* (Tokyo, Shinnami Shobo, 1996)
Reissue and re-editing of Tsuru-as-Butterfly revivalism by Noda Shizuko, Noda Hiranosuke's daughter.

Noguchi, Katsuichi and Tomioka Masanobu (eds) *Yoshida Shoin Den* (Tokyo, Noshidai, 1891)
Accounts of Yoshida of this period are interesting since, where today the joi influence is seen as safely distant, in the late nineteenth-century atmosphere of Meiji Conservatism the pulls of joi and internationalism were still both in action, and Yoshida was often seen as a nationalist hero resisting Euro-American hegemony.

Ota, Shoko, 'Suteibensun to Yoshida Shoin', *Tokyo Daigaku Kyoyogakubu Kiyo* 19 (March 1987), 87–103
An analysis of Robert Louis Stevenson's vision of Yoshida and Japan, published independently of Alexander McKay's research. Appears in an internal academic journal of the University of Tokyo.

Oxford University English Faculty History: www.english.ox.ac.uk/faculty/ Faculty-History.htm
Shows the solidifying of English Literature around the time of the set-up of the Indian Civil Service exams.

Paine, S.C.M., *The Sino-Japanese War of 1894–1895: Perception, Power, and Primacy* (Cambridge, Cambridge University Press, 2003)
Scholarly account of the war and its contexts. Like Ian Nish, goes into detail of the politics of the mid 1890s in great detail.

Paterson, Lindsay, et al, (eds) *New Scotland, New Politics?* (Edinburgh, Polygon, 2001)
Now inevitably dated, as is the nature of such research, but still an important study into who Scots thought they were during the post-devolution period. Useful here for thinking about the criteria for Scottishness, and what Scots' motives might be in creating national heroes.

Satow, Ernest, *A Diplomat in Japan* (London, OUP, 1968 (1921))
From Satow's own diaries. Satow is an indispensable source of information of the Restoration period, and also wrote a number of influential studies of the country. He is frustratingly silent on Glover.

Shewan, Alexander, *Spirat adhuc amor: A Record of the Gym* (Aberdeen, Rosemount, 1923)
A brief sketch of Glover's old school, including details of the progress of Nagasawa Kanae, youngest of the Satsuma Nineteen.

Shozan, Sakuma, trans. Tadao, Iijima, *Seikenroku* (Tokyo, Iwanami Bunko, 1986 (original date uncertain))
Edition of the thoughts of the mentor of Yoshida Shoin and in turn the many ronin joi samurai who made foreign traders' life a misery, and who were courted by Glover. Shows dual internationalism and defensiveness, along which lines mid nineteenth-century rebels were thinking.

Spence, Alan, *The Pure Land* (Edinburgh, Canongate, 2006)
Major novelisation of Glover's life.

Stevenson, Robert Louis, 'Yoshida-Torajirô', *Cornhill Magazine* (March 1880), 327–34
Stevenson's classic account of Yoshida.

Stevenson, Robert Louis, 'The Ebb-Tide', in *The Strange Case of Dr. Jekyll and Mr. Hyde, and other stories*, Calder, Jenni (ed.) (London, Penguin, 1979 (1894))
Story of the South Pacific, uncannily influenced by the North Pacific. Looks quite

critically at Victorian informal imperialism, more critical than Glover's. Stevenson's Pacific stories echo through later modern colonial literature, particularly Joseph Conrad's *Heart of Darkness*.

Stevenson, Robert Louis, *Letters*, Booth, Bradford A. and Mayhew, Ernest (eds) (New Haven, Yale University Press, 1994), four vols
Contains letters to Fujikura Kinjiro and other Japan-related correspondence.

Stevenson, Robert Louis, 'Records of a Family of Engineers': http://robert-louis-stevenson.classic-literature.co.uk/records-of-a-family-of-engineers/
Stevenson's autobiographical account of his childhood and family, particularly interesting for his ideas of the global reach of the mercantile empire drawn on by his family's lighthouse engineering, and for comments on social class and various other aspects of Scottish identity.

Sugiyama, Shinya, 'Thomas B. Glover: A British Merchant in Japan, 1861–1870', *Business History* 26.2, 1984, 122–38
Early and very detailed guide to Glover's business dealings of the 1860s. This account splits Glover's projects into the chronological periods of tea, arms and mining.

Sugiyama, Shinya, *Meiji Isshin to Igirisu Shonin* (Tokyo, Iwanami, 1993)
Fairly short but meticulously researched and telling account of various foreign influences on Meiji Japan, especially economic ones.

Tokutomi, Soho, *Yoshida Shoin* (Tokyo, Minyusha, 1893)
An attempt to account for Yoshida Shoin in relation to Meiji Conservatism, and to press Yoshida's nationalist ambition into imperial use. Soho produced a vast amount on Japanese history and was classed as a war criminal by the US occupying forces.

Van Rijk, Jan, *Madame Butterfly: Japonisme, Puccini, and the Search for the Real Cho-cho san* (Berkeley, CA, Stone Bridge, 2001)
Probably the most complete description of how *Madam Butterfly* came about, written by an ex-diplomat. Used here to corroborate some of the musical background to the opera.

Yoshida, Midori, *Retsuretsutaru nihonjin* (Tokyo, Shodensha, 2000)
Very general account of Yoshida Shoin's life, perhaps with high school students in mind.

Yoshida, Midori, 'Suteiibensun to Yoshida Shoin', *Kan* 5, 2001, 234–5
Rare discussion of the Yoshida/Stevenson connection, published in a heavyweight journal but in a freewheeling style which describes the author's discovery of Scotland rather than going into comparative Cultural Studies.

Yoshino, Kosaku, *Cultural Nationalism in Contemporary Japan* (London, Routledge, 1995)
Influential and brilliant discussion of the creation of 'Japanese uniqueness' in post-war Japan – which was itself reliant on the 1860s creation of uniqueness as encouraged by Glover and associates. A book to be read by everyone who imagines that there is a Japanese ethnic group which has timeless and naturally different characteristics.

Young, Robert, *Postcolonialism: An Historical Introduction* (Oxford, Blackwell, 2001)
Encyclopaedic discussion of colonialism throughout the world, and forms of resistance to it. Particularly important here for its account of China and of the domestic context of Victorian British imperialism, formal and informal.

Other works include:

Aberdeen Registrar's Office records

The Nagasaki Express, various editions, 1870–5
Rising Sun and Nagasaki Express, various editions, 1876–97

The Chronicle and Directory for China, Japan, and the Philippines [the *China Directory*] (Hong Kong), various editions, 1861–1923

Press and Journal (Aberdeen), various editions, 1945–2001

Evening Express (Aberdeen), various editions, 1969–99

Fraserburgh Herald and Northern Counties Advertiser, various editions

Thomas Glover Foundation Materials (Fraserburgh)

Aberdeen Maritime Museum records

Oral and diarised informal records of two Nagasaki families, accounts ranging from 1871 to 1923

Jardine Matheson corporate records 1859–70, Cambridge University Library

Foreign Office Records, 1860–1910

Statistical Account of Scotland, 1843, Part Two

Glossary

aikokuto	'love for the nation party' – one Meiji version of patriotism
Ansei	period of Japanese history from 1854 to 1860
Ansei Treaties	agreements to open four ports from 1859 – Nagasaki, Hyogo (Kobe), Hakodate and Yokohama, also known as the 'Unequal Treaties'
bakufu	military junta which nominally supported the emperor, overturned by rebels in January 1868
bakumatsu	period of bakufu rule before its collapse
besso	'separate residence', often a shack
bunmei kaika	idea of cultural opening, encouraged in Meiji times
bushido	samurai code of behaviour
daimyo	leader of a han
datsua	'escape from Asia': Meiji governments' policy of westernisation
en	yen, unit of currency
genro	senior advisers to the emperor
han	clan: often translated as 'feudal domain', the area controlled by a local leader before Japan was split into prefectures, or ken
higaisha	victim of the atomic bombings, also hibakusha
isshin	'steps forward': Meiji westernising reforms, and the generic name given to the period
Jiyuto	Liberal Party
joi	samurai desire to rid the country of incomers; often translated as 'Expel the foreigner!'
juku	training school, or today, 'cram school'
kana	phonetic Japanese characters
kanji	the most complex of the three scripts of Japanese characters, partly shared in adapted form with Chinese, and often mistranslated as 'Chinese characters'
kanpo	Chinese medicine
katana	long sword
ken	prefecture, set up after the abolition of the han in 1871. Originally they followed the pattern of around 300 han, but were eventually reduced to 47 (including 'metropolitan prefectures') in 1888

Kenpeitai	military, increasingly secret, police from 1881 to 1945
Komei	emperor from 1831 to 1867. Also means the time period during his rule, as in the Japanese dating system
koseki	official family registers
kyoryuchi	concessions allowed to foreign citizens in the Ansei ports from 1859
ku	district of a city
Meiji	emperor from 1867 to 1912. Also means the time period during his rule
rangaku	studies of Dutch culture and langauge
ronin	samurai without master. Typical of anti-bakufu rebels in western Japan in the 1840s to 1860s
ryugakusei	students abroad
ryo	unit of Japanese currency, valued at $1.1 Mexican silver dollars during the Ansei opening, but subject to huge fluctuations
Saccho	Satsuma and Choshu clans
sakoku	policy of complete closure of Japan between 1641 and 1853
samurai	member of the highest caste in pre-Restoration Japan
Satsuei	Satsuma and Britain: usually refers to the 1863 war
seigaku	studies of Chinese culture and language
seikanto	Japanese movement to colonise Korea
seppuku	ritual suicide by cutting the stomach
shokai	business company
shi	city, or urban administrative district
shishi	samurai elders, spokesmen
shigakko	religious-military schools based on joi principles
sonno	respect for the emperor, especially in rebel samurai, usually contrasted with the lukewarm protection of the shogun: often goes together with joi
Taisho	emperor from 1912 to 1926: also means the time period during his rule
tatami	straw mats used as flooring
to	metropolitan prefecture, Tokyo's version of ken
yujo	literally, play girl, companion/prostitute
yukata	garment covering the upper three-quarters of the body, of varying shades of formality, worn by samurai
zaibatsu	large government-supported company, often a virtual monopoly, the greatest early example being Mitsubishi

Place Names

Broch	Fraserburgh, north-east Scotland
Chuzenji	temple near Nikko in eastern Japan where the Glovers vacationed
Dejima	harbour area of Nagasaki, occupied by the Dutch during sakoku, then by various foreigners, now part of the city
Edo/Yeddo	today's Tokyo
Honshu	the central and largest of the Japanese islands
Hyogo	area in western Japan which opened concessions according to the Ansei Treaties: its main urban settlement of the Pacific coast later became known as Kobe
Hong Kong	city in south-eastern China, from 1842 to 1997 formally part of the British empire
Kagomshima	city on the southern tip of Kyushu, stronghold of Satsuma
Kyoto	until 1869, capital of Japan and home of the emperor. Samurai from around the country would travel to Kyoto to pay taxes
Kyushu	the southernmost and second largest of Japan's islands
Minami Yamate	mountain area of Nagasaki where Glover built Ipponmatsu
Nagasaki	city in the north-west of Kyushu. Until the early twentieth century, one of the biggest cities in the country
Nanoshima	island in Nagasaki, drawn into Glover's mining enterprise
Namamugi	town in today's Kanagawa prefecture. Site of a highly publicised conflict between the British and samurai in 1862
Oura	area of Nagasaki near the harbour
Ryukyus	island chain off the south-west of the country, once nominally a kingdom, but controlled by Satsuma. Today, Okinawa prefecture
Satsuma, Choshu, Hizen, Higo, Saga, Isahaya	some of the main clans and clan lands in Kyushu
Sakurajima	island in Nagasaki, drawn into Glover's mining enterprise
Shanghai	city on the eastern coast of China, and outpost of the British trading empire

Shimonoseki	city straddling the southernmost tip of Honshu and the northernmost tip of Kyushu, the Choshu stronghold of the 1860s
Takashima	island in Nagasaki which gave its name to Glover's mine
Tokyo	from the move of Emperor Meiji in 1869, Japan's de facto capital, now official capital
Toyoko	Tokyo and Yokohama
Yamate	the hills of Nagasaki, overlooking the harbour
Yokohama	city in today's Kanagawa, west of Toyko, joined in a single conurbation

Index